The End of Autumn

The End of Autumn

REFLECTIONS ON MY LIFE IN FOOTBALL

By Michael Oriard

DOUBLEDAY & COMPANY, INC.
GARDEN CITY, NEW YORK
1982

Library of Congress Cataloging in Publication Data

Oriard, Michael, 1948–
    The end of autumn.

    Includes index.
    1. Oriard, Michael, 1948–   . 2. Football players—
United States—Biography. I. Title.
GV939.O74A33   796.332′092′4 [B]
AACR2
ISBN 0-385-17798-4
Library of Congress Catalog Card Number 81-43426

Grateful acknowledgment is made to the following for permission to reprint
their copyrighted material.

    Excerpt from "A Shropshire Lad"—Authorized Edition—from *The Col-
lected Poems of A. E. Housman.* Copyright 1939, 1940, © 1965 by Holt,
Rinehart and Winston. Copyright © 1967, 1968 by Robert E. Symons. Re-
printed by permission of Holt, Rinehart and Winston, Publishers, The Soci-
ety of Authors as literary representative of the Estate of A. E. Housman and
Jonathan Cape Ltd.
    "Hey, Look Me Over," lyrics: Carolyn Leigh; music: Cy Coleman, from
Wildcat, © 1960 Carolyn Leigh and Cy Coleman. All Rights Throughout
the World Controlled by Edwin H. Morris & Company, a Division of MPL
Communications, Inc. International Copyright Secured. All Rights Reserved.
Used by Permission.

For Julie and Colin

Acknowledgments

ONE OF MY PLEASURES in writing this book has been to discover the many people—both friends and strangers—who offered their support. Mrs. Aubrey Briggar, administrative assistant for the Hamilton Tiger-Cats; Gordon S. Walker, director of information for the Canadian Football League; Judy Kachaylo, in public relations for the National Football League Players Association; Harley Wyatt, Jr., director of admissions at William Jewell College; and John Heisler, assistant director of sports information at the University of Notre Dame—all helped fill in the gaps left by a faulty memory. Timothy E. Bubb, assistant executive vice-president for the Newark, Ohio, Chamber of Commerce; James R. Allen, athletic director at Newark High School; Robert Worth, senior sports editor of the Newark *Advocate;* James Perry, sports information director at the University of Southern California; Ray Didinger, sports reporter for the Philadelphia *Daily News;* and Mr. and Mrs. Truman H. Cline, parents of Martha Tyrer—all provided information where no memory existed. To all these men and women who responded so generously to the questions of a stranger, I express my thanks. I owe special gratitude to my former teammates with the Kansas City Chiefs—Buck Buchanan, Ed Budde, George Daney, Willie Lanier, Jim Lynch, Larry Marshall, Kerry Reardon, George

Seals, Sid Smith, Bob Stein, Marvin Upshaw, and Clyde Werner
—for sharing with me their feelings about their football careers
and for reminding me once again how it feels to have teammates.

Friends and colleagues—Eric Solomon, Kerry Ahearn, and
Dennis Evans—read and criticized the manuscript at various
stages. Cheryl Watt cheerfully typed much of it. My editors at
Doubleday—Lisa Drew, Reid Boates (since departed), and
Charles Riley—consistently offered not just editorial expertise
but personal encouragement and warmth. Julie Voelker Oriard
somehow managed to be patron and critic as well as wife and
mother throughout the writing. To all, I add these public thanks
to my private ones.

This book gained much from all who helped—as I did. Other
debts of varied kinds will be obvious in the pages that follow.

CONTENTS

INTRODUCTION

My Last Game

A MINUTE AND SIX SECONDS showed on the clock the last time I took the field in a football uniform. I was a Hamilton Tiger-Cat in the Canadian Football League; across the line the defensive unit of the Ottawa Roughriders dug in for one more series. At stake was the Eastern Division playoff, the winner to meet the Montreal Alouettes for the right to play in the 1974 Grey Cup, Canada's version of the Super Bowl. The Riders led 21–18.

The lights in Ottawa's Lansdowne Park had been on for some time. On this chill, gray Sunday in November, fewer than 15,000 fans looked on—the smallest crowd I had played for since high school. They were just a blur on either side of me, an indistinct noise that enveloped us on the field, and that with the arc lights gave me the feeling I always had on the football field—particularly when the sun was down—that I was in a separate world, removed in space and time from the real world, which still existed, I supposed, somewhere out there beyond the stadium walls.

In the huddle I looked around at my teammates—barely familiar faces after two months. I had arrived in Hamilton ten games into the Tiger-Cats' sixteen-game season, the victim of a last-day cut from the Kansas City Chiefs at the end of a strike-

troubled training camp. We won just one of our last six games
but were still in the running for the Grey Cup. If we lost today,
I would never play another professional football game. If we
won, I would play one or two more until we lost, or won the
Grey Cup. This was my last season regardless; the only question
was whether it would end today or next week. As I looked
around the huddle, I really did not know what this game meant
to my new teammates. Thirty-six-year-old Garney Henley to my
left looked more like a scholarly chemist than a wide receiver,
but he had been one of Canada's best, was destined for the CFL
Hall of Fame. How badly did Garney want this victory? Across
the huddle, Dave Fleming flashed me a toothless grimace. "The
Fly" was the team character, a balding poor man's Joe Namath
who had gone straight from high school and sandlot football to
the Canadian professional league. At twenty-nine now, finishing
his tenth year in the CFL, was the Fly hungry for a victory, for
a shot at a fourth Grey Cup championship? Fleming barked
through his face mask, "C'mon, let's go after 'em. We can't let
these pussies beat us." Tony Gabriel, a Canadian tight end having a brilliant day, broke in: "We've come too far to let this one
get away. We've got time. Let's do it." All about me grunts of
agreement and determination answered Tony. I was determined,
too, out of my long familiar habits of competition. But, for a
change, I also felt remarkably calm, *professional* perhaps. I had
been in similar situations during the eighteen years I had played
organized football. With the Chiefs I had been involved in the
longest game ever played, a 1971 Christmas Day sudden-death
playoff against the Miami Dolphins, that ran nearly a full six
quarters before it was decided. When Garo Yepremian's field
goal sailed over the crossbar, I felt painfully deflated, my hope
for a Super Bowl dashed in just seconds. My career in college at
Notre Dame also ended on a drive such as this one about to
begin; down 21–17 with but seconds left, we had marched deep
into Texas territory before an interception crushed our dreams. I
cried in the locker room. In high school, we had pulled out a
last-minute victory to preserve an undefeated season, when our
split end made a diving reception for 28 yards on fourth and 21,
to keep our final scoring drive alive. The tension had been almost unbearable.

But now, as we broke the huddle, I looked at Wayne Smith across the line of scrimmage and felt no panic, no desperation, only calm anticipation. Quarterback Don Jonas barked the signals. At the snap of the ball, from my right tackle position I popped into my pass-blocking stance, feet wide, knees bent, padded fists and helmet ready to strike and parry. Smith leaped across the line, swinging his left arm for a roundhouse head slap. I blocked it with my right forearm, punching simultaneously with my left fist into his chest. With both hands he tried to grab my jersey, to yank me to one side, but I whipped my forearms from inside out, thrusting his arms apart before he could grip me, and rammed my helmet under his chin. He came at me again. This time I rotated my body slightly, giving him the outside, then drove my head and left shoulder under his armpit and assisted his own momentum to carry him deep into the backfield, well behind Jonas, who was setting up somewhere to my inside. With the roar of the crowd I turned upfield to see that Mike Walker, a local boy from Hamilton, had caught Jonas's pass for a big gain. Don quickly called time out as we hurried upfield to huddle again.

This had been Don's forty-second pass for the afternoon, and twenty-fourth completion. My man, Wayne Smith, was supposedly the best defensive end in the CFL that year. In an earlier game in Hamilton, won by Ottawa 33–21, Smith had almost single-handedly wrecked our passing game. I had played on the left side in that game, while Smith had run inside, outside, and over the top of our right tackle all afternoon. For the playoff, I had been switched expressly to stop Wayne Smith, and in more than forty pass attempts he had not once touched our quarterback. I did not feel the same exultation in this feat that I would if Smith had been Harvey Martin, and the opposition the Dallas Cowboys. The Canadian Football League has become in recent years a competitive bidder for some of the NFL's top prospects, but eight years ago it was a refuge for failed NFL players prolonging their careers, and for the younger athletes an intermediate step between college and their real desire, the National Football League. But the fact was, however much my teammates and opponents talked about making it in the States and dreamed of that happening, few were good enough to make the leap. Sometimes I wondered what I was doing there—playing with many athletes who could not have made my college team, seeming, I supposed, to my teammates just another former NFL player desperately warding off the end of my career. Was I desperate? I would not have wanted to admit I was, but I would readily admit that although Wayne Smith was not Harvey Martin, it felt damn good to whip him.

We lined up again—another pass, of course. Once more Wayne Smith reached and grabbed and butted and spun. Again I kept him harmlessly away from Don Jonas, who rifled the ball to Tony Gabriel. We scrambled to the ball, to run a play without huddling—another snap, another futile attempt by Wayne Smith to break down my protection, another completion to Tony Gabriel. Time out.

With one second showing on the stadium clock, Ian Sunter trotted onto the field to attempt a 37-yard field goal. We had moved the ball from our own 35 to Ottawa's 29 in three plays; now a tie and overtime hung on Ian's booting the ball through the uprights. We should never have needed this field goal. We had more than doubled the Riders' offensive output; only a deflected pass gathered in for a 55-yard touchdown and a 15–10 halftime lead, and four interceptions, one of which led to a score, had kept the Roughriders in the game. But that fourth interception, with 1:35 to go, had set up a 35-yard field goal for a three-point Ottawa lead—and set the stage for the final dramatics.

For what might be the last time ever, I lined up in my three-point stance, and on the snap of the ball turned head and shoulders to the inside to shut off any defensive penetration. Hearing the solid thump of an unblocked kick, I looked up to follow the flight of the ball. I could tell it would be close; with soccer-style kickers, it was the hook at the end of the ball's flight that told. But Ian's ball did not hook quite enough. It sailed just to the right of the upright, was conceded by Ottawa's kick returned for a one-point single, and the final score stood 21–19.

All about me my teammates slumped. Several of them muttered curses; one guy slammed his helmet to the ground while others kicked the turf. For their part, Ottawa's players were strangely subdued after their initial cheers: perhaps they felt undeserving, a bit like the kid who gets an A by cheating on a test.

I felt surprisingly detached. I was supposed to be crushed, right? We had just lost a playoff game, a chance to play in Canada's most prestigious football game. We had played better than Ottawa and deserved to win, but blew it. I should have been crying, swearing, groaning in pain over missed opportunities. I had reacted to similar defeats in past years in just that way. I had also decided weeks before that this was to be my last season. Now, my eighteen-year career would end with defeat. I had played well—but so what? Every coach I had ever played for taught me that the team was more important than the individual. Football was *the* team game. Teamwork and self-sacrifice were the essential requirements, especially for offensive linemen —the grunts who slogged away in the trenches while others took the glory. But we had just lost the biggest football game of our season, and I did not mind.

Entering the game I had been torn between a desire to go out in a blaze of Grey Cup glory and a more simple longing to just go home to my wife in California. After three years of marriage, commuting between Kansas City for the football season and Palo Alto for graduate school at Stanford—Julie finding whatever jobs were available for short-term employment—we had decided that if she could find a teaching job in California, we would put up with the separation for the sake of her career. She had been hired to teach in a private grade school in Mountain View, but this separation had proven more difficult than either of us had anticipated. Now, my compensation for losing to Ottawa was to go home. Five years before, I had felt as if I died a little when my Notre Dame team lost in the Cotton Bowl. I marveled now at how I had changed in just five years. I was not even wounded.

As I walked across the field to the visiting team's locker room, I passed Wayne Smith. As I nodded to him, he gave me a who-is-that-masked-man-anyway kind of look that capped my football career in the best kind of way. His look confirmed what I had felt for the last three hours—that I was dominating the best defensive end in the Canadian Football League. This was how I wanted to leave the game. When Hank Stram had cut me two months before, after four years with the Chiefs, I was angry, bitter, hurt. Had my career ended then, my last memory of the sport that had consumed enormous amounts of time, emotion, hope, and fear for eighteen of the twenty-six years I had lived would have been an unpleasant one. I had been resuced by a telephone call from the Hamilton Tiger-Cats after I had returned to the Stanford campus. Julie and I weighed the advantages and disadvantages. The money offered was not great, but it would see us through the completion of my doctoral dissertation and protect our savings account for a downpayment on a house when I found my first teaching job. We talked about money and separation and school and jobs, but we did not talk very much about the real reason I needed to fly away three thousand miles to play football for two more months. I did not want my last memory of football to be that unpleasant meeting in Hank Stram's office when he told me, "Mike, I've put you on waivers."

In the locker room, a few of my teammates slammed their helmets against their lockers or spurted curses in their frustration. I felt a bit traitorous, but I could not share their anger. I sat quietly before my own locker, unwinding the tape and gauze wraps from my hands, peeling my sweaty, muddy jersey over my head. The past two months in Canada had been good ones for me. I had not been totally unknown when I arrived. An old friend, Bill Etter, from Spokane and Notre Dame, was the Tiger-Cats' starting quarterback until injuries sidelined him, and he had an extra room in an apartment he shared with another teammate. Our other roommate had been drafted by the Chiefs the year before and I remembered him slightly from training camp. Another Ticat teammate, Lewis Porter, had been a teammate of mine on the Chiefs during my rookie season.

Because of my four years of NFL experience I had a certain amount of status among my new teammates. I had only to prove to them that I could drink, not that I could play football. I had spent much of my football life proving myself to my coaches and fellow players. I had been an outsider who had to fight my way onto the team, warring against my own teammates as much as against my opponents. In Hamilton, for a change, it was assumed I was a good football player. I only had to demonstrate that I could drink large quantities of beer to be admitted to full acceptance by my teammates. Dave Fleming, the master of ceremonies of our drinking marathons, made my welcome official on my second night in town, when I proved that my thirst could match my size. A few weeks of feeling twenty-one again, getting drunk once a week with the boys, was a refreshing diversion from my more orderly married existence. But my pleasure waned. For the last three weeks I only wanted to go home to Julie and my real life.

I untied my cleated shoes and slipped off my gold silk-and-elastic pants for the last time. Hot showers were running now, sending steam out into the locker area. Anger and frustration had given way to resignation and weariness among my teammates. Everyone spoke quietly, made small jokes, became gentle. Football in Canada had been a revelation to me. I had known a little about the game before I arrived—the longer, wider field, twelve men on a side, only three tries to make a first down. What I was not prepared for was the lack of hype surrounding the game. The local citizens looked upon the Tiger-Cats with much less awe than American fans showed toward players at home. Hamilton's crowds in 1974 averaged a little over 28,000 per game, and that was the second highest average in the league; the Kansas City Chiefs nearly filled 78,000-seat Arrowhead Stadium every week. My new teammates—particularly the Canadians—looked upon their own careers with proportionately less emphasis. Because many of them made very little money from football—$5000 to $10,000 perhaps—they had to have other careers. Garney Henley was a professor of physical education at a local college; a defensive tackle named Dan Dulmage spent his mornings and early afternoons at dental school. Most of the established players had second jobs even during the season. We were free until four every day, when we had a brief meeting and a short practice, finishing up by six-thirty. We had a coaching staff of three: head man Jerry Williams, a native of my own hometown of Spokane, who had coached in the NFL; and two assistants. In Kansas City we had seven assistant coaches. Football was simply not as important in Canada as it was in the U.S. While I was with Hamilton, the Canada—U.S.S.R. hockey series was taking place, and my Canadian teammates seemed more concerned about those games than our own.

I enjoyed this quieter version of football. My teammates felt more like a team to me because superstars were not possible in this environment. I found it ironic that compared to the NFL, these were second-rate players, but in many ways they were more fortunate. With their meager salaries and outside careers, they would leave football painlessly. In Kansas City I had seen former all-pros hanging on past their prime because they were unable to give up either the paycheck or the glory. They were extravagantly honored, but the loss of that honor created a monstrous void in their lives when age or injury finally forced them to retire. My teammates in Hamilton had not had many opportunities to play the hero, but neither would they have to live with the awareness of a magnificent past forever lost to them.

Under the hot, steaming shower I felt my muscles relax and all remaining tension from the game drain away. On either side of me, my teammates, too, had surrendered to the mellowing powers of warm water. Like every other Canadian team, we had our maximum allotment of fifteen "imports," or American players, and seventeen locals. Most of the Canadians had played college ball in the States but were not good enough for the NFL. Most of the Americans had been late cuts by NFL clubs in their rookie seasons, and had come northward as the only way to prolong their careers. Among such players I felt uniquely talented for the first time in my professional career. With Hamilton I felt like a gunslinger brought to town by homesteaders to clean out the desperadoes. I had been signed to play right guard, but I played left and right tackle as well—moved to the position where we needed the most help or the opposition was toughest. I had not come to Canada to prolong my career but to end it properly—still shooting from the hip.

I toweled myself off and began to dress slowly, resuming permanently now my identity as a civilian. Shorts rather than supporter, slacks rather than padded knickers, shirt and jacket without plastic armor in the shoulders. Dressing for a more normal life, not for combat.

At twenty-six, I could look back on only eight years when I had *not* played football, and as the earliest eight, those were the ones I knew least about. To conceive the kind of person I would have been had I not played football was as impossible as imagining myself at five six rather than six five. In trying to sort out the ways in which football had affected my personal development, I had a major chicken-and-egg problem. I was a disciplined, task-oriented person, but I did not know whether football made me that way or if already having those qualities had enabled me to succeed at playing football. I had high expectations of myself, but assumed success would come only against obstacles and with hard work. I loved to compete, was receptive to coaching, was physically and mentally "tough." Did football mold me, or had I always been suitable raw material for a football player? I had no way of knowing, but I did know that football had played a major role in my life. Yet I was ready to give it up not only willingly but gratefully. Football had helped me create an identity, but I now had a sufficient sense of myself to do without football. Like a good teacher, football taught me how to leave it behind. I had known men who ten years after retiring still could not accept the fact that they were out of the game. Football had once gripped me by the throat, too, but had loosened its hold.

I banged my locker door shut and followed my teammates out to the waiting bus, to be taken to Ottawa's airport. My teammates now were quiet, some murmuring words to each other I could not distinguish, most saying nothing at all, simply gazing sightlessly out the windows at the shadowy shapes that passed. This group of thirty-one other players was the last "team" I would ever be a part of. My sense of a team had changed over the many seasons I had played. For thirteen years, through five years of grade school, then high school and college, a half dozen coaches had taught me the ultimate importance of the team. But five years of professional football had impressed upon me a very different lesson. Hank Stram talked about the team as a "family," as Ara Parseghian had done at Notre Dame. But in Kansas City, unlike at Notre Dame, I was *owned* by an organization that, come income tax time, depreciated me as another firm might a piece of industrial equipment. I was bound by a contract that did not bind the organization reciprocally, that allowed me and other members of the "family" to be discarded when our usefulness had ended. In five years of playing pro football I had learned—at times painfully—that my primary concern had to be for my own welfare, not for the team's success. I had learned that winning and losing, success and failure, no matter what the public might think, were really personal matters. It was not just that there could be only one Super Bowl champion every year (or one Grey Cup champion); I had discovered in Kansas City, as every professional football player does sooner or later, that my team had corporate interests that did not necessarily accommodate the welfare of all the individual players. It was this understanding, coming late in my career, that enabled me to feel that I had "won" that day in the game against Ottawa.

In the airport, I joined my teammates in wandering through the shops and newsstands, and in buying hamburgers to hold us until the meal on the plane. At the gate, as we milled about waiting to board, Coach Williams came up to me.

"You did a fine job on Smith today, Mike. He didn't get to Jonas once."

"Thanks, Coach," I responded as he passed on. Although I had not needed to hear this, praise sounded good to me. I had always been my own toughest critic, but playing a football game was a different sort of performance from running alone for time, say, on a deserted track. Football could not have had the personal significance for me had I not played it in a public arena before the judging eyes of both familiar and anonymous spectators. A respected coach had always been my premier audience. I liked the sound of his compliment.

On the plane back to Toronto, I settled into my seat, stretching my legs as far as possible in the cramped space. A bus would meet us at the airport for the ride to Hamilton, depositing us at the Tiger-Cat stadium. I would clean out my stall and take one final look at the last of the locker rooms in which I had spent so many hours. One more night at the apartment, then collecting my final paycheck, settling my tax obligation to the Canadian government, and tying up any other loose ends would see me boarding a plane for my trip home to the Bay Area. I had only my dissertation to complete before I would finish my Ph.D. at Stanford and begin looking for a teaching job. The full range of new challenges that hovered in the future appealed to me. My life had not peaked, but was only changing directions. Eighteen years was a long time to do something and then give it up, but by the time I quit teaching I will have done that for almost forty. At twenty-six I was too young to feel my life had reached a pinnacle and would now begin a long decline.

My teammates' spirits had been largely restored by now. They, too, had tomorrows to think about. Some of the more boisterous ones were calling jokes across aisles to their friends. Others were dispassionately discussing today's game and its undeserved outcome. A few perhaps were dreaming futile dreams of future glory. I had dreamed those dreams, too, but had confronted reality as well. From one perspective my professional career had been a failure, but from my own it seemed now a success. I had completed an experience that would always be a part of me, that I could look back on with satisfaction, amusement— and pain, too. I was a survivor. Retirement for professional football players is a small death. The football player faces at twenty-six or thirty what the normal person confronts at sixty-five. For many football players, retirement does indeed seem like death, or slipping into a coma: nothing afterward will ever be as challenging or rewarding. But for me, retirement was merely the death of one phase of my life. I was a snake shedding its old skin. And I was leaving football in a satisfying way. I knew the alternatives: crippling injury, forced retirement, sudden release from the team. Had my career ended in any of these ways I would have felt a gnawing unfulfillment, a sense of something left undone, unfinished. Instead, I was physically sound—had the use of all my limbs and would be plagued only by the minor aches of a body made to do some unnatural things for eighteen years—and was emotionally sound as well. Had my last experience with football been the anger and hurt of being cut by the Chiefs, my entire relationship to the past two thirds of my life might have been very different. But I could look back on that period now as a positive experience—painful and difficult but also immensely rewarding, maturing as well as juvenile, both absurd and profoundly influential. But overall positive. I wondered how much I would miss the game in the months and years to come. Would I begin bouncing my wife off our apartment walls when September rolled around and I had no one facing me across a scrimmage line? Would I desperately miss the camaraderie, the physical exhilaration, the privileged treatment and special status that I felt as a football player? I didn't know, but I felt prepared for my life after football. Winging my way home three thousand miles away, reflecting on my long career, I marveled at the good fortune of my survival. I had not always been able to view football so calmly.

PART ONE
Seasons of Youth

ONE

Playing Games

FROM THE VERY BEGINNING, football was more than a game. Hide-and-go-seek was a game. Cowboys and Indians was a game. Softball and tag and red rover and kickball were games. Football was something more. I first played football in a large grassy field adjoining a neighbor's property around the corner from my house in Spokane, Washington. Most of the field was a hilly incline, but at the bottom, in a space perhaps twenty yards by forty rimmed by maple trees and pines, I first discovered football. The players in our games were the older kids in the neighborhood. Because I was big for my age I was allowed to play occasionally. The games themselves were ragtag affairs played with more enthusiasm than skill, but the quality of play was much less important to me than the mere fact of playing with the older boys.

Already to a seven-year-old, more was at stake in one of these football contests than in any of our games of hide-and-seek or cowboys and Indians. Football was somehow different. It was a game, too, and not unlike our other games in some ways: we were very conscious of rules, and we observed boundaries and regulations concerning downs, yardage, and eligible receivers as conscientiously as we regarded the conventions for falling "dead" when we were shot in the proper way on "Old Smokey,"

the wooded hillside where we played out our fantasies of the
Wild West. There were also clear ways of determining winners
and losers: in our football games it was by scoring touchdowns,
in cowboys and Indians by "killing" all the enemies or gaining
the top of the hill. But football was not make-believe, as our
shooting games were. Scoring a touchdown was a real event that
required no pretending to be meaningful. Already, playing football meant proving myself, even if only proving myself able to
play with the older kids. As the youngest player, much in awe of
anyone even three or four years older, I wanted to prove that I
could catch and throw well enough to be a worthy teammate or
opponent. Sometimes, when the others wanted to play tackle
rather than touch, my sense of intimidation was nearly overwhelming. A playmate who was four years older might have appeared to an adult onlooker to be only another kid, but to me he
was a creature of such awesome physical superiority that to hurtle my body against his seemed sheer folly. When we played
tackle, I leaped on my opponent's back and tried to bulldog him
to the ground with the least danger to myself. When we played
touch, I was less fearful, and tried to play well enough so that I
would not continually expose myself as the "little kid" allowed
to play by the others merely to even up the sides.

Of all the games I played as a child, football alone had such
potent significance. Growing up in a fairly typical small-town,
middle-class American neighborhood and home in the fifties, I
absorbed the obvious cultural values which made me understand
that, as a boy, I was to play cowboys and Indians or football,
not dolls. The girls in our neighborhood coerced us into playing
"house" occasionally. We grumbled and hedged—to do so was
expected of us, was virtually a required ritual—but we con-
sented in the end. Actually, sometimes we wanted to play house,
to play the father who came home to his wife's lovingly prepared dinner, or even to play the baby, fussed over by the dot-
ing mother. But we learned early on that as boys we were not
supposed to want to play such "sissy" games. We discovered this
the first time we were playing with the girls, and a boy, particularly an older boy, happened by.

"Look at the little girls playing with their cute little dolls and
dishes."

One such experience as this, reinforced by a few more subtle reminders, guaranteed that we would play domestic games with the girls only when we were assured that the rest of the boys in the neighborhood were occupied.

Among our boys' games, sports played a special role, because in them we acted rather than pretended. Even though I wore a coonskin cap and imitation deerskin leggings and fringed shirt, I was not actually Davy Crockett, and winning or losing at cowboys and Indians did not ultimately mean much. We enacted scenarios in which our parts were interchangeable. But a football or baseball game was a contest of skills that mere pretending could not give us. Someone might say, "I'm Crazy Legs Hirsch," but he still had to catch the pass by himself. My good fortune to be moderately competent from the beginning was just that—good fortune—but it has shaped my life, not just in initiating a long career of football playing, but in developing my expectation that committed effort will in time produce success. A kids' game played by seven-year-olds can have far-reaching consequences.

Among the sports we played, football's role was unique. I enjoyed backyard softball games and baseball in nearby parks when I was a little older. I competed hard at these other sports, wanting to win, wanting to play well. Baseball also consumed almost all of my inactive time devoted to sports. With my older brother, Flip, I read collections of baseball anecdotes, studied baseball record books and daily box scores in the newspapers, bought and traded baseball cards by the score. I could tell anyone who asked how many bases Ty Cobb stole in 1916, or name the lineup of the Gas House Gang in the thirties. I could repeat funny stories about Rube Waddell's zany antics chasing fire engines or shooting marbles with a group of boys under the grandstand while he was supposed to be pitching, or about the time Germany Schaeffer stole first base. My favorite athlete of all was Stan Musial; my brother's was Ted Williams, and we argued endlessly over who was the greater player.

But somehow football invaded my consciousness in a deeper, more lasting way than baseball did. Because baseball was a simpler game, both to watch and to play, I came to it sooner. I understood the game perfectly; it seemed I always had. Baseball was simple: one player pitched a ball, another tried to hit it, and nine more fielded it while the batter ran the bases. Football was more chaotic, less predictable. But many of baseball's simple actions became increasingly difficult as I grew older. By late grade school I had discovered that I was a great center fielder but a weak hitter, always late on a good fastball and helpless before any curve. What football demanded I was better able to deliver.

But football also grabbed my imagination and deepest longings in ways baseball never did. Football players seemed to me braver, more heroic, than other athletes. The risk of standing at home plate, facing a pitcher with a ninety-mile-per-hour fastball, seemed minuscule when compared to the danger of football's one-on-one collisions. As a player I actually preferred the dangers of football. As a boy facing a particularly fast pitcher, I felt more vulnerable than when I was aggressively attacking my opponent in a football game. I felt more control over my own fate simply because I was forcing the action. But the football players I *watched* also seemed much more heroic than baseball players. To see someone else face a hard-throwing pitcher evoked no dread in me, but to see Sam Huff and Jim Brown explode into each other on television was an awesome spectacle. Football players *looked* like the most heroic of men; the ones I saw on television with their massive padded shoulders and thighs looked all-powerful, invulnerable—the opposite of how I felt as a boy in an adult world. When I put on my own first football uniform at age nine, even *I* felt transformed into a mighty figure, to be reckoned with respectfully. Baseball had produced numerous heroes that I marveled over—vintage heroes such as Ty Cobb, Babe Ruth, Rogers Hornsby, and Walter Johnson; and more contemporary ones such as Williams, Musial, and Warren Spahn. But to me every football player more than two years older than I was a hero because he looked like one.

My first real hero was Hoppy Sebesta. Long before I had heard of Norm Van Brocklin, Jon Arnett, or Y. A. Tittle, I knew who Hoppy Sebesta was and that I wanted to be just like him. Hoppy lived across the street until I was seven, and he epitomized the magnificence of the older kids in the neighborhood. Although four years older than I, he treated me with a kindly condescension that perfectly met my expectations of so mature an individual. For his age he was not exceptionally big, but to me he was a colossus. His pleasant open-faced appearance was unremarkable to others, I suppose, but I read in it the look of greatness. Mostly, he *acted* heroically, particularly in football games. Hoppy was the leader in those pickup games in neighborhood yards, and he served the function that heroes have served since Hector and Achilles. Hoppy embodied the excellence in which I could share, and to which I could aspire in my own life. He seemed as unafraid as I was fearful, as skilled as I was inept, as graceful as I was clumsy, as powerful as I was weak. Yet he was not so different from me that I could never imagine myself in his role. He seemed both human and more than human; because I shared his humanity, I could dream, too, of one day sharing his superhuman qualities. Everything he did seemed connected to actions of great importance; his most casual comings and goings from the house opposite mine suggested significant actions in that larger world outside the tiny neighborhood to which I was restricted.

We all need heroes. They are more than role models; they teach us how to dream, what to aspire to. They tell us what our kind are capable of doing. A hero's accomplishments are ours as well, because he is one of us; he is our representative to the larger world. But in another way his labors are his alone; he both raises us vicariously to his level and remains beyond our reach—both a god and a man. We can find such heroes in the unlikeliest places. Maybe no one else responded to Hoppy Sebesta the way I did, but he was my Hercules and my Lancelot. The "worlds" in which we live can have very narrow boundaries—they can be neighborhoods, schools, football teams —but in each of these worlds we can find legitimate heroes. Hoppy Sebesta did ultimately receive wider recognition: he was a second-team all-city defensive back on the local Catholic high school team to which I knew I was headed. This was in 1961, when I was thirteen and had moved from the old neighborhood six years before. The local sportswriters had confirmed my choice of a hero made years before. And I hoped that Hoppy had blazed the way for me.

By the time I read about Hoppy's football success, I had discovered other, more widely acclaimed heroes as well. When I

was ten or eleven I could read the sports page, and had begun
watching college football on television. Billy Cannon was the
first great star I responded to. In 1959 he won the Heisman
Trophy as a running back at Louisiana State—during the years
in which LSU under Paul Dietzel sported the "Chinese Bandits"
on defense and Billy Cannon as the most glamorous back in the
college game. The figure I saw on the television screen beating
Ole Miss 7–3 with a spectacular 89-yard punt return in the
fourth quarter was a less real person than Hoppy Sebesta.
Hoppy was a great hero, but I could hope to someday play for
Gonzaga Prep as he did. Billy Cannon's heroism was of a
different sort. His exploits verged on the fantastic; the world of
LSU and Ole Miss and Heisman Trophies was a distant galaxy
peopled by demigods, a world that a young boy in Spokane,
Washington, could marvel at from afar but never hope to in-
habit. Except in his dreams.

I met Billy Cannon eventually; in fact, I briefly played with
him. In 1970, during my rookie year with Kansas City, I walked
into the locker room one day to see what seemed an old man sitting near my locker, in a tired slump suggesting relief that
movement was not necessary. I saw thinning hair, a face lined
with the evidence of hard labor and stress endured over many
years. Only his eyes and voice retained enough vitality to suggest that youthfulness had not entirely departed. I was shocked
to learn that this was Billy Cannon, just picked up from
Oakland. No longer the trim 207-pound halfback who had twice
run a 9.4 hundred in college, he was bigger, slower, and—*older*.
He was only thirty-two, but in the world of the National Football League he was already a senior citizen, and he retired at the
end of that season. Billy Cannon offered me one of my early
glimpses of mortality—of the aging of a hero, but also of that
particular kind of mortality that haunts football players and
other professional athletes, by which a man is old at thirty-two.
That season was a physically difficult one for Cannon, and
throughout those autumn weeks I could never consider him
without thinking how washed up he was compared to the
dashing hero I had first seen on television a dozen years before.
But Billy Cannon gave me another shock years later when I
learned he was a practicing orthodontist back home. He had

been reborn after his football career ended, and had obviously prepared himself. Now Billy Cannon was a hero who learned how to be just a man. My experiences in professional football came to teach me that this was the real challenge that faced each player. Billy Cannon truly played the game well.

This realization came much later, of course. My earliest experiences of professional football came in watching Sunday games on television with my father. Like all sons, I wanted to do things my dad did and like things he liked. I acquired early tastes for smoked oysters, Campbell's pepper pot soup, and hot chilies because these were some of my father's favorites, and I was going to make them mine. Watching Dad's favorite television programs with him was a particular treat. Because he enjoyed the Saturday-night Westerns—*Gunsmoke* and *Have Gun, Will Travel* —they became my favorite shows, too. He also liked Walt Disney's cartoons; so did I, but my greater pleasure was to enjoy his enjoyment. Whenever Goofy or Donald Duck did something I considered particularly funny, I would turn to look at my dad, to see if he was laughing. If he was, my delight doubled. Professional football games on Sunday were another pleasure for my dad, and they became important to me.

My father was no athlete himself. He had had polio for a year in his youth, from which he fully recovered but which discouraged any serious interest he may have had in sports. Music had been his passion from early childhood, and even after he abandoned his attempts to support his family entirely by his playing, he continued into my teens to perform professionally on weekends. He was the top jazz pianist in Spokane throughout the fifties—something I did not understand and fully appreciate until much later. Had I watched my father perform in the clubs around Spokane when I was growing up, I might have longed above all else to be a musician, too. But children don't go to nightclubs. I took piano lessons and practiced every day, but that was separate from my father's playing. What we shared was watching professional football on Sundays.

Often my father set up a portable TV on the front steps, so that we could watch the games while raking pine needles from the yard and weeding the flower beds. Triangular lines of connection were set up among my father, myself, and the television screen, where the Rams or 49ers played out their games. While I was in the yard with a rake and my father on his knees among the shrubs pulling weeds, the game pulled us back periodically to watch an important play or two, and for me to hear Dad's comments on the action. He was a quiet man, no raver at bonehead coaches or incompetent quarterbacks who failed to execute the play *he* knew could save the game. But his most casual comments were treasured by his young son, not for any insight they may have offered into the complexities of the game we were watching, but for the bond of communication and sharing they established between us. My brother, Flip, was part of these scenes as well, responding to Dad's companionship as I was, but he was not important in my own experience of these Sunday games. My relationship with my brother was a crucially formative one for me, but not on these afternoons when I felt Dad watched pro football games with *me*.

The games themselves were much less important than the watching of them. The only contest I remember with any distinctness from these very early years was the now-classic 1958 championship between Baltimore and the New York Giants, won by the Colts in sudden-death overtime, 23–17. Individual players stood out more distinctly than the games they played. My gallery of heroes became crowded from these Sunday afternoons. Jon Arnett, the Rams' running back, was my favorite player, but he had to compete for my loyalty with Jim Brown, Gino Marchetti, "Big Daddy" Lipscomb, Y. A. Tittle, and numerous others. As the only two teams west of the Rockies, the Los Angeles Rams and San Francisco 49ers were the most televised teams in Spokane, and the most likely candidates for my favorites. The Rams were my team for the perfectly understandable reason that I thought their helmets, with the curved ram's horn spiraling about the earhole, were just terrific. My great dream was to wear one of those helmets myself—strictly a dream, not a driving ambition, a dream that sustained itself best the further I was from any chance of its realization. At ten or twelve years old all things seemed possible, including the L.A. Rams. I could fantasize leaping high to make spectacular catches before 100,000 wildly cheering fans in the L.A. Coliseum, without troubling myself over the unlikelihood such an event might actually happen. My narrow child's world had no fixed boundaries; mine was a world of infinite possibilities, governed only by my ability to dream sufficiently grand dreams. When I thought about what I wanted to "be" when I grew up, I concluded an L.A. Ram, not a doctor or lawyer. But I was not working in my childhood toward that goal: I did not distinguish fantasy desires from real ones; all careers were equally possible and equally remote. With adolescence I encountered limits, discovering for the first time how much there was that I could not do, understanding many more of the realities that could make dreams mere illusions. I came to understand the difference between a desire to be a physicist and a dream to be a pro athlete. By the time I was a sophomore in college, struggling simply to make the team, not only the dream but even the thought of playing professional football had disappeared from my consciousness. When the possibility arose two years later, dreaming did not enter in except as a memory.

From watching those Sunday football games with my father I learned to argue with friends about the relative merits of Jim Brown and Jim Taylor, or Johnny Unitas and Y. A. Tittle, and to distinguish a linebacker from a cornerback. I also learned to associate football with masculinity. Those football players on the TV screen were ideal men, and my father who watched and enjoyed them was doing what a man did. Though my father was a nonathlete himself, the role model he projected included the importance of football.

But mostly I made a connection with my father through football that was sustained throughout my childhood and youth. My father was not a hunter or a fisherman who could introduce his sons to the wilderness. Self-employed, working seventy to eighty hours a week during most of this period to support a family that grew to seven children, he had little time to play ball with us, or to do many of the things that fathers do with sons. But it was the quality, not the quantity, of the time he spent with us that was important, and for me those football games watched together created a bond that I always felt through my eighteen years of playing football.

I came to appreciate that bond most fully many years after those Sunday-afternoon football games. As a child I did not real-

ize that fathers sometimes drive their sons to be the great athletes they themselves once—or never—were. I was not conscious
that football particularly is the sport into which some fathers
push their sons to prove the potency of the family gene pool. I
did not know that a father could alienate his son or make him
feel a failure or even deprive him of any pleasure from his real
success by imposing his own obsession on the boy. But I discovered these sad truths, as we all do.

As a teenager I knew one boy whose father had so pushed
him to excel from the time he was in grade school that at eighteen he had already peaked and burned himself out. He had
been a star at fourteen, a pretty good performer at eighteen, just
another player at twenty. And I never felt he enjoyed the game
much. Another boy, whose father had had a distinguished career
of his own and had continued in coaching, was neither interested nor skilled in football. He was a talented pianist, but in
committing himself to his music he had virtually to cut himself
off from his father, who saw no value in such pursuits. The
worst case I encountered was the former all-American who had
set up in his den a veritable shrine to his playing days. The walls
were lined with framed photos and certificates from various
awards; the mantel was weighted with trophies and game balls
from heroic moments in his past. When his son reached high
school age without demonstrating any comparable distinction,
his father led him into the holy sanctuary and demanded, "Okay,
when are you going to start getting some of these?"

I had no such father. He came to all my games, praised me
when we won and consoled me when we lost—but neither to the
extent that I was made to feel the one a triumph of extraordinary significance or the other a major tragedy. The games won
and lost were a quiet, unspoken bond between us, as the games
watched on television had been when I was younger. When my
successes became more notable—when I started for Notre Dame
and then was drafted by the Kansas City Chiefs—my father
never told me in words that he was proud of me or that he was
enormously pleased. But he made me *feel* it. It is a simple truth
that children give so much less to their parents than they receive, but it is an immense satisfaction to me to reflect that I did
give my father pleasure through my football career. It was not a

pleasure he demanded, or even sought, but it was a gift he accepted with the same quiet enjoyment that he gave to me on Sunday afternoons in the autumns of my youth.

My playing career in organized football began in the fourth grade when I was nine. We fourth-, fifth-, and sixth-graders of Sacred Heart Grade School formed the B squad, as opposed to the A squad of seventh- and eighth-graders. Our coach was the assistant pastor of the parish, a mild man named Father Sands who probably knew little about football but was an ideal first coach for other reasons. More and more stories have appeared recently in the media describing boys held back a year in school to enhance their prospects for playing on the local powerhouse high school team. No such pressure accompanied my introduction to football. Father Sands taught us the basics: how to line up properly in a three-point stance; how to block and tackle with our padded shoulders, keeping our hands close to our chests; how to execute simple running and passing plays that gave us the semblance of an offense. We were taught that if we kept our heads up and tackled low with our shoulders, we would not be hurt. We were *not* taught by Father Sands that we had to be mean and want to hurt our opponents, or that the big game with St. Augustine's was the most important event in our lives.

From the fourth grade into my first year as a professional, I was to look to my coaches as figures of wisdom and authority whose pronouncements were gospel and whose expectations of me were to be met at whatever cost. One of my first major adjustments to professional football was the discovery that my coach was an employer, not a father figure. In grade school, Father Sands seemed more priest than coach, but the one role simply reinforced the other in my perception. After Father Sands, the elder brothers of one of my teammates coached us through our grade school years. Carl and Marty Ota were elder brothers rather than fathers, but they were sufficiently older than the players to wield the special authority of coaches. Carl in particular was intense, but not with the unreasoning intensity of a frustrated ex-jock reliving his youth. He emphasized fundamental to us—blocking and tackling—and would not let us flinch from physical contact. But he did not belittle those of us who shied away, as I have seen some coaches do, and he made certain that every boy played in every game. On one occasion several years ago, I stopped by a practice field on a walk home, and stood appalled as I watched a red-faced, paunchy young coach of about my age, screaming at one of his players that he was a "pussy" for not sticking his nose into the ball carrier's middle when tackling him. The boy appeared to be twelve or thirteen, and he looked like the kid I remembered from my own grade school days as the one everybody picked on. He had a look in his eyes of both a caught rabbit and a cornered rat, terrified and hating at the same time, as he fought back his tears. Around him, his teammates registered a variety of emotions. Some were smugly snickering; a few looked on with obvious pity, and I suspected identification, combined with a fear of defending their teammate to the fuming coach. Finally, the attacked boy burst into tears and outrage.

"I quit, you sonuvabitch! I quit, I quit, I quit," turning to run off the field.

The coach was briefly taken aback. Then he stormed after the boy, loudly demanding an apology for the affront to his dignity. They disappeared behind a school building.

My coaches were not of this type, but by praising our good solid hits and criticizing, however constructively and calmly, less effective ones, they nonetheless helped to instill in us a veneration of "toughness." We understood from very early on that to be football players we had to be tough. To be tough meant approval in the eyes of our coaches; to be tough was the sign of a special kind of worthiness. Among all the games from five years of grade school football, one stands out most clearly as the earliest test of my own toughness. In a practice game between the A squad and the B squad when I was in the fifth grade, I found myself repeatedly having to tackle one of the biggest kids in the school. He was only a solidly built 150-pounder, but he looked enormous. I was large for my age myself, and accustomed among my peers not to be physically overmatched, but now I was confronting a physically superior opponent for the first time. He should not have been a running back at all—in our grade school league, the rules limited backs to 110 pounds—but in this practice game the seventh- and eighth-graders were determined to make us youngsters feel their superiority as fully as possible.

From my defensive end position it seemed I was having to tackle the monster on virtually every play. I was afraid of him, but my greater fear was to show my fear, and I kept hurling myself against him, dragging him down with the help of teammates. Writers such as Stephen Crane and Ernest Hemingway have described how "courage" can be an ironic kind of fear. By not quitting and not flinching from contact I proved my "courage" to myself on that day—the particular kind of courage that is necessary to football players—and that became a major part of my subsequent experiences. In college as a sophomore walk-on with what seemed to me the dimmest prospects of ever playing, my sticking it out was at least in part fear of admitting I had failed. In the National Football League to play with pain and injury was universally applauded as the sign of courage. More often than not it was more truly motivated by the player's fear of losing his job to a talented substitute. It was the fear of mortality.

However ironic this kind of courage is, to the ten-year-old confronting an intimidating opponent its significance was positive and real. As I fought through my physical fear to tackle my antagonist on play after play, I discovered that I was not hurt, that I could meet the challenge—that I could survive. I made no impact on the guy with the ball. He slammed into me as hard on the tenth play as he had on the first. I saw no new respect in his eyes after I had dragged him down a dozen times. I did not even actually fear him any less when lining up for the last play of the scrimmage than I had on the first. But I feared my fear a whole lot less. I realized that it did not paralyze me, and that the reality of what I feared was less terrible than the expectation. I learned that I could live with my fear of getting hurt, of being overwhelmed by a superior opponent—that I could become surprisingly comfortable with such fear and even turn it to my own advantage. My fear actually gave me the power to deal with the fear. I received my own version of a red badge of courage when I split the entire leg seam of my jeans on one tackle. Here was the physical proof of the force of our collisions, and I wore those jeans the rest of the day with pride. They gave me bragging rights, but they also more privately signaled to me that what I had feared had indeed been fearful, but that I had not flinched.

That afternoon taught me lessons that served me during my entire football career. Through high school I was physically overmatched only a few times, in college and the NFL quite frequently. I performed best when I felt I was an underdog, when my opponent was bigger or faster, or when my opposition in a practice scrimmage or drill was the very teammate who was starting ahead of me. The fear I felt in such a position gave me added strength; the need to prove once again I was not incapacitated by the fear gave me even more. It even became my regular strategy in mentally preparing for a contest to construct the coming game in these terms. If I had no good reason to fear, I manufactured one. If my opponent was smaller than I, I told myself he was going to be so quick I would have a hard time just catching him. If he was bigger, I told myself he would completely overpower me unless I was prepared. When I entered the game, and handled my man on the first couple of plays, I experienced a surge of confidence that carried me through the day. This was the same confidence that I first experienced in discovering I could tackle an eighth-grader who outweighed me by twenty pounds.

On that afternoon in the fifth grade I also discovered for the first time what a private experience playing football was. For me the real drama of that scrimmage was the inner one in my own psyche that involved essentially just me and a single opponent. I was aware of the presence of ten teammates and ten more players on the other side, but they were immaterial to the real contest. I did not know if any of my teammates felt about the opposing running back in the same way I did. I did not know if that scrimmage was as significant to them as to me. Football may be *the* team game, in which the cooperation of a group is essential to successful play, but football never stopped being for me an intensely private experience as well. It was not just that I had my own responsibilities on any given play, which I had to execute successfully for my role to mesh with those of ten others. In addition to that obvious fact, and in addition to the distinct pleasures that playing with a group of teammates produced for me, my involvement in football was also intensely private. The sport in all its phases—practices, games, off-season training—meant things to *me* that I did not share with all those I played with. The game might have had a very similar importance to many of my teammates, but those private pleasures and pains were not the ones we talked about.

Already at that early age I began to think of "toughness" as my dominant quality as a football player. In their own ways many of my friends on the team were working toward a similar understanding of their relationship to the peculiar fears and kinds of courage that were a part of the sport. Unfortunately, there was a negative side to this discovery of what we considered courage. In our self-satisfaction over having passed certain tests, we could too easily feel ourselves superior to those we decided were not tough enough for football. In the eighth grade my team had only thirteen players. We were well coached by Carl and Marty Ota, but practices, obviously, were a problem. While the offense ran its plays, the two remaining team members lined up on defense at the point of attack. Not ideal preparation for games.

A major reason for our paltry number was the fact that many players had quit the team. Or had been driven off. On one occasion after the season was already under way, we convinced two classmates to try out as running backs. They were both part of that nondescript group in our eighth-grade class undistinguished for athletic, academic, or social abilities. Now, we wanted their help, but perhaps we wanted more to prove that they were not worthy to join our elite thirteen. The initiation of our two classmates was meant to discover their toughness, and consisted exclusively of tackling practice—with us doing the tackling. The thirteen of us lined up and one after another took our shots at the two newcomers. We faced each other about six yards apart; on the signal the coach flipped the ball to the back and the defender sprang forward to tackle him. We cheered each other's good hits—the ones in which shoulder pads met thigh pads with a resounding pop and dumped the runner on his back. We were waiting for our new recruits to cry out, to feign an injury, grabbing an ankle or knee and announcing they could not go on. But

a strange thing happened. They did not quit. In their eyes we
did not read fear but determination. When they were solidly
popped, they got up again to await their next turn. They broke
tackles and drove through the defensemen as often as they were
driven back. We grudgingly came to admit to ourselves that we
were not such an exclusive group after all—that these two
fellows to whom none of us paid much attention on the school
grounds were every bit as tough as we were.

The next day, however, the time for practice arrived with no
sign of either of our new teammates. No one was able to report
any reason for their absence, but deep inside we were confirmed
in the opinion we had wanted to hold all along. They could not
take it as we could.

Our two running-backs-for-a-day disappeared back into their
anonymity at school. They disappeared, too, from my own
awareness, only to return years later when I could wonder about
what damage we may have done in our immature machismo. At
an age at which the truly or supposedly untalented began to be
more clearly weeded out from the talented, the achievers from
the nonachievers, we found through football an arena to pass
such judgments on ourselves, but on others, too. I do not know
what happens afterward to those who become relegated in our
minds—and more unfortunately in theirs—to the slag heap of
the poor or nonathletes. It seems always the fate of such persons
to be ignored or unknown. Maybe they are toughened by adver-
sity, as we platitudinously like to assure ourselves. But maybe
not.

Proving or not proving physical toughness is not the only self-
discovery young boys make on football fields. Through football I
learned many things about that fascinating machine I carried
around with me: my body. In wind sprints during practices I discovered I was pretty fast for my size, but not as fast as a couple
of others. In tackling drills I learned how my body could be
used as a force—how my shoulders, back, hips, and legs driven
in a straight line against a ballcarrier's thighs could topple him
easily. As early as nine years old, I began to know my own body
in ways that only an athlete or dancer knows it. I discovered
limits—how I was quicker or faster than these particular players
but slower than those, bigger and stronger than some but not

than others. For eighteen years I continued to discover and to test such limits, learning to compensate for weaknesses and exploit strengths. An athlete's body becomes a mechanism which he views with some detachment, conscious of any malfunction no matter how minor, always aware of what the body can and cannot do. At ten, eleven, twelve years old I was discovering primarily what I *could* do; maturity, which came later, involved learning and accepting what I could not.

Both limitations and overcoming limitations can be discovered on the football field, and on occasion the surpassing can be so extraordinary that the only possible response is wonder at some mystery fleetingly glimpsed. Athletes in all sports experience moments of almost mystical transcendence. Friends in other sports have told me about their days of perfection, their games or parts of games in which they were virtually superhuman. One, a basketball player, has described how at times that little hoop, barely wider than the ball's diameter under normal circumstances, seemed as large as a peach basket. He saw everything with perfect clarity; from any spot on the court, whether he was open or tightly defended, he saw that circular rim gaping out to him, ready to swallow up any ball he should throw at it. The game that often seemed frantically confused became utterly simple; his play became effortless. Golfers, baseball players, gymnasts, all have such moments when they seem to transcend human limitations. The better athletes have many such moments; all have some. Even offensive linemen. In college and the pros, I tended to think of pass blocking as the equivalent of a dogfight. I was to obstruct the defensive lineman's path by whatever desperate means were necessary, until the quarterback could release the ball. But at times, not at all as frequent as I would have liked, I felt impregnable as a pass blocker. In the flurry of arms grabbing and heads butting, I saw every move coming as if in slow motion, with plenty of time to parry each blow, to counteract every tactic. To an onlooker all that could be seen was four or five seconds of frantic combat ending in stalemate, but my inner clock on these rare occasions kept different time.

My first experience of this type happened in the sixth grade. We were nearing the end of a routine practice session in the public park where we played for lack of our own school field. Other local kids had been playing a pickup game of touch football nearby, but had departed as dinnertime neared. Behind one end of our practice field, the slides and swings and jungle gym for the younger children had stood abandoned for some time. The entire playground—baseball diamond, football field marked out in the outfield, children's play area—was left to us alone as we scrimmaged well into the growing darkness. The October weather was ideal for football, crisp without coldness, dry with just a hint of humidity. As often happened, our coach, Carl Ota, had taken over as quarterback for the last series of downs. He had been a fine player at Gonzaga Prep, and at twenty-one was in excellent physical condition, still lean and strong. As a coach of eleven- and twelve-year-olds, he must have been frustrated on occasion by our inability to reproduce on the field the plays as he conceived them in his imagination, or remembered from his own recent playing days. In the last few plays of the scrimmage, he played quarterback, perhaps trying to match conception and execution a little more closely.

In the faint light of an expiring day, I lined up at right end for what had to be one of the last downs. In the huddle, Carl had not called one of our set plays, but had told me simply to run straight down the field on a fly pattern, and he would loft me the ball. Perhaps in his mind's eye he was going to be Y. A. Tittle for just one play, even if his supporting cast was only a bunch of sixth-graders. As I glanced down the scrimmage line I could not even clearly distinguish the ball, but in the stillness of coming nightfall I had no difficulty hearing Carl's signals barked out above the faint sounds of passing traffic. On "two" I sprinted out of my stance, racing down the field oblivious to any pass defenders, seeing virtually nothing at all. But somehow I was not troubled by the lack of visibility. I simply ran and ran. After several seconds I stretched out my arms . . . and the ball dropped neatly into them from forty yards upfield. The feat seemed nothing short of miraculous. But more astonishing yet was the fact that I had *known* I was going to catch the ball. I had reached out my arms, without ever having seen the ball in flight, at just the instant before it floated over my shoulder. I had known it was there. Without seeing it. But knowing it. That play ended practice for the day and left me stunned by an unarticulated awareness of some mystery in which I had just participated. Only "mystery" could describe it. I knew my catch had not been merely lucky, yet I knew no other way to describe it. Football can be explained by the laws of physics—by trajectories of balls, angles of impact, laws of force and momentum. But football, like other sports, is also an art, and sometimes the sweaty muse that presides over the game inspires inexplicable wonders. That ball dropping surely into my outstretched arms gave me my first fleeting experience of the mystery that is simply a part of athletics, one of the major reasons for many individuals' commitment to their sports. As a sixth-grader I had not yet fully discovered the limits that my own body had placed on me, but already at that early age, on grade school football fields, I was becoming dimly aware both of physical limitations and of the possibilities of transcending them, if only momentarily.

The following year, another incident on the football field—in which I gained another badge of courage, this one truly red—was memorable for very different reasons. In the seventh grade, in a game against archrival St. Augustine's, I felt a sudden pain in my left knee after tackling the opponent's quarterback. I was startled to see a red splotch appear on my white football pants, but I was too dazed at first to tell anyone. Finally, a teammate, wondering why I had not joined the defensive huddle, noticed the blood and called time out. Two friends helped me limp to the sidelines, where my injury could be checked.

Peeling back my pants revealed a quarter-sized hole next to my kneecap. The back I had tackled was missing a cleat from his football shoe, leaving an uncovered metal screw that had punctured my knee. By this time, after several minutes on the sidelines, I had sensed that my wound was only superficial, and I began to experience a certain odd pleasure. My teammates hovered over me in concern, marveling at the glimpses of white ligament and bone exposed by the injury. In their eyes I read fascination, horror, compassion, and disgust. One teammate turned away visibly sickened; our coach issued sharp orders to another player to bring a towel that could be torn in strips for a bandage. Never before had I been the center of attention in quite so conspicuous a way; *I* was the owner of that nifty little hole in the knee.

The best was coming. My wound bound, again with two teammates supporting me under my shoulders, I was helped across the field, past the stands of anxious spectators, to the parking lot beyond for a ride to the hospital. As I neared the stands I heard perhaps the sweetest sounds that can strike the ears of a twelve-year-old—*my own cheer*, chanted by those most lovely of older women, the eighth-grade cheerleaders. "Two, four, six, eight, / Who do we appreciate? / Oriard, Oriard, Oriard!" Sweet ecstasy! I played the part of a fallen warrior well —bearing up uncomplainingly under what I hoped others would assume was intense pain.

The only hitch was my mother. I was set down next to the school building while my father was sought to drive me to the hospital, when I looked up to see my mother bending anxiously over me. Into my masculine world of coaches, teammates, opponents, and pain—with those feminine cheerleaders lending support only from a proper distance—now appeared the ultimate female in my life.

"What happened? Are you all right? Where's a doctor? Is it serious?"

It was difficult to maintain my illusion of epic grandeur with my mother hovering over me, asking such reasonable questions. In all the movies I had ever seen in which stricken warriors were carried away from battle, or football games on television in which injured players were helped to the sidelines, no mother had rushed in to offer comfort. Her presence made my condition less heroic, more domestic—and I wanted no part of it. Had my father alone driven me to the hospital, we would have discussed the game and my injury as men. Sharing a common understanding of football. With my mother along, I became just a hurt child.

My resentment at my mother's intrusion was unfair to her. But at twelve years old I had long ago absorbed the notion that football was a man's world for which I must prove myself worthy, and whose sacred mysteries were incomprehensible to females. Girls in general played no role in our football world, except as cheerleaders at the games. We did not even think of impressing them as a major reason for playing. The masculinity whose codes we were exploring was a particularly asexual kind, dependent most essentially on its freedom from feminine intrusion. My mother had to be excluded from my football world simply by virtue of her sex. What could she know about my manly sport? Having borne seven children over a twenty-year period, and largely raised us while my father worked impossibly long hours, she demonstrated a strength every day that was hidden from my awareness until I was much older. But to her football-playing son, my mother represented an opposing principle to my athletic world. She insisted that I practice at the piano for an hour *before* I could go to football practice, even if it meant doing so at six-thirty in the morning. She was concerned more about silly things such as my health than about my playing a starring role or winning the game. She even unknowingly embarrassed me five years later in high school, when she called my crusty old coach on the phone to express her anxiety about my injured hand, which had been stepped on during a game and had swelled to twice its normal size.

My mother has mentioned recently that she used to talk to me about Notre Dame when I was first becoming interested in football. And apparently she induced me to watch the movie *Knute Rockne, All-American* with Pat O'Brien and Ronald Reagan, which led to my fantasies of playing for Notre Dame. I remember none of this. At Notre Dame I could not recall how I had come to dream of going there; I thought I was the only student on the campus who had not seen the Great Movie. Football was what I watched with my dad and played with my male friends; it was much later that I realized my career gave my mother as much pleasure as it gave my father.

Neither of my parents pressured any of their children to meet certain expectations, whether in academics, music, or sports. Nor did they reward us with bribes when we earned this or that minor distinction. As a consequence we pursued our activities as our own interests dictated, and invested them with as much importance as we saw fit. Football became the great passion of my grade school years, but my parents' low-keyed response enabled me from early on to realize that it was not the sum of what was

important in my life. I have known too many football players
who did not understand that simple fact. In high school, in college, in the NFL I have known individuals for whom life was
just marking time between football games. But football always
ended for them much sooner than life did. They were left just
marking time. As a young athlete I did not always see so clearly
the proper relationship between football and the rest of my life.
I cried over lost games and forgot occasionally that success on
the field could not satisfy all of my desires. But my parents provided a stable environment which always brought me back to a
more balanced perspective, one that lingered with me as I grew
older and left home: football had to be fit into my life, not my
life around football.

My last grade school football game is the only one I remember very clearly. The opponent was St. Francis Xavier's and
at stake was the Catholic grade school league city championship.
We were confident. We doubted there was a grade school team
in the state that could whip us—an attitude based on imagined,
not real, ability and on an absolute ignorance of the way football
was played anywhere outside Spokane. At thirteen all things
seemed possible—to middle-class white kids anyway. The real
world would disabuse us soon enough; perhaps it began to do so
on this day. Xavier's had two ends, John Bowman and Al Naccarato, who were faster by several steps than anyone on our
team. St. X.'s strategy was simply to dump the ball to either of
them a few yards beyond the line of scrimmage and let them
run. At our level of competition, superior athletic ability was obvious, and Bowman and Naccarato made us look inept all afternoon. They scored only twice, but it seemed that my view of the
entire game was from a sprawled position on the turf as I
watched their receding heels.

The loss was not devastating. My grade school career ended
as my college and pro careers would end. Only in high school
did my team win its final game. But of all the levels I would experience, it was only in college that the final loss delivered a
crushing blow. As eighth-graders we quickly found excuses for
our defeat to restore our sense of invincibility—in the time-
honored way of immature losers everywhere. My teammates
were no more fully aware than I of what was truly at stake in

our football playing. For myself, I had completed five formative years playing a game that was beginning to assume a large role in my self-identity. My life encompassed much more than football: I was a serious student who loved to read and learn; I had become a competent pianist, even winning an award in the Greater Spokane Music Festival for playing a Beethoven sonata; and I enjoyed a full and normal home life with parents, five brothers and sisters at this point, and neighborhood playmates. But football was becoming more than a hobby to me. I had played end and tackle with reasonable proficiency, and was considered by my classmates a good athlete. I took some pride in that recognition. Less obviously, the clarity of the football world was already exerting its appeal. My peer relationships troubled me at times; as a top student I felt sometimes admired, sometimes resented. At times I was full of excessive self-importance, at others I felt myself a rejected outsider. Even on the football field I could feel estranged from certain of my teammates. During one period in the eighth grade, I became involved in a silly rivalry between the right and left sides of our line that masked deeper animosities and bad feeling. But on the football field I could deal with such anxieties, resentments, and insecurities in a direct way. Once I donned my shoulder pads and helmet, I knew what was expected of me. The game was more "real" than reality. Blocking and tackling, however difficult at times, were neither confusing nor complicated. The object in our football games was never as ambiguous as it often was in our everyday world. We were simply to try to win the game, playing by straightforward, clearly understood rules. For all of its spiked knees and egos, football created a comfortable world to grow up in for one who could meet its requirements. My reasoned plans for the future vaguely included college, graduate school, a profession. But my *dreams* for the next few years were more immediate and clear: I wanted to star for the Gonzaga Prep Bullpups.

TWO

Hey, Look Me Over

I WENT TO GONZAGA PREP to play football. I also planned
from the beginning to study hard, get good grades, become involved in a variety of extracurricular activities, lay the founda-
tions for college. But those things I could take for granted. Having been a good student in grade school, and having a brilliant
older brother as a model to follow, I would have been surprised
had I not found myself somewhere near the top of my class. But
football was different. Football offered the challenge of uncertainty, an answer to self-doubts perhaps, a possibility of achiev-
ing some kind of heroic distinction. Hoppy Sebesta had been my
first Prep hero, but others had followed him; this was big-time
football in my book. There was no guarantee that I would be
able to cut it.

Football also was particularly important because my brother,
Flip, two years ahead of me in school, did not play it. Football
at Prep was what *I* did, not what my brother and I both did.
Part of my motivation to succeed at football was a desire to establish my own identity separate from my brother's, to stake out
my own little territory in which I could be lord instead of vassal.
We had competed incessantly as kids, but Flip had always won.
All those childhood experiences of losing to my brother at races,
losing at cards, losing at any number of sports, from Ping-Pong

to bowling—but continuing to hope and to try again—disposed
me to expect success only with difficulty and not to be surprised
or overly disheartened by temporary failures. I had never de-
spaired of ultimately competing equally with my brother, because somewhere I had picked up the idea that, because I was
big for my age, it was just a matter of time before I overcame
Flip's advantage in years. This confidence in ultimate success became habitual with me, and carried over onto the high school
football field.

Success did not come immediately. In my first year I did not
even earn a starting position on the freshman team; as a sophomore, I remained a backup lineman for half the season. My high
school career began with a death—the heart attack of my B-
squad coach. The first act of his successor, who was one of our
Jesuit teachers, was to assess his material through a full day of
"slaughter practice." That term was applied to any number of
blocking and tackling drills; the particular one on this day was
set up in this manner: Four blocking dummies were laid lengthwise in a row three yards apart. The spaces between the dummies represented the holes through which a ballcarrier could run
—up the middle, off guard, off tackle, and around the end. On
one side of the bags were lined up a blocker and a ballcarrier,
who were given a signal to send them through one of the holes.
Opposing them, on the other side of the dummies, was a
defender who had to mirror their movements until they committed themselves to a hole, at which point he was to take on the
blocker and tackle the runner. Such drills were intimidating in a
way, because failure was obvious and embarrassing. But they
became one of my greatest pleasures, for I had no fear of contact, and I loved to dominate my opponents physically in a public arena. Such dominance was a salve for the many wounds my
adolescent ego received during my high school years.

I played my fiercest, most determined football in such drills
when I was pitted against teammates playing ahead of me. I was
never ostentatious, grunting and growling or exulting in good
hits. Rather, I was as tight-lipped as a religious fanatic, my crusade to prove myself every bit as holy to me as his faith to him.
On the football field I could project onto my opponents all of

my own frustrations and angers and self-doubts. I didn't like my long gangly body or the acne-marked face I saw in the mirror. With my Catholic scrupulosity I was troubled by my emerging sexuality. I felt awkward around girls, too unsure to seek out their company, but frustrated by my retreat into the sexless environment of my all-boy high school. I envied my peers who seemed self-assured, who appeared to share none of my own anxieties and insecurities, who were more socially successful than I. On the football field I was licensed to vent my troubled feelings in unambiguous, carefully regulated physical actions, and I could do so without guilt. Behind my face mask, encased in concealing pads and uniform, I could remain anonymous while working out my most deeply personal frustrations, compensating for them by dominating others if I could. In playing football in high school, I was continually enacting a basic psychic drama: the need to prove my significance.

On that first day in my sophomore year under our new B-squad coach, I made my initial impact on the consciousness of my peers and coaches. Moderate rain continued uninterruptedly throughout practice, as we went through blocking and tackling drills for two hours. The more it rained the muddier grew the field, and the muddier we became until we seemed ourselves simply masses of the slimy earth infused with life. We were no longer separate from the elements but part of them—part of a conflict of natural forces. I was invincible that day. In my first turn, I lined up opposite a classmate of about my size, a starter at tight end. On the coach's signal, I pulled sharply parallel to the bags, turned into the hole, and drove into the would-be tackler, forcing him to one side while my ballcarrier ran untouched through the other. Coach Albrecht told us to go again, revealing little emotion. We took our positions, dropped into our stances, awaited the signal. As I sprang out of my stance, I felt a sense of control over my life that eluded me off the field. No one existed for me but myself, the defensive player preparing to meet me, and the disembodied voice of the coach waiting to pass judgment. As I moved, my eyes never left the midsection of my opponent, into which I would bury my head and shoulder. I was an eagle intent on a rodent hundreds of yards below as I swooped in for the kill. I felt powerful, utterly confident, unstoppable. As I turned into the hole, I dipped my shoulder and drove it directly into my man's breastbone, following through with my legs until I dumped him on his back. The moment of impact did not produce a physical sensation so much as a psychological one—triumph, superiority over a teammate who was supposed to be a better player. Vindication. As I picked myself up off the ground, shaking mud from my hands, I knew that should we have repeated the play twenty times, the outcome would have been the same.

After the play, I switched over to the defensive side. Other teammates took their turns before me, but I watched their successes and failures through the detachment of my self-absorption. I felt alone, not part of a team; I was trying to prove my right to that role. Finally, I came to the front of the line. Opposite was a tackle, another first-teamer. I felt loose, invigorated, anxious for the play to start. My wet, muddy uniform felt wonderfully heavy and comfortable; I was well beyond the point at which the rain and mud felt unpleasant and unfamiliar. I dug my feet and hand into the soggy grass. On the signal, I jerked out of my stance, moving down the line, mirroring the blocker's actions, itching impatiently for him to commit himself, so that I could leap forward, throw him aside, and drive the ballcarrier to the ground. When he turned upfield, I charged low, drove under his shoulder pads using my leverage to neutralize his force, then stuffed him into the runner's path and wrestled the ballcarrier to the turf. Although I was on defense, I took the offensive; I was a force, not just an obstacle.

"Good job, Oriard," the coach yelled.

I did not even shake off the mud this time. I wanted to wallow in slop, to spread my arms and expose as much of me to the rain as possible—to be drenched with water, coated with slime, enveloped by the elements.

I went back to the offensive side. Waiting in line between plays was torture. I wanted to go on every play, to prove to every person on the field that I was the king of the hill who had been ignored too long. I listened to the sounds of football practice all around me: the grunts of the players, the shouts of the coach and those waiting in line, the thud of pads and suck of cleats leaving mud and occasionally the smack of a body hitting wet turf. But the sounds did not seem so much around me as *in* me. I had absorbed them all.

In my next try on offense I repeated several turns in a row, as I embarrassed one of the starters. The first time, I moved him easily out of the way for my running back to skirt through the hole untouched. The next time, I drove squarely into the tackler, raised him slightly, as if impaled on my shoulder pad, and dumped him heavily, burying him completely with my block. The coach barked his approval, then growled at my victim to do it again—and again and again until he did it right. But no one could do it right against me on that day. If the footing was slippery, I didn't know it; if I was growing tired, I didn't feel it; if the temperature was dropping as dusk came on, I was oblivious to it. There was only I and that single individual across the line.

My teammate was forced to line up against me five or six times, while I overpowered him on every play, feeling no compassion, only exultation. After the last, I looked into his eyes and saw helplessness, resignation. I was only more satisfied. In the classroom, in the school hallways, he was a person, an individual, not a friend but at least an acquaintance. But here on the football field, he was only a reminder that I was on the second team, he on the first. In the hallways I could not show my resentment and envy of the fact that he seemed self-assured while I was insecure, that he was "cool" while I was not. On the football field, I could express those resentments without even admitting that I was doing so. We confronted each other as football players, not as human individuals, but the resulting satisfaction fed my very human needs.

I became a starter on the B squad and our new coach passed on the word to the head varsity man that he had a prospect for next year. This was how I earned my early status on the football team; such afternoons and such drills became a primary experience in playing football. To outsiders there may have seemed something inhumane, almost inhuman, about individuals simply attempting to overpower one another by brute strength, trying to *dominate* one another as if we were animals in a pack. All our finer human qualities—intelligence, sensitivity, compassion— were minimized in what may have seemed merely a struggle for animal superiority. But the competition of football was both more and less than such animalistic behavior. The dominance that I sought was psychological and private—only expressed in physical terms. The controlled environment of the football world channeled such needs into a relatively harmless outlet. Both blocker and tackler were protected by pads, what we could do to each other was clearly set out in rules, and the clash rarely resulted in real physical damage. We were competing for dominance in an ordered game, not in interpersonal relations or in social standing. I sought on the football field solutions to the anxieties of my adolescent life. Success in football did not transform my life off the field, but it provided a parallel existence in which I could feel myself a little more fully the kind of person I wanted to be: confident, powerful, impressive.

I was not always so invincible in slaughter practices as I was on that rainy afternoon. During the preseason of that year, while the sophomores were still practicing with the varsity, I had felt incapable of handling opponents whose superiority was so obvious and real. The top varsity linemen weighed only 190, but to me at twenty pounds less, that seemed a prodigious difference. Instead of moving confidently down the line to bury my shoulder in the other's midsection, I had carefully picked my way, then dived at the tackler's ankles, hoping to trip him up with little risk to myself. What I would have seen in the opponent's eyes I never knew; I never raised my own high enough to find out. On defense, I faced the doubly formidable task of shedding a 190-pound blocker, then tackling an equally large back. One running back in particular, Ted Gerela, whose brother Roy later became the Pittsburgh Steelers' placekicker, had frighteningly powerful legs. On one play I lined up in my defensive position, facing a blocker who was not among the team's stars, but who had Gerela behind him. On the signal from the coach, I pivoted out of my stance to move down the line, not with salivating anticipation but with uncertainty, even reluctance. As the blocker turned into the hole, I managed to meet him squarely and fend him off with my arms. But there was Ted Gerela nearly upon me. Half because I thought my only chance to stop him was to trip him up, but half because I feared those massive thighs, I dived for his feet. Big Ted ran right over me.

Yet, on the whole, I proved myself in contact drills to a series of coaches, and became a good football player by physical toughness and determination more than by innate ability. And I acquired a sense of my own powerfulness in doing so—a sense of power that gave me emotional and psychological security. Football offered a refuge; while I was trying to discover who I was off the field, at least I knew a little more clearly who I was on it. And I liked that person on the field pretty well. Physically dominating other football players was the basis of that feeling of self-worth; for all its possible unattractiveness such physical dominance had the virtue of being unambiguous. My triumphs had to be at others' expense, their successes at mine. But individuals humiliated on one day may triumph another; defeats as well as victories help us to fashion a clearer sense of ourselves. One friend of mine at another school quit football in his sophomore year with great anguish. He had an older brother who physically resembled him in every way, except in size. The brother was six five, 220 pounds by the time he graduated; my friend was five eight, 140. The brother was a great football player; my friend wanted desperately to be a great football player but he was simply too small. Our friendship became a little strained during our high school years when I was playing football but he was not. Whether he envied and resented me or not, I feared he might. We saw each other less frequently than formerly, and when we did, we studiously avoided talking about sports. But if his adjustment was a struggle, he bore no long-term scars. Having given up football with painful reluctance, he continued on in school as a top student and eventually achieved notable professional success. He compensated for whatever sense of failure football gave him, perhaps even turned it to his advantage.

Others undoubtedly fare less well from adolescent failures. Whether football has a positive or a negative impact on young athletes is impossible to judge by any sweeping generalization. Success or failure at football can have a more pronounced effect than similar experiences in other activities, because our culture invests the game with particular importance. But the variety of possible experiences and the adaptability of the individuals involved make football's impact on the players as diverse as they

are. Football neither transforms boys into men nor destroys
moral character. It neither guarantees future happiness for the
athletically successful nor dooms to misery those who fail. It
teaches different lessons to each participant; for me it created
important possibilities for self-discovery.

Joe Albi Stadium. Here, in the arena in which Hoppy Sebesta
and others had proven themselves before me, I was to debut in
my first varsity game as a junior before 8000 fans. To succeed or
fail in public.

Because two games with four different teams were played on
each Friday night in the fall, we could not use the limited locker
rooms at the stadium; our preparations for the contest began
back at our own schools. I ate an early dinner at home, anxious
to escape the familiar domestic scene for an environment more
appropriate to the seriousness of the evening. Driving the family
car across town to my school, I may have been a strange sort of
knight in this modern, technological world, but I had left home
with the exalted purpose of a crusader. As I drove through
traffic, stopping and starting as the lights dictated, mechanically
following the conventions of traffic safety, I felt that I must
somehow look different from the other motorists, that observers
could not help but notice in my steely gaze and tight-lipped expression a sign of my important mission. Surely they could tell I
was to start on both offense and defense tonight, as Gonzaga
Prep took on John Rogers High School.

Parking in the school lot, I strode purposefully into the familiar building. In the locker room, the strained silence of forty-five
self-consciously hushed individuals was broken only by stifled
clashes of metal lockers and shufflings of bodies and clothes, and
occasionally a terse whispered question. I was shocked to see
two teammates laughing secretively over some private joke, but
was reassured when I saw that the expressions on the rest of my
teammates' faces were properly serious. I undressed before my
narrow locker, taking off the reminders of my ordinary citizen-
ship in an everyday world, preparing to become reincarnated as
an inhabitant of a more exclusive, enchanted society where heroic deeds and martial courage were common. My shoulder

pads, hip pads, and other equipment were familiar from years
of playing football, but I also put on the unfamiliar blue-and-
white uniform that identified me for the first time as an honored
representative of my school. I had never before put on the over-
the-knee blue nylon socks. We were issued a pair of socks and
two thick rubber bands to hold them up, but no one had instructed me on how to put them on. Did my regular white cotton socks go over or under the blue ones? Was I to secure the
blues below or above the knee? Trivial questions, but crucially
important ones as I prepared for the coming contest not as a
game but as an entry into a longed-for world. Putting on my
football uniform was the ritual by which I could be transformed
into someone worthy to enter that world. To be improperly
outfitted would be shameful; to have the appearance of a hero
was the necessary prelude to performing heroically. I fumbled
with the socks, worked out a method that seemed reasonable to
me, but, glancing around me, I realized they were all wrong. As
quickly but as unobtrusively as possible I took everything off,
and began again, covertly observing how the seniors managed
theirs.

Our pants were solid blue, as were our jerseys but for the
white satiny numerals. The material was exceptionally heavy—
no light-nylon perforated jerseys like some teams wore. Our jerseys were ten or fifteen years old, and had been bought to last.
They were heavily mended; in a dozen places or more, snags
and tears had been restitched and holes patched, until each jersey became a historical artifact. Who knew how this jagged tear
on the left sleeve had been acquired, or this particularly large
patch on the back? How many touchdowns had been scored by
players in times past wearing this very jersey? How many game-
saving tackles had been made? How many game-winning
blocks? Despite the fact that my positions were tackle on offense
and end on defense, my number was 15; my school had not yet
entered the modern era in which backs wore numbers 1–49,
linemen 50 and up, ends 80–99, and so on. Although I was unaware how many illustrious 15's there may have been in the
past, I knew very well who had worn that shirt the year before.
His name was Fred Schultz and he had been an all-city tackle
and prominent member of our state championship team—facts

of great significance to me. Would I become another Fred Schultz? I had no way of knowing, but I fervently hoped so.

I also prayed that it might be so. Once uniformed, I padded on stockinged feet with the rest of my teammates to the school chapel, to pray for whatever favors we hoped to gain from the coming contest. The chapel was a small one, with twenty rows of pews on either side of a center aisle, before a simply ornamented altar. It was ideally suited for meditation on the eve of a heroic undertaking. I knelt briefly before a small shrine at one side of the altar, then took a place in one of the front pews. I prayed for victory, for a clean game, and for distinction. I feared that, having reached the threshold at last, I would fail the test that would mark me among the elect. I did not acknowledge my fears, but I prayed that I would meet the challenge that lay before me. Suddenly I was startled by the booming report of someone's gassy dinner—of a loudness possible only in the quiet of a church. Repressed giggles and laughs came from several of my teammates, shocking me with their irreverence. My concentration broken, I noticed for the first time that not everyone in the chapel seemed as intent as I was. One teammate who had been the grimmest of the grim-faced ones in the locker room, through which Coach Frazier occasionally wandered, was now joking with a friend in the back, where no coach could be expected to intrude. A few other twosomes and threesomes were engaged in quiet conversation; one pair seemed to be snickering at a teammate several rows ahead of them who was as solemn as I had been. I tried to brush these distractions from my mind. If the game tonight had not the same importance for all my teammates that it had for me, I could not let them deflect me from my own preparations. Nothing in my life seemed as important to me as the game that would start in two hours. I wanted all the divine help I could get.

On the walk back through the halls to the locker room downstairs, I was acutely aware that no one was in the school building but football players and coaches. We alone would represent Gonzaga Prep on the field in less than two hours. The honor of the school and the continuation of long-established traditions of excellence rested on me and my teammates—but particularly on me, I believed. If I should fail, I would be letting down my teammates, my coaches, my fellow students—even the many heroes of past Gonzaga teams. The charge, I felt, was a weighty one—and uniquely mine. My teammates would play well as a matter of course; only my own performance was questionable, it seemed to me. Back in the locker room I finished dressing by putting on my shoes and grabbing my helmet. Talk was still forbidden, but the noise level rose as four dozen pairs of cleated shoes clicked on concrete, and an equal number of metal lockers slammed in erratic sequence.

Our coach, who had been secluded from us in the coaches' locker room, now appeared, and gathered his young athletes about him. Bill Frazier was fifty-seven years old, in his twenty-sixth year of coaching at Prep. He was a cliché—a living stereotype of the crusty old coach who must have dominated football teams all over the country thirty years before, but he now was one of the few survivors of a nearly extinct species. His craggy face was deeply furrowed, he had a habit of baring his teeth in a thin-lipped grimace that seemed at times almost a snarl, and he growled rather than talked in a way that commanded instant attention. We called him "Fox" behind his back, but were coweringly submissive to his face. He was the quintessence of authority, and if we could not always like him, we understood that he was a teacher more than a coach, and a disciplinarian interested in imparting a way of life more than a way of playing football.

Coach Frazier's pep talk before this first game was of the same vintage as his grizzled countenance—the kind that Knute Rockne had immortalized four decades earlier. He reiterated the cardinal truth he had impressed upon his players for twenty-six years—that football was blocking and tackling, that if we went out there tonight and blocked and tackled, we would win. The message was already a familiar one to me, but it spoke directly to my hopes and fears for that night. Blocking and tackling were what I had to do; they had been what I had had to do in the fourth grade, the fifth, the sixth, the seventh, the eighth, the ninth, and the tenth, and they were what I had to do now to prove myself worthy of wearing the blue uniform I had put on

for the first time moments before. Blocking and tackling would
be the test of my toughness; I grimly vowed I would not be
found wanting.

Then the coach told us a story—about one of the small, hard-
nosed athletes who played for him in the thirties, the kind of
player he loved above all others.

"They didn't wear face masks in those days," the coach told us
in his raspy voice. "On one play Pete made the tackle, but he
caught a knee that splattered his nose all over his face. The
other guys on the team rushed over to him, and waved to the
bench to send in a substitute. But Pete shook them off.

"'Leave me alone,' he growled, jumping to his feet. 'That's the
way I like to play.'"

I listened with awe. The message was clear. My only doubt
was whether I would be as tough as Pete when the occasion
arose. But I swore to myself I would be. All around me, I sensed
a similar intensity charging up my teammates. As Coach Frazier
finished, we burst into a collective growl, leaped to our feet,
and, still shouting, clattered out of the building to the waiting
bus.

The twenty-minute bus ride to the stadium along darkened
streets allowed time for more meditation. As we pulled out of
the school parking lot I was leaving the security of the familiar
behind me, to encounter unknown challenges from an alien foe
in the stadium across town. A few of the bolder players broke
the hush with occasional grunts: "C'mon, we gotta do it!" "It all
starts tonight!" "We're gonna kick their butts!"—incantations to
call down the powers of the universe to our cause and to stir
ourselves up to the proper frenzy. There was a certain amount
of earnestness here, but also some posturing—players sending
signals to the coach, to let him know they were ready to play.
One of the players who had been most casual in the locker room
and irreverent in the chapel now appeared the most intense of
us all, growling with determination, taking upon himself the responsibility for inspiring his teammates. How phony, I thought,
but I dismissed him from my mind, to be alone with my own
thoughts for a few minutes longer. As I stared out the window,
seeing a faint reflection of myself and my teammates superim-
posed over passing scenes, I ran through the same litany of

thoughts and feelings with which I had been preoccupied for the past few hours. It was warm in the bus and cold out. Secure inside. Safe. While the bus continued to move I would remain in the anticipation of the coming game; once it arrived at the stadium I would be spewed out, to win or lose, succeed or fail, dependent only on my own ability and determination. Part of me was impatient to get there; the other part wanted the bus ride to continue forever.

As the stadium lights came into view my nervousness grew intolerable. Now I simply wanted to be off the bus, on the field, in the game. A long ramp led down to the field; at the bottom of it we huddled for a moment, then burst into a run onto the grass to the exploding cheers of our supporters. My first impression was of the expanse of white-lined greenness illuminated by banks of towering arc lights. For me there was always a slightly unreal quality to a football game played at night—the unnatural brilliance of the artificially lighted green grass, the vaguely indistinguishable rows of spectators behind both sidelines, and the darkness beyond surrounding the arena with peaceful nothingness, making the stadium seem the only center of life on an alien planet. To overcome feelings of puniness in a space so large, we filled it with our noise, not just the noise of our supporters clustered in the stands behind our bench, but *our* noise. During calisthenics we barked out the rhythmic counts, clapped and shouted between drills, asserted our presence in as many ways as we could. From an initial wide-eyed sense of the vastness of Joe Albi Stadium and of the rows of seats, crowd, cheerleaders, and concession stands, my focus now became intensely narrow. I concentrated on what I was doing as the sole orderly action within a bedlam of images and sounds. My teammates were a sea of blue around me, more than clearly differentiated individuals; the purple-and-gold-clad bodies at the opposite end of the field seemed more a sinister force than fifty separate opposing players. As I became accustomed to the sights and sounds of the pregame activity from my new perspective on the field, I was able to filter out the many distractions around me. I began to recognize the familiar. The lined field with goalposts at either end was the same field, after all, on which I had played grade school, freshman, and B-squad games. The opponents,

however more exalted they seemed as varsity players at a rival
school, were simply the eleven players who would oppose us
once the game started. The ball was the same, the rules the
same. I drew inward, blocking out the distractions, understanding even in this strange place the nature of the contest I
was about to engage in.

One particular sound did burst into my consciousness from
the surrounding noise. Our band and cheerleaders had broken
into the song, "Hey, Look Me Over," that had become part of the
standard repertoire of high school cheering sections in Spokane.
For some reason, the first two lines of our local version—"Hey,
look me over, / Give me a cheer"—grabbed me powerfully during my high school years. The catchy tune and my own personal
taste in music could not account for the song's appeal. The lyrics
sung by cheerleaders may have been mildly provocative to a six-
teen-year-old who could imagine no woman more alluring than a
high school cheerleader. But the real appeal of that song was
more personal and more deeply buried in my psyche. *I* was the
one about whom those words were chanted, as high school football provided the first occasion when I consciously placed myself
on public display. "Hey, look me over," I was saying to all those
people in the stands.

The game was a blur. It began with a team prayer on the
sideline, final instructions from Coach Frazier, a coin toss, a
whistle, and a kickoff. After two twelve-minute quarters we clattered up the ramp to the locker room for haranguing and encouragement, then clattered back down. After two more twelve-
minute quarters it ended with a gunshot, and the scoreboard
revealed that we had won, 28–7. The play itself—the object of so
much anticipation, of so much hopefulness and uncertainty—
was a blank space between clearly orchestrated buildup and aftermath. It was forty-eight minutes of actions and reactions
rather than of impressions and meditations. We ran the old belly
series off which we had essentially four plays to the strong side
and three plays to the weak. The quarterback could give the ball
to the fullback off guard, or he could put it into the fullback's
stomach and pull it out again to give it to the halfback off
tackle. Or, he could pull it out of the halfback's stomach and
keep it himself around end. Or, finally, instead of running with

it, he could throw a short sprint-out pass. The plays were called simply 11, 12, 14, and 15, and were run off basically just two formations. We operated out of a line unbalanced to the right—as left tackle I lined up next to the center—but for a little razzle-dazzle we could bring our split end to the left and line up in a conventionally balanced formation. Ours was the simplest offense in the city but over the years the most effective, because we executed it well. Our blocking assignments were as simple as our formations: we always blocked away from the hole and with an angle; whoever had no one to block pulled and blocked the first man outside the hole. This was the system of a coach who truly believed that blocking and tackling were the essence of football.

The bus ride back to school was marked by both jubilation and calm. Sweaty, grimy, grass-stained, I sat in the warm confinement of the bus, feeling a peace very unlike my nervousness of two hours earlier. The atmosphere was as boisterous now as it had been tensely quiet before: fierce warriors were now become boys again, laughing, shouting, and pounding the seat backs. I shared a little of the general exuberance, but my feeling was more a quiet satisfaction. I felt neither a star nor a failure; I simply knew that I had blocked and tackled well enough to compete on an equal footing with other sixteen- and seventeen-year-olds in the city. But that was enough.

After changing and showering I drove home not believing myself a hero, but feeling a new confidence and self-assurance. For now, that was all I needed. Later I would want more.

Toward the end of my junior season, playing against the best running back in the city, I broke free across the scrimmage line on one play, and met him head on. Someone had missed a blocking assignment, and I was so startled to find myself untouched in the backfield that I barely had time to react. But I lunged low with my shoulder into his knees, wrapped my arms behind his legs, and dumped him on his back. It was a most clear-cut meeting of force with force, and the fact that my force prevailed over so powerful an opponent filled me with intense pleasure. If I could tackle Rob Young, I could tackle anyone. For a moment I felt capable of doing anything I chose to do. After the season, when there was no longer any danger I might prove myself a liar, I began to imagine my coming renown as not just possible, but likely.

Thus my senior year began with great expectations. As a junior I had not felt fully accepted by the seniors, but now as a senior myself I had no superiors. I was a returning letterman and starter; that I would be a starter again and a key figure on the team was a foregone conclusion. My only uncertainty concerned the plateau of excellence I would attain this year in the climax of my high school career. I had now grown to six four and 195 pounds—very good size for Spokane high school football. On offense I had been moved from left tackle to left end; in our unbalanced formation this position made me as much lineman as receiver, but I would be included now on a few pass patterns. My possibilities for fame and glory had increased considerably. When my teammates voted me captain just before the season opened, I was not surprised. The selection confirmed my sense of destiny.

It lasted approximately eighteen minutes into the season. Midway through the second quarter of our opening game, I charged from my defensive right end position to stop a sweep. When the back tried to veer wide of me, I planted my left foot to sprint out to meet him. My knee turned but my foot remained planted. With a sickening pop, my plans for an untroubled year of successes crumpled with my body in a heap.

I did not know if the injury was serious. I tested my knee and felt a peculiar sensation of something missing under my kneecap. Or loosened. Like a door on a loose hinge that can swing open and shut but wobbles and grinds as it does. It hurt, but pain had already become a common element in football and my inclinations were to ignore it. Coach Frazier had an unambiguous response to any minor injury. "Rub a little dirt on it and get in there," he would growl. He indulged no one. "If it isn't broken, you can play on it," was the dictum we heard over and over again. Aches and pains were part of the experience of playing the game, and anyone who could not endure them was a mollycoddle who had no place on his team. Coach Frazier's attitudes confirmed my own code of mental and physical toughness;

I had borne many minor injuries uncomplainingly in the past. I now had one that I sensed was more serious, but everything in me was trained to treat it in the same way.

I played out the game. The weakened knee hampered my movements and remained a constant distraction. In the locker room at half time I told no one of the injury, but quietly nursed it myself, paying little attention to the coaches' instructions for the remainder of the game. The second half passed as the last few minutes of the second quarter had. Routine plays became frustrating challenges again as I hobbled through my assignments, playing respectably despite the handicap, but feeling no elation or powerfulness. On the bus back to school after the 46–14 victory, I shared in none of the hilarity. I sensed only doom.

By the next morning my knee was swollen to twice its normal size, and a visit to an orthopedist confirmed my fears: torn cartilage. As I hobbled from the doctor's office to the bus stop, dragging my swollen and bandaged left leg behind me, tilting my body to the right and hopping to lift my stiffened left leg over the curb as I crossed the street, a confusion of emotions passed through me. My dreams of glory were as deflated as my knee was swollen. I had been exhilarated by the preseason write-up in the local newspaper, that referred to me as "a pleasant surprise" in my conversion to end, and as "a good target" and "a good receiver, too." I had read those simple phrases over and over, savoring them like a favorite candy. I had been on the brink of stardom. Now, instead, I had toppled back into oblivion. Twenty-four hours ago fame had been mine for the taking; now I could barely take a walk.

On the other hand, I felt a sort of peculiar pride—perhaps not really pride, but distinction—in that of all my teammates *I* was the one who had torn cartilage in my knee. In the seventh grade I had sat on the sidelines while my teammates and coaches hovered over me, marveling at the puncture in my knee. Now I would be the first Prep player in my memory to have torn cartilage—a fairly glamorous injury since it regularly befell college and professional stars, and received much attention from the media. I would join the ranks of wounded soldiers in John Wayne war movies, of fallen warriors in Greek and Roman

epics, of stricken heroes everywhere whose value is felt even
more highly by their followers because so painfully and poi-
gnantly taken from them. I would join dying Patroclus, El Cid,
and the Gipper in the pantheon of mourned and inspiring casu-
alties. In my romance of martyrdom part of me was strangely
complacent.

I also felt just a little relief. All pressures—self-imposed or
otherwise—were now removed. There was no longer any possibility I could fail to meet the expectations I had set for myself,
and that my teammates had created by voting me captain. My
failure to be named all-city, to be a defensive terror and an
offensive juggernaut, would now be excused by the appallingly
bad fortune of my untimely injury. I could live out the season on
what-might-have-beens, receiving consolation and regrets over
lost opportunities from all those around me. And I would have
to do nothing else to gain their tender regard.

I appeared at school on Monday, despondent, resigned, and
tragically self-pitying. I dragged my leg through the hallways
from class to class, responding to solicitations, "I don't know, it
seems pretty bad. Torn cartilage, you know." Passing by the faculty lounge, however, I was stopped abruptly by Coach Frazier's
bark.

"What are you limping for?"

"I tore cartilage in my knee on Friday, Coach. I thought I'd
come out to practice today to see how it feels." (I was playing
the stoic, realizing that anyone could see it was *very* serious and
that I was acting heroically to be upright at all.)

"Well, that's real big of you," Coach Frazier spat.

"Well . . . but . . ." I was dumbfounded. With a single comment my coach had reduced me to a sniveling whiner.

Starting that afternoon, my senior season followed none of the
scripts I had fantasized. Instead of unalloyed triumph or tragic
resignation, my last year of high school football became simply a
frustrating struggle. Monday began the longest week of the year.
In the training room my knee was poked, probed, twisted, and
examined—then wrapped heavily with elastic bandages and
tape. Coach Frazier and the trainer decided I would not practice
for a few days, but I would be present on the field to watch and
listen, to prepare at least mentally for the week's game. With my

awkwardly wrapped leg I hobbled along the practice field, hovering at the periphery of the groups of players receiving instructions from Coach Frazier and his assistant, Joe Waltner. As the groups broke, the players to return to their positions, I limped back to the sidelines or behind the huddle to be out of the way. I felt extraordinarily lonely and alienated. Watching my teammates doing what I could not, I became more acutely aware of my condition. I was not just a casual observer; that would have been easier. I was supposedly a member of that team on the field, but I felt less a part of it than if I had been only an interested outsider. I felt guilty for not having to endure another two-hour practice session as my teammates were doing. Even in my achingest, weariest moments as a player, I had the pleasure of sharing my physical tortures with the group around me. Now, my discomfort was very different from theirs; there would be no bond of shared experiences at the end of this afternoon. I felt physically helpless, but, even worse, I felt emotionally estranged in being forced to involve myself in practice in a way that only pointed out more clearly my noninvolvement. That evening my parents drove me to the home of a local beer distributor, who also provided therapy for injured athletes in the area. He treated my knee with ultrasound equipment and hot packs, but at the conclusion of the session I noticed no improvement. The bandages that I wore continuously had made the swelling subside to some extent—simply by forcing some of the fluid down my leg into my ankle. I saw my left leg as a grotesque *thing* grafted onto my body—like victims of elephantiasis I had seen pictured in *Time* magazine. Walking, sitting, lying, I remained acutely aware of my own fragility. The slightest twist sent pain shooting through my leg, but, worse, it left me conscious of my physical incapacity. Normal movements that I had taken for granted all my life were now severe tests of my capability simply to do them or to withstand the pain.

Tuesday, Wednesday, and Thursday passed as Monday had—with me hobbling forlornly through an afternoon practice, then trying to notice some improvement during my evening therapy sessions. Friday morning, I arrived at school feeling little healthier than I had felt five days before. At noon, three hours before game time, I stood on a table in the training room while Coach

Frazier, my therapist, and our school trainer examined my knee and pronounced me able to play.

That game was the first of eight I played that season on my heavily taped knee. The feelings of joyful anticipation and mastery with which I had begun the season the previous week had entirely disappeared. The game was played not under the cool lights of Joe Albi Stadium, but under an unseasonably hot afternoon sun on a parched high school field. Dust, glare, bulkiness, and sweat created the sensations of that game. Not the comfortable sweat of joyful exertion, but the unpleasant, prickling sweat of overheating. My week of inactivity had taken the edge off my conditioning; I was transported back to the first unpleasant week of preseason practice. My knee was still swollen, and the protective elastic wraps and tape created an elephantine mass at the end of my hip, which I was conscious of dragging about the field all afternoon. At my positions, barring pass plays, I was accustomed to operate in a fairly restricted space. As long as I could maneuver within a five-yard radius of the spot where I lined up, I could function adequately both on offense and defense. But I could never feel firmly planted in the earth as I dived to make a block or tackle; my fragile base made me feel more vulnerable, more detached from the ground, from which under normal circumstances I could push off for stability and power. More noticeably, any play away from me on defense might as well have been run on an adjoining field, for any chance I had of pursuing and helping on the tackle. And I was not even considered as a possible pass receiver; I could not have outrun any defensive back in the city. Never did a victory mean so little to me.

That first game after the injury was the worst, but it set a pattern for the others. My knee improved—the swelling subsided, and the pain grew less severe—but the heavy bandaging and the knee's weakness and susceptibility to reinjury continued to hamper me. I lumbered rather than flowed through that season. On offense I was an asset to my team on running plays, but on passes I offered little help. I caught five passes all year (three for short touchdowns, when I had sneaked underneath the coverage), but near the end of close games, the coach increasingly began to substitute for me—a severe blow to my ego. I had to watch from the sidelines as our split end made a diving catch for a 28-yard gain on fourth down and 21 from the opponent's 49, in a game we were losing 26–23. Three plays later we scored to salvage a 29–26 victory in the most suspenseful game of the season. Before the game for undisputed first place, Coach Frazier had delivered his most moving pep talk of my two years of playing for him. He told us about Ma French, a seamstress who lived near Gonzaga University when the high school was part of the same campus, mending band uniforms, the priests' cassocks, and whatever else needed repairing. Ma French, the coach told us, never went to a football game, but she stayed home saying her rosary and praying for the team as long as the game lasted. His eyes began to mist and his voice to choke up as he continued.

"Ma French died not too long ago. She won't be at home by the radio tonight, praying for you during the game. But I know that Ma French will be watching. When things get tough and you've got to have a little bit more, I want you to remember Ma French. Ask her for a little help. She'll be up there praying for you."

As Nick Scarpelli gathered in the 17-yard pass for the winning score with just over a minute to play, we on the sidelines began beating each other on the back and chanting, "Ma French, Ma French, Ma French!" She became our patronness for the rest of our games, the focus of an emotional season. In this first instance of her miraculous intercession, I shared my teammates' jubilation, but also felt lonely there on the sidelines, watching the drama in which I should have been a participant.

The cruelest hurt of all came in a midseason meeting in which we were reviewing films of our previous game. On one play our opponent had run a sweep away from me for a sizable gain. As we watched the film, my form appeared in the upper right-hand corner of the screen, lumbering across the field to help out on the tackle. "Here comes Lucille," chortled Coach Frazier as my teammates joined in his laughter—as if I were a hippopotamus in a tutu performing in an animated Disney film. The coach did not believe in the seriousness of my injury all season.

I played well at defensive end and was named all-city at that position. My dream was realized, but it had been tarnished; I did not *feel* as I had planned to feel in all of my fantasies. I had assumed that an all-city player was powerful and strong; instead I had felt anxious and cumbersome all season long. I probably deserved the award; in real terms my performance was not severely affected very much by my injury. I provided a solid front on the right side of our defensive line and stopped most of whatever came my way. But I did not feel like a dominant force; I felt vulnerable. I did not play effortlessly as I imagined great athletes played; I had to work hard, to struggle. And I could never forget about the crippled leg that seemed like an anchor always dragging behind me.

In the last game of the season, Coach Frazier planned to showcase my talents. He never told me this, but I realized after the game that he had decided to give me an opportunity to increase my chances for a major-college scholarship by producing an impressive game film to show recruiters. I had been an infrequent target as a pass receiver all year—partly because of our offensive system but more so for my obvious limitations—but in this last game, play after play was called on which I was the primary receiver. But the coach's good intentions toward me were frustrated by my own bad luck. That morning at school I had lost a contact lens in the washroom and had no replacement for it. In addition, I strained my knee again during the warm-ups before the game, and was more hobbled than I had been for weeks. Coach Frazier must have watched from the sidelines in disbelief as he saw pass after pass soar just over or through my hands, while I flailed away at it. I must have looked like a one-eyed, one-legged imposter, rather than a pass receiver. From *my* perspective, it was the most bizarre game of my career. I should have removed my second contact; instead of clarity *or* fuzziness, through my one lens and one naked eye I saw clear fuzziness, which made everything seem unnatural. As I ran on my reinjured knee, my left leg felt several inches shorter than my right. From my end position I wobbled through my pass routes, then managed to pick up the flight of the ball just as it sailed by, within easy reach. My personal clock ran several seconds slow all day. Finally, I suspect in exasperation, Coach Frazier substituted for me, and I played little offense for the remainder of the game. He had planned to make me a hero; instead I had played the fool.

On a Monday in late February, Coach Frazier barked at me with his customary disgust.

"Oriard, are you still limping like that?"

For once I had a satisfactory answer.

"I had surgery last Thursday, Coach. I had torn cartilage removed."

It was he who was speechless this time. He mumbled something incomprehensible and passed on. At last I felt vindicated.

Coach Frazier may have insisted on a little more toughness than was healthy, but he was even more adamant about the morality of playing cleanly. In many ways that did not become clear to me until long afterward, the frustrations of that season contributed significantly to the good fortune that attended my football career for eighteen years. In the nine seasons I had completed by this time, I had had few opportunities to develop an inflated sense of my self-importance. My parents had not driven me to expect spectacular achievements on the football field for their pleasure. My grade school coaches had not made the winning of football games the sole justification for my existence. Coach Frazier, for all his crustiness, regarded football as part of the education of his players, not as an end in itself.

The national press in recent years has revealed that such is not always the case in high school football programs. One Los Angeles team in 1980 built a 63–0 half-time lead, partly by seven on-side kickoffs to create more scoring opportunities, apparently to avenge a 49–0 pasting the year before. The opponents refused to return for the second half, claiming they feared for their physical safety. A high school coach in Austin, Texas, experimented with hypnotic tape recordings intended to build team morale, but perceived by some parents as "mind control." The voice on the tapes whispered into the receptive ears of the young players, "When you're playing on that football field you have such aggressiveness it's absolutely unreal." Another high school coach in Wisconsin awards one player after each game for the "Hit of the

Week"—the most vicious hit he can find on the game film. Such
incidents suggest a severely distorted perspective on the role of
athletics in the high school curriculum. Other, more bizarre
events defy explanation. In Dubuque, Iowa, in 1977 a high
school coach spray-painted a chicken gold to represent the
"Golden Eagles" of a rival team, then threw it onto the field to
be kicked around by his players. "Get the eagle" was the name
of the game. The topper of them all was the coach in Eau Gallie
(Oh Golly?), Florida, who psyched his players by biting off the
heads of live frogs, and by cutting his own shaved head with a
razor. According to the coach, "Our kids love it. They say, 'Look
how wild the coach is; let's get wild, too.'" The coach apparently felt unjustly criticized for his tactics. "Last year we
were winning," he explained. "People would have loved it. But
now we're losing, and certain intellects will use this as an excuse
to pick on football. We didn't have a kid over two hundred
pounds last year, but we screamed and hollered and we beat the
hell out of everybody we played except Merritt Island." I guess
it's okay then. The most unfortunate note in the entire incident
was the justification by the school principal. After defending the
coach personally, the principal put the entire matter in perspective: "A lot of coaches have their own crazy way of doing things,
and I'm sure there are things that go on every day at a lot of
schools that wouldn't go on if they were made known to the public. Coach Canaday's status here is just what it has been. We
dedicate our efforts to our kids, and that's what we'll continue to
do—frogs or no frogs." It is reassuring to know that the kids'
welfare came first.

"The kids" in such situations may have little control over their
perspective on the importance of football in their lives. For me,
the entire support system during my early football career guaranteed that the sport would be a *part* of my life, not its primary
purpose. In high school, the rigid discipline with which Coach
Frazier ran his program was consistent with the educational philosophy of my Jesuit teachers. Because a major element in their
approach to schooling insisted on the training of the whole person—mind, spirit, and body—sports such as football were not
perceived as activities separate from the academic curriculum
but as an integral part of it. My senior class graduated five

straight-A students; two of us were starters on the football team and three played tennis. There was no separation in my class between jocks and scholars. The fact that I was valedictorian of my graduating class and captain of the football team was entirely consistent with the goals of my Jesuit education. My teachers insisted on an intellectual rigor in the classroom that matched the physical rigor demanded by the coach on the football field. *Discipline* was a key element in both spheres.

Young players must be allowed to determine football's importance without excessive external pressures. Small-town newspapers in particular can far too easily feed an unhealthy overemphasis on high school sports. As the school's football team becomes the focus for the town's identity, the local papers commit more and more coverage not just to the games but to profiles of the individual players. This tendency may be worst in those football hotbeds in the South and elsewhere that have gained notoriety in recent years, but I cringe when I pick up the newspaper in my own town, and see yet another full-page story-with-photo on the front of the sports section, profiling a local high school athlete. The boy's clichéd feelings about the upcoming Big Game with a nearby rival are chronicled in as much detail as is given the President's last press conference. His most banal observations are treated with the same seriousness accorded the statements of SALT negotiators. One recent article focused on a rival running back who had moved away from town and was returning to play his old friends. His comments were reported as major pronouncements—his desire to avenge last year's defeat, his expectations for the coming game, his plans for his former teammates. About his best friend, who would now be an opponent, he observed: "I hope I get to play a lot of defense against Crescent Valley because I want to get after Troy. I want him to know I'm around." All boys playing high school football have such attitudes; they are entirely appropriate to juvenile sports. But to showcase such adolescent chest-thumping in the local press invests the games with a distorted significance. That same season saw articles about the opposing quarterbacks of the crosstown rivals—emphasizing what good kids they were—and portraits of a wide receiver and a converted fullback (who vowed he would "try to hit people and run

over them"). And so on. The worst was an article in early summer about the outstanding prospects from the *freshman* class.
Making celebrities of fifteen-year-olds!

Such newspaper stories seem innocuous, and they serve local
interest in high school athletics, but they are potentially dangerous to the profiled athletes. A seventeen-year-old boy who sees
his picture and several columns of copy about him on the front
of the sports page is liable to begin thinking of himself as a very
important person indeed. The danger here is what I have come
to think of as the *Rabbit, Run* syndrome, after John Updike's
novel of that name. Rabbit Angstrom in the novel is a twenty-
six-year-old failure—a failure at marriage and in his other personal relationships, and a failure in his career—whose life
peaked when he was eighteen years old and a small-town high
school basketball star. Having been a hero at eighteen, he sees
the rest of his life as a long painful decline. The number of Rab-
bits multiplying each year is depressing to consider. Young athletes must assume some responsibility for their own lives, but
they can achieve balanced perspectives only with great difficulty
if they are constantly bombarded by reminders that athletic stardom is the most meaningful of all accomplishments. So many
factors—pushy parents, fanatical coaches, rabid fans, effusive
sportswriters—conspire to create a culture in which American
adolescents, desperate to discover who they are, decide they are
first of all *football players*. But with graduation, what follows?
College perhaps, and for a limited number a continuation of
their football playing. What then? A pro career? For only a very
few—and even for those a small number of years before they,
too, must accept the end of the game. Whether at eighteen,
twenty-two, thirty, or forty, *every* football career ends early. But
life goes on.

In high school, football became even more important to me
than it had been before. My culture made football seem important, but my parents and coaches allowed me to determine the
nature of that importance for myself. The game offered me
above all else my primary means of self-discovery. In the classroom I discovered new ideas and reconfirmed my commitment
to learning. I read Latin and Greek and Shakespeare, discovered
the fundamentals of chemistry and physics, studied history and

religion. But through football I discovered myself. And proved that self in a public arena. The world of my mind was a private one in which the risks I took and the advances I made were known to few outside myself. On the football field I bore public scrutiny.

If my football career at Gonzaga Prep did not transform me, it did contribute significantly to my developing sense of worth. But the frustrations and setbacks of my high school career also kept me rooted in the real world. I was vulnerable as well as powerful, lucky as well as unfortunate, neither as good as I hoped nor as bad as I feared. Football had played a crucial role in my high school life, and I wanted to continue playing. More specifically, I wanted to play for Notre Dame.

PART TWO

Under the Golden Dome

THREE

In the Land of Legends

THE PRESS GUIDE to the 1969 Fighting Irish football team included a particularly dramatic portrait of one of the seniors:

> Three years ago a gangly, seemingly uncoordinated sophomore-to-be walked onto the spring practice field, uninvited, unheralded and unknown by coaches and players alike. The lanky youth merely wanted the opportunity to "try-out" for the Irish football team. He was given the chance and, not illogically, he spent the next three springs and fall practice sessions on the preparation team. Suddenly last September, however, he began to catch the eye of coach Wampfler who noted some happy changes in the young man, both physically and artistically. And before the 1968 season was over, Mike Oriard not only was a member of the varsity, he was the team's starting center. . . .

Readers of this little scenario must have been reminded of nineteen thirties college football movies they had seen on Sunday morning television: the kind of movies that starred Jack Oakie as Boley Bolenciewicz, star halfback for old Clayton, who must pass his exams and foil the kidnapping plot of the mobsters to win the Big Game for his alma mater. Our hero this time is a gawky hick from a *Saturday Evening Post* magazine cover by Norman Rockwell who blossoms into a brawny football star. The final scene would find our still-modest lad carried off the field on

teammates' shoulders after a bowl-game victory, protesting
weakly, "Aw, shucks, fellas, it weren't nothin'.""

Unfortunately, the reality of my career at Notre Dame was
not so cinematic. I was a walk-on, yes. Gangly, perhaps. Seemingly uncoordinated, I shudder to think I so struck the coaches
or other players. After my modest success in the Spokane City
League, I was no blue-chip prospect, no member of a *Parade*
magazine high school all-American team. A Notre Dame alum-
nus in Spokane—the dermatologist who was treating my acne
(not exactly the stuff of Hollywood epics)—informed the coaching staff of my interest in playing at Notre Dame. I sent in an
application, together with some game films, and received a polite
reply that the team's scholarship quota had been reached. But
when Coach Parseghian invited me to come without a scholarship, and my father said he could afford the tuition, I accepted
the offer.

Over the next four years I worked my way through the ranks,
finding in my small success on the freshman team a measure of
encouragement that was quickly squashed by my first varsity experience. I did not even suit up for a game as a sophomore,
remaining on what was called the "prep team," the third- and
fourth-string units which played the role of the week's opponent
for the varsity. Just when my discouragement was becoming ter-
minal, I was switched from defensive end to center and given a
chance to play. By the start of my junior year I was on the second team; by the fifth game I was a starter; by my senior season
I was offensive captain. I was pleased to feel these accomplishments impressive, but they hardly defined the storybook career that the sports information office concocted.

However overdone, in many ways that cinematic publicity
blurb was entirely fitting, for football at Notre Dame has for
seven decades been played in the realm of myth and legend as
much as on the fields of intercollegiate competition. From the
autumn day in 1913 when a quarterback named Gus Dorais and
an end named Knute Rockne first revealed the possibilities of
the forward pass in upsetting a vastly superior Army team, to
the Four Horsemen, Johnny Lujack, John Lattner, Paul
Hornung, and countless other ND "immortals" in subsequent
seasons; to historic wins over Ohio State in 1935, Oklahoma in

1957, and Alabama in 1973; that little school in South Bend, Indiana, run by the Holy Cross fathers, has created more football history and nurtured more legends than any other university in America.

Two years before my own coming to Notre Dame in 1966, Ara Parseghian demonstrated that those legends, which had lain dormant for a decade, were not dead. Taking a team that had struggled through a 2–7 season the year before (spared a possible eighth loss only by the cancellation of the game following the assassination of President Kennedy), Parseghian unveiled a previously unknown passing combination of John Huarte (later my teammate in Kansas City) and Jack Snow, and guided the team to a 9–1 record—losing the national championship in a season-ending upset by USC. Ara's arrival on the ND campus had been greeted by several thousand cheering students who stood outside Sorin Hall in knee-deep snow and freezing February temperatures to hear the first address from the coming savior of their hallowed traditions. "We will win football games," he told them. They did indeed.

My first experience of the Notre Dame campus immediately impressed upon me the continuing vitality of those traditions and legends. Riding in the back of a taxi cab down Notre Dame Avenue toward the campus, I was entering a world that had seemed until then to exist only in my imagination. Dozens of towering maples stood on either side of the street—an honor guard at attention before the entrance to a magical kingdom. Through the trees on the left was a cemetery, whose gravestones and monuments suggested the resting places of heroes and fallen warriors from Notre Dame's past. Straight ahead, above and through the leaves and branches of several layers of protective trees, I saw the Golden Dome, crowned by a statue of the university's patroness, shimmering as brightly in reality as it had in my imagination. Any major university campus has its sacred shrines and holy places, but Notre Dame has them in abundance. There are literal holy places, such as the Grotto, where Dr. Tom Dooley liked to pray and meditate as a student before his self-sacrificing career in Southeast Asia—and a Tom Dooley Room in the student center commemorates the life and death of one of the university's most revered graduates. But there are other, in many ways more prominent, *secular* holy places as well. At one end of the South Quad stands Rockne Memorial, a red-brick structure built in 1937 to house handball courts, a basketball gym, and a swimming pool. "The Rock" is more than a site for classes in physical education, however, as Yankee Stadium is more than just another baseball park. To the eighteen-year-old freshman from Spokane, Washington, "the Rock" was a reminder that even lowly mortals from obscure regions of the country might tread the same ground over which the great Rockne himself once strode. Some sacred objects on the Notre Dame campus have been transformed into secular shrines to the football team for which the university, despite its other excellences, is universally known. Outside the library a sculpture of Moses with the right arm extended and index finger raised in an admonishing gesture is said by students on occasion to be indicating their team's number one ranking in the country. On the front of the thirteen-story library stands an immense mosaic of Jesus with arms upraised in benediction; to fans looking north from the stadium during a football game those arms could only be signaling a score. "Touchdown Jesus," he is somewhat irreverently called.

The stadium itself is the holiest place of all. A perfect oval constructed of red brick in 1930, Notre Dame Stadium is a monument to the heroic deeds and legendary players who created history on its grassy field. On my first view of the stadium I was awestruck—as one is awestruck at his first glimpse of that other Notre Dame in Paris, or of other edifices which stand as monuments to a fabled history. The stadium is in some ways more impressive in the absence of fans and players than it is on game days. Amid the cheering voices of 59,075 loyal domers, and the grunts and thuds of twenty-two players on the field, the noiseless presence of ghosts is more difficult to feel. But in its repose, as I saw it for the first time on a September afternoon in 1966, the stadium's walls seemed to reverberate with echoes of long-departed heroes. In the shadows of the spartan locker room, with its rows of plain benches and simple green metal lockers, I could imagine lingered the benevolent spirits of Bertelli, Hart, Sitko, Guglielmi—who used the very same lockers in which I would soon be hanging my clothes. In the tunnels under the stadium I could look up and see the beams added in recent years to support the sagging weight of the tons of brick and concrete completing their fourth decade, but holding up also much more —seemingly the legendary history of Notre Dame football. From my solitary seat on a wooden bench behind one end zone I could look down upon the flawless green of the playing field, and create in my mind a more perfect game than had ever been played. Lujack hands off to Gipp, who follows the block of mighty Leon Hart into the secondary . . . Sitting by myself as a freshman in that end zone seat, I dreamed of becoming a part of that Notre Dame legend.

How is it that a simple oval structure of red brick, and a boys' game played by undergraduates at a small Catholic school named in 1842 for Our Lady of the Lake, could come to mean so much, not just to me but to millions of my countrymen? What moved Grantland Rice to compare a foursome of pretty good running backs to the Four Horsemen of the Apocalypse? What moved a Hollywood producer to make a film about a football coach whose plea to his players passed on from a dying teammate to "win one for the Gipper" has become as famous as "I have not yet begun to fight," "Remember the Alamo," and other immortal calls to heroic action? If we add up all the games and all the players and coaches who have been part of Notre Dame football since 1887, the sum cannot account for the total impact Notre Dame football has had on American culture.

Football to a great many Americans is more than just a game. We tell dejected losers and coaches who believe that they must win at all costs that "it's only a game," but really we lie when we say that. Maybe hopscotch is "only a game," or perhaps hide-and-seek, but not football. It is possible, actually, that no *competitive* game—no contest between two individuals or groups of individuals in which a loser and winner will be determined—is "only a game" in the sense in which that phrase is used. Competitive games by their very nature are significant events in which one person's human capability is pitted against that of another: a winner or loser inevitably wins or loses something of value. This is certainly true of football. The opponents in a collegiate football game often represent different regions, different conferences, different traditions, different value systems, different religions perhaps; the winner of such contests wins more than the winner of "only a game."

Football is also more than just entertainment—no matter what players and particularly owners at the professional level would sometimes have us believe. Circuses are entertainment; movies are entertainment; opera, ballet, situation comedies, Grand Ole Opry—these are entertainment. Despite what Woody Allen claimed in a routine several years ago, the ballet *Swan Lake* could never be fixed. There could never be heavy money laid on the swan to live. Viewers of movies may temporarily accept the illusion that the characters and conflicts they watch are "real," but audiences always understand that the performers are actors and actresses, and that the outcome has been determined already and cannot be altered. The audience may not know if the hero is going to escape with his life, but it knows that the producer and director know. And it knows that even if the hero should die, the actor who plays him will rise to act again. Viewers of football games (or other sporting events) truly do *not* know who will win, even if Nebraska is playing St. Mary's College; and for the fans of both teams winning and losing matter. No watcher of a cop drama yells at the TV screen when the hero unwittingly walks into a trap, but countless football fans groan with real anguish when their team's star halfback fumbles in the last two minutes of a close game, and roar wildly when the winning field goal clears the crossbar as the final gun goes off. Even in his living room before his television screen, a real fan does not watch his favorite team from a lounging position on the most comfortable sofa, but literally from the edge of his seat, with a white-knuckled grip on the arms of his chair.

A football team gives fans something to identify with, and heroes to admire and emulate. In a society of complexity and rapid change, football is stable. One can be the fan of the same team for a lifetime; one can feel ties to history, to a tradition, to timeless values that are difficult to find elsewhere in our turbulent world. Ultimately—at some deep, unconscious level—football is mythic. It pits the forces of good against the forces of evil, with the outcome in doubt. America is too new a nation to have had mythic heroes: we look to no Achilles or Odysseus as our forebear. But Jim Thorpe and Red Grange, Jim Brown and

O. J. Simpson, perform the same heroic deeds that cultural heroes have always performed. Slaying dragons and monsters of more human proportions, they embody traits and achievements with which in our modern age we are still reluctant to lose contact.

Notre Dame football has a larger share in the mythology of the game than does any other college or university program in the country. Football *is* merely entertainment unless the spectator *cares* who wins; only then does it become more than "only a game." Quite simply, more people care about Notre Dame football than care about football played anywhere else. Football teams represent particular regions—usually states or parts of states. Notre Dame alone among major colleges belongs to the entire country. Unaligned with any conference, Notre Dame has long played a truly national schedule. Army, Georgia Tech, Iowa, and USC—or schools of similar geographical distribution—are on the schedule every year. Notre Dame has played often in all of the major media centers; Grantland Rice did not have to travel to South Bend to immortalize the Four Horsemen. Notre Dame's strongest appeal is to the Catholics who reside in every town and city in the land, but non-Catholics, too, at an early age become aware of Notre Dame, simply because Notre Dame is seen by more people in more parts of the country. In the South, those Yankee Catholics from South Bend are less appreciated than elsewhere, but even in the heart of Dixie diehard alumni and subway alumni keep the faith.

Undefeated seasons, all-American players, and thrilling victories have been necessary for the creation of the Notre Dame mystique, but legends are made in peculiar ways in modern technological societies. It was perhaps fortuitous that the unveiling of the forward pass by Dorais and Rockne in 1913 and of the Four Horsemen in 1924 took place in New York, where the top sportswriters wrote. The pen is uncontestably mightier than the sword in creating legends. Rockne as a coach was a genius at publicity. Who else in his era had one of his famous locker-room pep talks recorded for posterity? Coaching in the nineteen twenties during the Golden Years of sport in America—the decade of Babe Ruth, Jack Dempsey, Red Grange, Bobby Jones, even Man o' War—Rockne perhaps better than anyone else understood how to exploit the media. The Rock's untimely death in a Kansas cornfield in 1931 was tragic, but it assured his own immortality and that of the football team he had coached for thirteen seasons. Frank Leahy and other successors merely had to keep winning football games to perpetuate the legends.

However self-consciously the legend of Notre Dame football has been created over the years by reporters and publicists, the power of the legend is real and self-perpetuating. No school has been involved in so many classic games and historic upsets as Notre Dame. Whether ending Oklahoma's forty-seven-game unbeaten string in 1957 by a 7–0 score, or losing 19–13 to SMU the year before on a touchdown in the final two minutes, Notre Dame arouses emotions in her own players and in opponents that produce truly memorable football games. The series with USC has been particularly notable, but before Southern Cal there was Army and in recent years there has been Alabama. Somehow, more seems to be at stake in any game Notre Dame plays than in other intercollegiate contests.

As an eighteen-year-old freshman I came to Notre Dame fully conscious of the school's mystique. Whoever plays at Notre Dame becomes a part of Notre Dame history, and even if the press guide exaggerated the drama of my four years there, I was not unaware of the role I was playing. If the drama of my career at Notre Dame had much greater interest for me than it could have for any Hollywood movie mogul, it nonetheless had its drama—which was created less by what I did than where I did it.

I was introduced to Notre Dame much as other freshmen are. The campus itself provided the first overwhelming impression, with its two tree-lined quadrangles perpendicular to each other, forming an L along whose borders stood the academic buildings and dormitories; the pair of lakes on the north end, across which lay additional buildings and the road to St. Mary's, our "sister school"; and precisely in the center, the Golden Dome. Once I drank in these scenes, I began to encounter the people, and the first Notre Dame students I met were football players. With five friends from my high school, I had come to the university early for freshman orientation. The only other students on the campus were the football players who had already begun preparing for the season. One of my friends from Spokane reported that two of them lived across the hall from him, while two more were a few doors down. More amazingly, he claimed that one of the players had invited him into his room to chat, and to welcome him to the school. The rest of us had to investigate this astonishing story. Trooping down the hallway like so many giggling schoolgirls with a map to Burt Reynolds' house, we arrived before the ballplayer's door with some trumped-up question to ask as a way of meeting him. When our knock received a "Come in," we found ourselves in the presence of a normal-sized but well-muscled fellow in glasses, reading a book. We mumbled our excuse for being there and introduced ourselves.

"Pleased to meet you," our host said. "My name's Rocky Bleier."

The name meant nothing to us yet, but his playing on the team did. We talked for only a few minutes longer, torn between a desire to remain and our embarrassment over having really nothing to say.

"What position do you play?" one of my friends asked.

"Halfback."

"Oh, really. Uh . . . well, good luck; hope you have a great season."

As we said goodbye and shuffled out of his room, he invited us to stop by anytime he could help us. The entire exchange took all of three minutes, and never rose above the inconsequential. But we left impressed. If he was not as awesome in his physical proportions as we might have expected, it was even better to discover that he was entirely human and in some ways one of us. Already we felt we were a part of his world and he of ours. I walked away from Rocky Bleier's room feeling a little less insignificant. I knew a Notre Dame football player now. I could say hi to him on campus and feel good in his recognizing me. He was immeasurably more important than I, but we were fellow students and even residents of the same dorm.

Our next discovery was that three doors down from my own room lived two more athletes, Pete Duranko and John Horney. We knew that they, like Bleier, were starters on the team and we were anxious to see them. For several days this did not happen, until, coming up the stairs one day, I received my first astonished glimpse of Duranko. He was walking downstairs—on his hands! Now here was the stuff of legends. As a six-two, 235-pound defensive tackle, Duranko was not exceptionally large, but most of those pounds were bulging out of his T-shirt, and with his square jaw and darkly bearded face he seemed truly a hero, chiseled out of the granite of my imagination.

Meeting Duranko in this manner confirmed the sense of my own smallness and inconsequence that I had already developed, despite Rocky Bleier's welcome. Bleier had seemed much more human and ordinary than I had expected a Notre Dame football star to be, but Duranko was clearly outside the realm of my experience. More intimidating yet, I had by now met my fellow freshmen footballers and was beginning to fear I would not measure up.

Shortly after my arrival on the campus, I had reported to the locker room to check out equipment. Another freshman was there before me, an impressively muscled black guy about three inches shorter than I but obviously heavier. He looked every bit the athlete, broad in the shoulders and chest, narrow in the hips, powerful in the legs. I felt intimidated at once. I had played against no lineman in high school who looked so strong, and something told me that he was fast as well. I hesitantly introduced myself and was pleased to discover he was quite friendly. He said his name was Larry Schumaker, and that he was from East Orange, New Jersey. I asked him what he played. "Running back and linebacker," he answered. Running back? My God, the backs were bigger than I! I had grown to six five and an even two hundred pounds over the summer, reaching a plateau that impressed me. Now here I was meeting freshmen running backs who outweighed me by ten pounds!

My shock was worse when I reported for my first practice. I had been prepared for the varsity players to be awesome physical specimens, but my fellow freshmen astonished me. As I walked through the gates onto the practice fields, I felt I had stumbled accidentally into someone else's bad dream. All around me I saw monstrous bodies that made me feel as if I had shriveled up like an inflatable toy with all the air sucked out of it. I could not take my eyes off one of the freshmen in particular, supposedly just an eighteen-year-old like myself, but the largest human being I had ever seen. His arms looked as big as my legs, his legs as big as my waist, his chest as big as . . . There was nothing about me that could even compare. I learned that he was Mike McCoy, from Erie, Pennsylvania, and that he weighed 270 pounds. I had never played against anyone who weighed over 215 and was not a blimp with a thyroid problem. Here was a person no older than I with a fifty-four-inch chest and times as fast as mine at 40 yards. And he was not alone. Each of the other linemen I met at those early practices outweighed me by at least thirty pounds. One of them, a tackle from Cleveland who weighed 240, told me he had weighed that as a high school senior, and had played against only one opponent in his league all year who was smaller than he was. My world view was undergoing a drastic redefinition. I winced to think how we Gonzaga Preppers, with our 160-pound guards and big 195-pounders such as myself, had felt we were a real powerhouse. With a sinking feeling I also realized that my chances of playing for Notre Dame were, to say the least, bleak.

And then there was Alan Page, whom I was to "meet" the first time we freshmen were called to run plays against the varsity. This was the team that would win the national championship that year. From that team no fewer than fifteen players would go on to pro careers, including Terry Hanratty, Jim Seymour, Nick Eddy, Rocky Bleier, Bob Kuechenberg, and George Kunz on offense, and Pete Duranko, Kevin Hardy, Jim Lynch, Mike McGill, and John Pergine on defense. Also Page.

The first time I lined up against him, I was certain doomsday had arrived. At six five, 238, Page was not extraordinarily big by football standards, but he seemed bigger than his measured size, and more particularly he was the biggest *black* man I had ever seen. Being black, he was somehow less comprehensible to someone coming from a largely white community such as Spokane. As I trotted from the huddle to the line of scrimmage to face Page, I knew real fear on a football field for the first time since fifth grade. I settled into my stance as if I really were going to run a football play, then threw myself at his feet on the snap of the ball, protecting first of all my face and head, and praying he would not crush me like a roach. As it turned out Page was a gentle soul. Bearing no animosity toward that skinny freshman opposite him, he stepped over, not on, me. The rest of practice passed uneventfully. I had survived. But I had not played football against him.

Fortunately my cowardice faded. As I began to reorient myself to the new level of football at which I was trying to compete, I came to see more clearly the physical disparity between myself and some of the other players, and the advantages and disadvantages I faced. Knowledge was less terrifying than the unknown. My most serious shortcoming as a prospect obviously was my size. At six five, two hundred, I looked like a split end. The only hitch was that I had the hands and speed of an interior lineman. I thought of myself as a defensive end, but the freshman coaches would not accept this fact until they had tried me at wide receiver and tight end for several days. They discovered I was right.

My second handicap, my lack of a scholarship, proved to be a less serious obstacle than I had feared. Together with three of my freshman teammates I had been invited to try out. We were issued green practice jerseys as the scholarship players were, which distinguished us from, and raised us slightly above, the white-jerseyed other walk-ons. I do not know how much the coaches expected from me—I suspect very little—but I at least had a small measure of status from the beginning. I felt partially in and partially out. While the scholarship players were paired together in the freshman dormitories, I lived with other ordinary students across campus. While the scholarship players had contacts with the coach and varsity players through the recruitment process, I was unknown and felt it. While the scholarship players were assigned an adviser who gave them their books, helped them fill out their schedules, and directed their academic careers in numerous ways, I pursued my degree as the rest of the student body did. I felt like an outsider, but I was also given opportunities to prove I could play football. It was all up to me.

I made my initial mark on the Notre Dame practice fields in the same manner that I proved myself in high school and in grade school—in contact drills, where I proved my toughness against bigger and supposedly better players in versions of our old "slaughter practice." The drill this time was simpler than our four-bags, four-holes exercise at Gonzaga Prep. An offensive and defensive lineman faced each other across a line of scrimmage, with a running back and a defensive back behind them. On the signal, the offensive lineman was to block his opponent to one side or the other, while his back cut off the block, beating the defensive back himself. The two defensive players were to prevent any of this from happening.

This drill provided my finest moments as a freshman at Notre Dame. In a way, it captured the essence of football—power against power for a clear-cut decision. But in other ways, such a drill is not football at all. Football is a complex game. A defensive player can be attacked by any number of players from at least three different angles: he must play the pass as well as the run; he must also be alert for screens, draws, and other gadgety plays whose purpose is to fool, not overpower, him. A good defensive lineman must be strong and tough, but he also must be quick to read the play, to react, and to move—and he must do all of this without being blocked out of the play in the meantime. My favorite contact drill, on the other hand, reduced all of this complexity to a one-on-one matching of strengths and determination. In an actual game, my rangy frame and lack of bulk would make me vulnerable to blind-side blocks. In the drill, I did not need to be a physics major to know that leverage was the key to overcoming my physical disadvantage. If I drove under my opponent's shoulder pads and lifted him upward, he would be helpless. And my motivation to do well was spurred by the realization that my opponents were on scholarship while I was not. They represented the belittling forces against which I had to prove myself.

I gloried in those one-on-one collisions of bodies. We freshmen practiced in the areas not needed by the varsity, most often in out-of-the-way places at the outskirts of the practice fields. Wherever we lined up was the center of my private universe. I was vaguely aware of the Pages and Durankos and Bleiers somewhere off to my right or left, overseen by Ara Parseghian and his assistants. Parseghian was just a presence to me, not a real person. He was a voice, not deep or particularly strong, but intense —like a harsh, raspy whisper bellowed through a microphone. With that voice he controlled those giant athletes as completely as a chess master moves his pawns and knights—yelling criticisms and occasional approval that floated over to me as a reminder that the *serious* activity was taking place over *there*, not where I was. Parseghian was the sun and we freshmen but minor distant planets, and as a walk-on I was among the most insignificant satellites of all. I had talked to the coach only once, when he asked me my name as I passed him on my way to practice.

"Oriard," I told him.

"Oriard? Oh, yes. Well, keep working," he responded as he turned away.

I did not feel rebuffed; I hadn't earned any greater notice yet. My world was not yet his. I had to prove myself among the freshmen first, and my greatest opportunities came in the blocking and tackling drills that took place well beyond the range of the head man's observations. But somehow, Ara Parseghian was always the coach I was trying to impress—even if he was not actually present.

On the periphery of the practice fields, directed by a single assistant coach named Don Hogan, I was given my chance to prove I could hold my own against the scholarship players. Hogan seemed a bitter man. Only three years before, his own promising career as a Notre Dame running back had ended in a crippling auto accident. I did not feel that he liked me, but I forced him to notice me. Standing in line on crisp October afternoons, I took my turns on offense, driving low into the player across the line, scrambling, rooting, struggling, until the whistle blew. Nothing beautiful here, but usually effective: the back would make a few yards. But on defense—that was a different story! As I waited in line, all my concentration narrowed to the single play on which I would prove to some scholarship ballplayer that I could whip him. I counted the players waiting their turns on offense to see who my opponent would be. I watched the others going before me, to see who stuck his head into the play and who shied away from the contact. These were not really my teammates but my opposition, and I wanted to understand their strengths and weaknesses as fully as possible.

At last it was my turn. Across the line was a big tackle from Chicago, full of the self-assurance that I wanted to have. He outweighed me by forty pounds, but I knew that would not matter. I dropped into my four-point stance, coiled to explode. Coach Hogan called signals. On his whistle I lunged out, driving my head and shoulders under the other's shoulder pads, standing him up in the ballcarrier's path until I glimpsed the side the runner had committed himself to. I rammed my helmet into the ballcarrier's stomach, driving him to the ground. I loved the sweet sounds of my shoulder pad popping and my helmet crunching with a harsher note, of my own grunt of determination and my opponent's grunt of pain when I slammed into him. I felt powerful. A mean sonuvabitch.

"What kind of a block do you call that?" Hogan bellowed. "Get in there and do it again."

We lined up a second time, awaited the signals, lunged into a second collision. Again I neutralized his weight advantage by getting under his shoulders. The back tried to run wide but I pushed the blocker away and dived into the ballcarrier's legs, getting help from my defensive back to bring him down. Damn! that felt good.

"That's pathetic!" screamed Hogan. "That's just awful. Get someone else in there to do it right. You go again, Oriard."

My new opponent was a sloppy, not solid 240-pounder I knew I could handle with embarrassing ease. We took our positions while Coach Hogan called signals one more time. On the count I exploded with my helmet right under my opponent's chin, and followed with my hands under his shoulder pads. I stood him straight up, and ran him backward into a humiliating tangle with his running back. The back was smothered before he even had a chance to pick a hole.

Hogan was livid.

"What's the matter with you clowns! Are you going to let this guy push you around? How much do you weigh, Oriard?" (I answered quietly.) "How much do you weigh, Romanski?" (Mumbled reply.) "Maybe he should have your scholarship; someone else get in there and show me something."

I felt no compassion whatever on these afternoons. When I glanced into Romanski's eyes, I saw the look of a whipped dog, but I did not look long. In my obsession, I did not care how Romanski felt; if anything, his dejection only fueled my satisfaction. These were not *people* I was playing against but obstacles to my desires. They represented everyone who said or felt I was not good enough. When Romanski later quit the team, and school, I felt no share in the responsibility. I did not know what he went home to. Such things did not matter.

On my next turn I drew Jim Reilly, which meant that my easy domination was over. Jim was a tackle from Yonkers, New York, who seemed quiet and relatively unheralded compared to a handful of other scholarship freshmen. But when we lined up, I was facing the best blocker on the team. Knowing what to expect, I dug in more intently, planting myself to draw strength from the earth beneath me. On Coach Hogan's signal I slammed into Reilly, aiming under his shoulder pads to gain leverage. Even at my forty-pound disadvantage I had handled the others in this way, but Reilly was too good. He drove low, too, keeping his head down and his neck, back, hips, and legs in a straight line. We collided, forehead to forehead, shoulder to shoulder, stalemated at first. I grunted and strained, but Jim's superior size exerted itself. I kept my feet planted, but could neither drive through him nor deflect his strength with my hands. Jim kept churning with his stronger legs, and gradually bent me backward just enough to turn me slightly for the back to slip by. I was not embarrassed, but Jim Reilly controlled me as no one else had been able to do.

My own inability to handle him proved prophetic. He became a three-year starter on the varsity at left tackle, far and away our best offensive lineman. Fortunately for my own reputation, Jim Reilly was only one of many opponents I faced in the drills, and the net result for me was that I at least caught the coaches' attention. Once again, I had demonstrated my toughness. If I had not yet proven my ability actually to play the game, at least I bore watching as a candidate for the future.

We freshmen provided a preparation team for the varsity defense, scrimmaged against the varsity reserves, and had two games against outside opponents—Pittsburgh and Michigan

State. This was before freshmen were eligible for varsity play. For the Pitt game I was a second-team tight end and defensive end, but by the time of the MSU freshman game on November 18, an injury had made me a starter at right defensive end. Our coaches must have made this decision with some reluctance.

"At left end, six seven, two hundred and fifty, from Perth Amboy, New Jersey—Jay Ziznewski."

"At left tackle, six five and two hundred and seventy pounds, from Erie, Pennsylvania—Mike McCoy."

"At right tackle, six three, two hundred and sixty pounds, from Peoria, Illinois—Bob Jockisch."

"At right end, at six five and two hundred pounds???, from Spokane, Washington—Mike Oriard."

That trip was a memorable one, though the game was no impressive debut for me. We rode the train to East Lansing with the varsity players, whose game was the day after our Friday-night contest. We watched the epic Irish–Spartan 10–10 tie from the sidelines, seeing the two best football teams in the country struggle to a stand-off that left sportswriters and fans disgruntled but that impressed me as one of the great football games of recent years. Our Hanratty, Eddy, Duranko, Page, and Lynch were matched by Michigan State's Bubba Smith, Charlie Thornton, George Webster, Clint Jones, and Gene Washington. Unfortunately, Nick Eddy injured himself in a freak accident stepping off the train; George Goeddeke, our brilliant center, badly hurt his ankle in the first quarter and had to be replaced by a sophomore, Tim Monty; and Terry Hanratty separated his shoulder in a first-quarter collision with Bubba. Michigan State attempted to exploit our weakness up the middle by moving six-foot-seven, 285-pound Bubba over our six-foot, 220-pound Monty. Coach Parseghian had to call on Hanratty's sophomore backup, Coley O'Brien, to direct the offense against one of the most physically intimidating teams of the decade. The game was epitomized by one play in particular, on which Jim Lynch intercepted an MSU pass, but fumbled on the return when Clint Jones upended him so violently that for a brief moment he stood perfectly upright on his head before crumpling back to the turf. Despite our fifteen all-Americans, from my concerned view we seemed physically mismatched, but we clawed back from a 10–0 deficit to tie the score. Coach Parseghian was later criticized for settling for the tie, despite his explanation that O'Brien, a diabetic, was too weak to throw long at the end of the game. Whatever Ara's reasons, I felt fortunate we had survived.

The night before, we freshmen had pulled out a stunning victory with a 32-yard field goal in the closing seconds that gave us a 30–27 edge. My first road trip, my first hotel, my first visitors' locker room, left me in a daze that unfortunately I did not recover from until the game was over. I did not play well. The Spartan freshmen were nearly as physical as their varsity, and they wisely decided that the weakness on our defense was that two-hundred-pound end on our right side. They sent sweep after sweep my way, and more often than not I was inundated in the flood of green-and-white bodies. An athlete has days on which the actions around him seem to happen in slow motion, when he sees everything so clearly that he can respond with invincible ease. And he has days on which all is a mass of confused shapes and sounds. My game against Michigan State was of this second type. Finally I was replaced, to return to the sidelines and wonder if it were not, in fact, proper that the others on the field had scholarships while I did not. I tried to console myself with reminders of how far I had come since the beginning of the fall. But I was not very convincing.

Football was only a part of my life as a Notre Dame freshman. Except for the hours between three and seven each afternoon, when I had an ambivalent sense of belonging on the football field, I was no different from the other six thousand undergraduates on campus. My dormitory and classroom world was not peopled by linebackers and halfbacks, but by physics majors and premeds. Notre Dame had no jock dorm. I had read in *Sports Illustrated* just the year before about Tommy Nobis living in the captains' suite in the luxurious athletic dorm at the University of Texas, and had heard of similar arrangements at Alabama and other colleges. But at Notre Dame such special privileges did not exist. The football players lived in the regular dormitories, ate the same food as the other students except for dinners during the season (when we ate the same food but more of it), and were expected to be students as well as athletes. Because all freshmen at the university took a laboratory science, the coaches accepted the fact that freshmen players would come late to practice on the days of their labs. As a physics major I had two afternoon labs each week. No problem.

As a freshman I felt much more a student than a football player. I roomed with an engineer from Austin, Texas, next door to a premed from Los Angeles and a math major from Chicago. This was more truly my world than was Cartier Field, where the football team practiced—and where I always felt something of an imposter. More of my time went into studying physics, chemistry, calculus, English, and theology than into stopping sweeps and rushing the passer. My primary mentor was not Ara Parseghian or even Wally Moore, the freshman coach, but Joseph Duffy, my English professor. Mr. Duffy epitomized for me the scholar-teacher—a learned man deeply committed to the literature he taught and to the individuals who took his classes. Mr. Duffy had no interest in football: he had not been in Notre Dame Stadium in years, since he had been a new faculty member who felt certain obligations to the university. He had long since discovered that attending football games was not necessary. He was also not accustomed to having many football players in his classes. But he never made me feel anything but his support for this funny obsession I had about rooting around in the grass with a leather ball during my afternoons. He was more interested in the papers I wrote than in the tackles I made, but he made me feel that he respected my desire to excel in the game I took so seriously. I switched majors from physics to English after having Mr. Duffy both semesters of my freshman year, and by the time I graduated, after taking two more classes from him, I wanted to teach English, as he did.

In my social life as well I was an ordinary student, not a football player. My friends off the field were my fellow freshmen on the third floor of Dillon Hall. I felt no connection to anyone at all on the freshman team. They remained a group apart throughout my first year. I did not court the girls of St. Mary's—our sister school across the road—as a budding Notre Dame football star, but as a tongue-tied physics major from Spokane, Washington, trying to meet girls in a strange place. For the most part I

led the dull life of a studious freshman, breaking away from my
studies for an occasional movie in downtown South Bend or a
pizza at Frankie's or Luigi's. The only difference between me
and my engineering roommate was that I spent my weekday afternoons in football pads and cleated shoes.

But as a Notre Dame student, I found football to be a major
part of my life whether I played the game or not. Through six
days of classes (including Saturday mornings) and six nights of
studying in the library, we looked forward to football weekends
for the liberation of our spirits. On football weekends the campus and the city of South Bend were transformed. A town of
130,000 at the time, South Bend swelled by a third on those five
Saturdays in the fall. The stadium's capacity of 59,075 was sold
out for every home game that year (and every year since), and
40,000 of those came from out of town to fill ND's campus with
color and excitement for the afternoon. Instead of 6000 drably
attired males walking to classes and the dining halls, the campus
was alive with women as well as men, all in holiday mood,
streaming through the bookstore doors to buy T-shirts and other
souvenirs, and parading about the grounds to enliven every
corner of the campus. It was as if a monastery had suspended its
rules to celebrate Mardi Gras. The Golden Dome seemed a mag-
net drawing all the vitality from miles around to this one loca-
tion, where a football game was to be played.

The game was the high point. From the student section in the
northwest corner of the stadium, my friends and I joined with
the nearly 60,000 others in a single desire to see Notre Dame triumph. The section for St. Mary's students was to our left, and
during breaks in the action on the field, if the level of tension
was not too high, the two student groups chanted insults at each
other, believing ourselves extremely clever as we released our
frustrations over the 5:1 male-female ratio. Another pastime involved grabbing a student and passing him back on a sea of
upraised hands toward the uppermost row, while the rest of the
students chanted, "Over the top, over the top, over the top."
Sometime later, a student who came to be called "the stripper"
stood and began removing article after article of clothing, sway-
ing to the chants of his fellow students. Take 6000 mostly studious, celibate males and turn them loose for three hours on a

crisp sunny Saturday afternoon, and any number of things could happen. Freud would have enjoyed sitting among us with a pencil and notebook.

While Freud was jotting notes, the rest of us would have been focused primarily on the game. The football game did not just provide the excuse for packing into the stadium to indulge our rowdiness; it was the center of our passionate involvement. As a student in the stands I felt a closer bond to the athletes on the field than I did as a quasi-member of the freshman team. They were representing me, as they represented all of us, to the world outside the university. And they represented us well. The first game I saw as a freshman was the season opener against Purdue. Most of the stars from the year before were returning—from a team that had been brilliant except at quarterback. Bill Zloch had been a fine ball handler, but he was more famous for his end-over-end passes. This year, our hopes were placed in a sophomore, Terry Hanratty. Purdue was led by senior Bob Griese, a quarterback who had troubled the Irish for two years. The Notre Dame–Purdue rivalry was an intense one, and Griese held the records for completed passes and yards gained passing against the Irish—and had engineered a 25–21 upset of Notre Dame the year before.

This day belonged to the Irish. For me in the stands, the game was a dizzying exhibition of everything Notre Dame had come to represent in my fantasies. From the moment the players, huddled at the end of the tunnel, burst into the playing field in a stream of blue and gold, I was tingling. I had seen these same players on the practice field during the past week, but in their game uniforms they were more magnificent. The blue and gold of their jerseys and pants were deeper and richer than anything I had yet seen, and their helmets were truly dazzling. Other teams embroidered their helmets with numerals, stripes, and insignias; Notre Dame simply spray-painted them with a fresh coat of gold before every game. The Golden Dome was reproduced on sixty football players, each helmet flashing in the bright sun. The Irish played as well as they looked. The game started disastrously when Leroy Keyes returned a punt 94 yards for a score. But Nick Eddy countered by returning the ensuing kickoff 96 yards for the tying touchdown, and the fireworks were not finished. Hanratty completed 16 of 24 passes, 13 of them to fellow sophomore Jim Seymour, including touchdowns of 84, 39, and 7 yards. The defense held Griese to 178 yards, compared to Hanratty's 304, while the offense piled up more than 450. The net result was a 26–14 victory that started ND toward a number one ranking in the polls, and even a cover story in *Time* magazine. Hanratty and Seymour became the darlings of the early season—players just a year older than I on the cover of *Time!* This was football as I had always dreamed it should be played. To see it in person rather than on television, and to see it as a Notre Dame student rather than as a fan two thousand miles away, gave the game an immediacy and significance such games had never had before. Each time we scored and the band burst into "The Notre Dame Victory March," I got goose bumps. The fight song had been familiar to me for some time—my high school had borrowed it, after all—but now it was altogether different. It represented all the history and legend of Notre Dame, of which I was now a part. I was watching my first game in the stadium dedicated thirty-six years before, at the beginning of Knute Rockne's last year as coach. This was *my* football team now.

Football invades the consciousness of the receptive Notre Dame student in many ways. In addition to the official history, of which he is much aware, there are unofficial legends that permeate the campus. Paul Hornung's spirit lingered on in Dillon Hall, where I lived. We laughed enviously over the stories told by upperclassmen—who had heard them from other upperclassmen in previous years—of Hornung's escapades in the room across the hall from mine. The room was part of a suite with a private bath that four students shared. Hornung was said to have installed a pool table in one of the rooms, and to have entertained a whole series of famous beauties in defiance of university regulations. We wide-eyed, big-eared freshmen, so conscientious in our respect for rules, were deeply, enviously impressed. Other unofficial legends were more outrageous. A senior told us about a traveling sideshow that sported a gorilla and a challenge to any two people who could last three minutes with the animal and not be thrown out of the ring. Supposedly two football players accepted the challenge and nearly killed the poor gorilla. While one held the beast's arms, the other reputedly kicked him in the groin; then both stomped all over him as he crouched in agony as any male—even a gorilla—would do. Someone else told the story that I suspect circulates on every college campus, of the football players who, for a prank, deposited a dead horse in a buddy's room over spring break. In their cruelty and violence, such probably apocryphal stories were our primitive folktales. They invested our football heroes with nearly superhuman power to control life and death, which we vicariously shared when we watched them play football on Saturdays.

Our bond with the players also developed in part from the pep rallies on Friday nights before home games. They took place in the old field house, a massive barnlike structure with a dirt floor and a balcony at one end where the football players filed in to take their seats above their admirers thronging and cheering below. The players were raised up as on an altar. We 2000 or so students and visitors on the floor were celebrants at a sacred rite, offering homage to our gods elevated above us. We praised them with our cheers, offered thanksgiving for previous victories, and pleaded for continued triumphs. From my position on the floor I viewed the varsity players from what seemed to me the proper perspective. If they were not truly godlike to me, they at least represented human perfection. They stood for a level of excellence for which I longed, but which seemed as far beyond my reach as they were literally above me on the balcony.

Occasionally a guest speaker appeared at the pep rally. One time, Pat O'Brien rendered Knute Rockne's famous half-time speech as he had done it in the movie. For a few minutes I was transported to the Notre Dame locker room just moments before the game is going to begin. The opposing team is a powerhouse, but the great Rock will inspire the Irish to a courageous effort. His sonorous but urgent voice grabs me:

> We're going inside of them, we're going outside of them; inside of them, outside of them—and when we get them on the run once, we're going to keep them on the run—and we're not going to pass unless their secondary comes up too close. But don't forget, men, we're going to get them on the run; and we're going to go, go, go,

go; and we aren't going to stop until we go over that goal line—and don't forget, men: today is the day we're going to win. They can't lick us, and that's how it goes. The first-platoon men go in there and fight, fight, fight, fight, fight!!! What do you say men!

With 2000 others, I yell a resounding, "Yeah, yeah, yeah!" Somehow the Rock never really died.

On another occasion, Bill Russell rose to say just one sentence: "For many years now it has seemed to me that there are two major examples of excellence in sports: Boston Celtics basketball and Notre Dame football." We roared our agreement.

A player or two usually spoke next—Jim Lynch, perhaps, the team captain. Clear-eyed, square-jawed, dignified in an unselfconscious way, Lynch seemed to me the epitome of what a captain should be. He seemed so self-assured, so capable, so poised whether in front of 2000 screaming admirers or eleven angry opponents—everything I felt I was not but hoped to be. I watched him in the dining hall and on campus, going to classes (where I had heard he was a good student), with a mixture of respect and envy. I listened to him now as he mouthed familiar clichés about what the mighty Irish would do to our hated rivals tomorrow. I drank them in as if they held the secret to perfect happiness.

The next speaker might be Pete Duranko, who offered a striking contrast to Lynch's more serious appearance. Duranko stood above us, rugged and powerful, looking as if he could drive rivets with his chin.

"You're probably standing there thinking how much I look like Gary Cooper," he began.

I was incapable of irony in my own attitude toward Notre Dame football, but I roared with delight together with the 2000 others as Duranko proceeded to tell a series of achingly bad cornball jokes.

When George Goedekke stood up, he did not have to speak at all. The six-three, 230-pound center with a shaved head simply stood with folded arms across his chest, while we burst into frenzied cheers, crying, "Mr. Clean, Mr. Clean, Mr. Clean."

Finally, High Priest Parseghian always concluded the sacred ritual with the familiar litanies, punctuated by our jubilant roars, rather than by "Amens."

He rises before the congregation, dressed in coat and tie instead of the customary sweats he wore on the field, but his suit has now become the sacred vestment of his office. His deep-set dark eyes burn with the conviction of the true believer and his prematurely lined face expresses all the wisdom and deep concern of his calling. He is a short man who is the tallest person in the field house. My first football coach in the fourth grade was a priest; now, the coach I most want to play for seems even more priestlike in the aura through which I see him. Standing magisterially before us, he intones the litany.

"Tomorrow we've got a real challenge out there in that stadium." We roar our agreement. "We need your help." Someone to my left cries, "You've got it"; several others roar a prolonged "Yeah"; we all cheer wildly. "We need every one of you out there in the stadium tomorrow, making just as much noise for the entire sixty minutes as you're making here tonight." We bellow louder than ever to demonstrate our intentions for tomorrow; a knot of celebrants who dipped a little early and heavily into the sacramental wine whirl into a stumbling Irish jig.

"Purdue"—our cheers turn suddenly to loud boos—"is going to be tough." Even louder boos. "They've got a great quarterback in Bob Griese." Our disagreement crescendoes; Griese can't touch Brother Hanratty, our violent booing tells him. "They're going to be ready for us. I hear from Lafayette, they think they can beat us." Our outrage peaks with deafening boos; numerous cries of "Hell, no!" and "We're gonna kill 'em!" spontaneously burst from pockets throughout the crowd; a group in one corner begins chanting, "Screw Purdue, screw Purdue, screw Purdue. . . ."

"But these young men behind me"—abruptly we explode into cheers, as we focus again on our heroes sitting passively above us—"have been practicing hard for several weeks to get ready for this game." We send prolonged cheers of gratitude up to the balcony. "While you were enjoying the end of your summer vacation, these young men have been running, hitting, sweating, and doing everything necessary to get ready for this season and for tomorrow's game." We roar our blessings on them, stamp our feet, clap wildly. "And I'll tell you one thing"—pause; after a few seconds we have become uncannily still, breathlessly await-

ing the sacred mystery—"They are *ready!*" We explode into
cheers for several minutes until the Reverend Parseghian raises
his hand. "And I'll tell you another thing"—pause; pin-dropping
silence again—"we're gonna beat those Boilermakers!" We
unleash all restraint in thunderous cheers; spontaneous chants of
"Beat those Boilermakers, Beat those Boilermakers, Beat those
Boilermakers" fill the field house until the band bursts into the
fight song while we rock the building with singing and rhythmic
clapping.

After several minutes of prolonged cheering, stomping, and
impromptu dancing, we in the congregation settle down as the
band now plays the sacred hymn—"Notre Dame, Our Mother."
Instantly a more tender emotion reduces us to solemnity, as our
2000 voices sing the alma mater. At its conclusion, our spirits
just as suddenly become more martial again, as we burst into
wild cheers once more, while the players file out across the front
row of the balcony, down the stairs, and to the outside. Drained
almost to exhaustion, but anticipating tomorrow's game more
than ever, my friends and I troop wearily but happily back to
the dorm.

Not all of the students attended the rallies, but a large percentage did. Because the overwhelming majority of students
lived in the dormitories that were part of the central campus,
Notre Dame functioned as a self-contained community separate
in many ways from the town of South Bend, within whose borders the school was situated. As a student I often passed through
entire weeks without leaving the campus—attending classes, eating meals, and even finding my entertainment within the school's
boundaries. In that enclosed community the football team
served a particularly vital function, and the pep rallies were one
emblem of it. The team not only provided the best game in town
on Saturday afternoons, and generated the social activities that
surrounded the games, it created our link to the outside world.
We knew that Notre Dame football was followed by every major
newspaper and television network in the country. It was that
media attention in part that had brought the school to our notice, that had helped make it seem the place above all others we
wanted to attend. Now we were in the fold and felt through our
football team a part of the special mystique that Notre Dame

alone among universities in this country had. The players were our ambassadors, proving weekly to the rest of the country the excellence of which all of us in the student body were able to feel a part.

To some Notre Damers the football team is an embarrassment. The university, they point out, offers an excellent undergraduate education, has a fine law school and several other first-rate academic departments. Notre Dame graduates have gone on to notable careers in politics, law, literature, medicine, science—all outside the National Football League. It belittles the university to be known primarily for its football team.

Such objections are pertinent. I received a fine education and was influenced by a number of professors who were deeply committed to liberal education and to the university as a community of students and faculty united by a common goal. But at Notre Dame the football team is a major part of that community. The athletic department is not an embarrassing independent institution that recruits illiterate superstars in defiance of university guidelines, for the sole purpose of winning football games. The football program is more fully a part of the total university at Notre Dame than at most major universities, particularly at universities which compete successfully on the football field. Not all Notre Dame football players have been brilliant students, but a great many have been good ones, and the program as a whole has long been successful in graduating virtually all its seniors each year.

Equally important, the football team is in many ways the heart of the university. Not the brain of the university or merely the brawn, but the heart—the center of student enthusiasm and emotional involvement. Given the high-minded quality of the program, that is not a bad function for a football team to serve. There are many universities as fine academically, but its football team makes Notre Dame unique. The academic excellence of the school is not diminished by this fact, but can be enhanced. What distinguishes Notre Dame as a university most of all is nothing tangible. It is the sense of community a student feels, the sense of belonging to a place and a group of individuals as a sort of extended family of which he can be immensely proud. Many elements contribute to that sense of prideful community, but the football team is not the least among them. At pep rallies and in the stadium, the football team evokes that communal feeling among the students. It provides the clearest links to the university's past, particularly to its heroic past. It is Notre Dame history as an ongoing process—a history with which all the students can identify themselves.

As a freshman at Notre Dame, I discovered early that football would be an important part of my life as a student. The game provided not just relief from a week of workaday dullness and hard studying, and an outlet for pent-up adolescent restlessness, but a clear expression of excellence that became a part of me. For an aspiring player, the football team also provided more specifically the object of my dreams and desires—a goal more exalted than football at any other university could be. Were I at Washington State near my own hometown, to become a starter on the football team would be satisfying, but I would not feel transcendently honored. At Notre Dame dreams could come true. Whether I made the team or not, I would be affected by my association with Notre Dame football. But if I should make the team despite my obstacles, I could become not just a sharer in but a maker of legends.

FOUR

Aches and Pains . . . and Dreams Come True

"ACHES AND PAINS ARE SIGNS OF GAINS." That motto had been posted on the wall of my high school weight room, where I saw it each time I entered. I took it to heart when I was in high school, and I continued to take it to heart at Notre Dame beginning with my first off season. When I ran for conditioning, I ran until I hurt. In the weight room, I pushed myself to lift heavier and heavier barbells more and more times, so that next day my muscles would ache. I took those aches and pains to be the surest sign that I was developing more strength and endurance. The end of the football season meant no more organized practices, no more team meetings, no more weekend games. But the long months of my first South Bend winter drove me inside the weight room or under the stadium for an hour and a half each day, leaving more time for other interests but still keeping my focus on my ultimate goal. My daily progress was hard to measure, but each workout made me feel I had inched a little closer to my dream.

After my freshman season, I felt both discouraged and hopeful. I had not played well against Michigan State's freshman team, yet the fact that I had started the game at all indicated to me that the coaching staff had seen something in me that it liked during those many weeks of the fall. When I looked at the var-

sity roster for the coming year, I saw that Tom Rhoads and Alan
Page, the two starting defensive ends, were both graduating. Of
their backups, only one, Chick Lauck, was returning; my calcu-
lations foresaw a place for me on the second team—with a
chance of becoming a starter if I could only improve enough.
Counting players at one's position is one of the more futile
games indulged in by football players who are trying to make it.
While I was busy adding up defensive ends, the coaches were
rearranging their depth charts, moving players from one position
to another. I knew no coach well enough to discuss my prospects
with; as a walk-on I was not called in for an off-season review of
my status on the team. I had no way of knowing that I was not
prominent in the coaches' plans.

I worked hard during that off season. Three days a week I
bench-pressed, dead-lifted, curled, and squatted in Father
Lange's gym, the dilapidated weight room behind the administration building—attempting to add strength and bulk to my
slender frame. On alternate days I met with other team
members under the stadium for conditioning drills. NCAA regulations allowed no supervision of such workouts, but we had a
program of exercises that Rocky Bleier, next year's captain, led
us through. We did calisthenics, climbed ropes, went through a
variety of drills, then ran laps around the oval under the stadium. Our last exercise was the most grueling one. We ran the
stadium steps—up one aisle and down another, working our way
eventually around the entire stadium. We hated Paul Hornung
for this. He had said publicly on one occasion that running the
stadium steps at Notre Dame had been responsible for his powerful legs. Our coaches decided we could benefit as much. At the
end of one of these workouts, my legs were often so wobbly I
could barely stand. But aches and pains were signs of gains, and
I was preparing myself for spring ball.

The team that reported for spring practice that year was not
as imposing as the previous fall's national champions. Nick
Eddy, Larry Conjar, Tom Regner, Paul Seiler, George Goeddeke, and Don Gmitter were gone from the offense; Tom
Rhoads, Pete Duranko, Alan Page, and Jim Lynch from the defense. But Hanratty and Seymour were back, plus Bob Kuechen-

berg, Dick Swatland, Rocky Bleier, Kevin Hardy, Mike McGill, John Pergine, Dave Martin, Tom O'Leary, Jim Smithberger, and Tom Schoen. Hanratty, Seymour, Hardy, Schoen, and Pergine had all received all-American recognition in 1966. In addition, George Kunz, who started the first two games that fall at right tackle as a sophomore, before tearing a ligament in his knee, was back and more massive than ever. I saw George in particular as the image of what I needed to be. He was my height, and we shared a similarly rangy frame, but he packed 240 pounds on his, to my 210. All in all, it was an impressive group of returning athletes with whom I hoped to find a place.

One major weakness appeared to be in the defensive line, where Kevin Hardy was the only returnee. Here surely was my opportunity. For all my supposed intelligence, I had not considered very carefully the fact that the coaches of an undefeated national champion were not liable to place an excessive amount of confidence in a six-foot-five, 210-pound walk-on freshman. When I reported for spring practice, I discovered that Bob Kuechenberg had been moved from offensive tackle, where he had been a starter, to left defensive end, making room for George Kunz at his old position. Two other backup offensive ends and a linebacker from the previous year were also moved to the defensive end spots. Suddenly I found myself not on the second team battling for a starting berth as I had foolishly imagined. I was listed fourth at left defensive end (my position in the past had always been on the right side), behind not just the six-two, 245-pound Kuechenberg, but even other freshmen. The message was clear: walk-ons worked their way up from the bottom.

I toiled that spring with the other defensive linemen. In one drill we formed two parallel lines a few feet apart, with one man facing the heads of the two columns. The players in the lines were to run at the lone defender, one at a time from alternating rows in quick succession, popping him hard with their shoulder pads. The defender was to hit each man with shoulder and forearm, shucking him off as he would blockers in a game, always holding his ground and maintaining his readiness for another blocker. One after another we took our turns. Joe Yonto, our defensive line coach, a fireplug with a crew cut, a booming voice, and a fiery intensity to handle the athletes who towered over him, bellowed his reproaches.

"Get lower, McCoy. If someone your size comes along, he's going to bowl you over."

"Do you call that a football position, Kuechenberg? Keep your shoulders parallel and your butt low."

When my turn came, I took my position facing the two columns. As one after another of my teammates approached, I chopped my feet steadily, hitting and shedding one, then another. Then Kuechenberg appeared and staggered me with his blow; McCoy followed, knocking me back a couple of feet. I was not quite reset when 250-pound Eric Norri rocked me again, then 260-pound Bob Jockisch. By now I was not a defensive end but a child's top, spun whichever way I was struck. Coach Yonto did not scream at me. His silence was more damning than anything he could have yelled. It said, why bother?

When we scrimmaged, the first- and second-teamers saw most of the action. I usually played a few downs near the end. One on one with a lineman I held my own, but in the swirl of bodies coming from all angles, my lankiness made me fatally vulnerable to blind-side hits and cut blocks at my knees. I had fashioned an image of myself with the freshmen the previous fall as a rugged defensive end who compensated for physical limitations with toughness and determination. Now I was beginning to recognize myself as the coaches saw me—an underweight, unproven walk-on who was clearly not good enough to play for Notre Dame.

This realization was a painful one. I had never had illusions that I was spectacularly talented, but I had perceived my earlier setbacks as challenges that could be overcome, and my lack of recognition more a failure in my coaches' understanding than a true reflection of my ability. Now, I had to face the possibility that maybe I was just not good enough. I did not despair entirely, and I did not seriously consider quitting. Nine years of grade school and high school football having ingrained in me a scorn for quitters, I had not yet realized that quitting might take more courage than sticking it out.

I was under no pressure from home. My parents had not sent me off to college with the expectation that I would become a

star on Notre Dame's football team, and my slipping out of town
to play football in the Midwest rather than at Washington State
or some other local school had received no notice in the Spokane
press. But I nonetheless felt in some vague way that I would be
letting my parents and friends down were I to quit. Had I had
no personal attachments to anyone anywhere, I might have resolved right then that my prospects were hopeless. But I could
not afford such despair. I realized that success, if it were to
come, would not come soon or easily. In the meantime I would
work hard and try to give myself as much satisfaction as I could
—in the way that had become traditional for me. I would try
physically to dominate my opponents on the practice field, to as-
suage at least my own ego.

In this way, I began my career on the prep team. Through
that spring of my freshman year, the entire 1967 season, and half
the following spring I joined with other third- and fourth-string
players in providing opposition for the varsity offensive units.
We played the role of the week's opponent, presenting the defensive formations that the coaches expected to see on Saturday,
simulating as well as possible the techniques favored by individual players. During that 1967 season I impersonated Southern
Cal's Tim Rossovich, Michigan State's Rich Saul, Miami's "Mad
Stork" Ted Hendricks, and other, lesser opponents. It was all im-
personation, however. Come Saturday, I was sitting in the
stands, while my teammates faced the Rossoviches and Hen-
drickses on the field.

As a prepper, I did not really feel that I was a teammate of
Hanratty, Bleier, Kunz, and the others. My teammates were my
fellow members of the prep team. Most were good athletes, but
a step slower, a few pounds lighter, a bit less agile than those
who played ahead of us. Some had been injured too seriously to
recover fully their skills; some had "bad attitudes." A linebacker
named Denny Kiliany was known as a "hitter." From a nose-
guard position or as a middle linebacker, he used his forearms as
clubs that left opposing heads ringing. But Denny had had a
particularly bad knee injury which surgery had failed to correct
entirely. He was healthy enough to play football, but had lost
too much of his speed and quickness to be any longer looked to
as a possible starter. Brian Stenger was a second-team defensive

end one year, but had fallen out of the coaches' favor, and found himself down on the prep team the next. (After graduation he made the Pittsburgh Steelers roster as a free agent, vindicating preppers' self-conceptions for years to come, I suspect.) Some of us accepted our roles on the prep team with surliness; others, such as a defensive tackle named Tim Swearingen and a line-backer named Tom Reynolds, clowned through practices as much as possible, lightening the psychological burden for the rest of us as well. My attitude was more stoical, perhaps because I had not yet accepted my current role as my final fate. I en-joyed the camaraderie of our defensive prep team—it was the only bond I felt to any group on the roster—but it was a strange sort of cohesiveness. What we all shared was frustration. We wanted to be playing and resented those who played ahead of us. We showed our frustration in many different ways—in anger, in seeming not to care, in contempt—but we drew together as well, united against those around us who failed to esteem us.

Our combined frustrations gave us remarkable power at times. We were not just the dregs of the team, we were also survivors, hardened and embittered to varying degrees. Many others had entered the program with us as freshmen, but had fallen away for various reasons. In a highly competitive program such as Notre Dame's, many fail. The all-state halfback has his teeth jarred one time too many; the three-year starter and All-Star finds himself sitting on the bench for the first time in his life; the high school phenom discovers that football is not fun anymore. All drop football, most leave school. To transfer to other colleges? To go to work? In most cases I never knew; they disappeared from my consciousness altogether. Those of us who were left on the prep team had nothing to lose. The varsity offense was ex-pected to handle us, to open large holes in our line and complete passes against our secondary. If we were knocked down, the coaches applauded the offense rather than denigrated us. We could afford to be reckless, not to worry about draws and screens and all those other possibilities that keep a defense "hon-est." We could unload on the men in front of us and ignore any need for caution. Our only pleasure lay in making the varsity players look bad.

Our moods on the field were varied. One day, listless. Let the

offense look terrific, slicing through our line with little resistance.
The hell with them, and the hell with their coaches. What did
we care? We had nothing to lose. . . . Another day, irreverent.
In defiance of the coaches' obsessive seriousness and the offensive players' grim efforts to satisfy them, we would be loosey-
goosey—having fun, cracking jokes, perversely enjoying the
agonies of the people across the scrimmage line. We would have
swapped places with them in a second, but unable to, we turned
our frustration to parody. . . . On some days, though, we were
fiercely combative. We were going to prove to those sons-
abitches across the line—coaches and players alike—that we
were every bit as good as they were. We fused into a unit,
welded by our stubborn pride. Each play was a challenge and
an insult thrown at us by those lousy prima donnas. We wanted
to stuff them into a heap in their own backfield, humiliate them,
hurt them. On such days, fights broke out. The coaches let them
go for several seconds, then stormed in to break them up and
chew out the scrappers for unfootball-like behavior. But the
coaches never stopped the fights immediately. Those seconds of
trading punches were the best unscheduled practice they could
wish for their players—sharpening toughness and fierceness for
the coming Saturday. The coaches didn't particularly like fights,
but they liked fighters.

Morale could obviously be a serious problem for players on
the prep team. If we were spared criticism, we were also spared
praise. The offensive players received both the congratulations
and the browbeating. We were periodically told that we served
a vital function in the team's success. If we prepared the varsity
well for the upcoming opponent, stimulating the opposing
team's defensive strategy as well as possible and providing
enough physical resistance to keep our own team sharp, we
would make a significant contribution to the victory. So we were
told. Football was a team game, and every individual in the organization, from the head coach and every player on the practice field to the managers and trainers, contributed his share to
every victory or defeat. This may have been true, but we did not
believe it. No one could convince us that if we exerted maximum effort during the week of practice before a game, we were
truly as valuable to the team as the offensive and defensive

players who performed on the field. We wanted to believe what the coaches assured us about our importance, but deep down we felt it was just talk.

Low morale could be a particular problem for athletes who had been spectacularly successful earlier in their careers, but who now were forced to do the anonymous drudge work of the football team. Players such as Denny Kiliany, Tim Swearingen, and Tom Reynolds had been great high school athletes. To have been recruited by Notre Dame, they had probably been at least all-state in high school, and were most surely wooed by dozens of other universities. To have come to Notre Dame with expectations based on such credentials, then to have found themselves two or three years later on the hamburger squad, could be utterly demoralizing. In many ways I was fortunate. I could not feel I had fallen so low, because I had never been so high. I could at least hope that my tenure on the prep team was preliminary to better things, not the final result of my decline.

Given such potentially demoralizing conditions, one can easily imagine that the prep-team players might simply give up—might take the attitude, "I have nothing to gain, so why bother?" But in our own ways we were still proud. However much those players across the scrimmage line might be exalted above us, we were not convinced they were truly our superiors. If we could not prove it to anyone else, we would at least prove it to ourselves.

We did have one advocate for our cause. We had our own coach, Brian Boulac—the low man on the coaching staff as we were on the team. His responsibility was to provide the best preparation possible for the first- and second-team offensive units, but his sympathies were clearly with *us*, and he probably enjoyed the days when we could make the offense—and offensive coaches—look bad. When we played well he praised *us* rather than abused the offense. Perhaps more important, when we played badly he chewed us out, implying that we were actually good athletes who ought to play better. I cannot say for certain that Brian Boulac's support was important to my prep teammates, but I do know it was vitally important to me. It was important to me to feel that at least *someone* besides myself was noticing if I played well or badly. My own self-judgments could not entirely satisfy my need for confirmation that, however anonymous I might seem, I was in fact an individual. Brian was a northwesterner as I was, having attended my own high school for two years in the mid-fifties before moving to western Washington. He recruited in the Northwest, and probably had reviewed my background when I had originally applied to Notre Dame for a scholarship. Having also witnessed a couple of my afternoon drills on the freshman team, when I had manhandled offensive linemen who outweighed me by forty or fifty pounds, he was convinced of my potential.

Brian was a big man with a voice that carried well, and he used it to champion his prep-team players. If I made a particularly good play, Brian would bellow, "Great job, Oriard. Helluva play, Oriard. Way to go, Oriard." Such praise was pleasant to my own ears, but I realized even then that he was not yelling those compliments just for my sake. He wanted to reach the ears of the other varsity coaches preoccupied with other matters, even those of the head man, Parseghian, standing on his observation tower above us. Brian always repeated and elaborated the compliment, and used our names several times. If, over a period of time, Coach Parseghian heard a certain name often enough, that name might pop into his head the next time he was fiddling with the depth chart. It was clear to me that at least Brian Boulac believed I might have a future, and his belief helped sustain my own.

I felt Brian Boulac, not Ara Parseghian, was my coach, but Parseghian was still the godlike figure I was ultimately trying to reach. He greeted me more frequently now than that one time when I was on the freshman squad, but I never knew if it was because he was really aware of me as a member of his team, or simply that he could read the name taped across my helmet. Our exchanges were never more than the perfunctory few words traded in passing. *I* longed for a different relationship, but I knew I could not expect it yet. My sense of the man had changed in subtle ways. Parseghian was no longer the disembodied voice floating to me from an adjoining field, but the all-seeing eye stationed on a scaffold fifteen feet above us. On a raised platform perhaps three feet by six, Ara paced back and forth, or turned from side to side to watch either the offense or the defense. Mainly he watched the offense—which meant I, too, had a chance to catch his notice. It seemed that he saw everything the offensive players did—the left guard's block, the right half's fake, and the wide receiver's pass route on every play. If he saw all that, perhaps he could see me, too. Perhaps if I did a good job often enough, he would come to know me. Maybe once every two weeks, after Brian Boulac had shouted my name several times, I would hear that well-known voice above me.

"Yeah, good job, Oriard."

No beggar embraced alms as greedily as I did those few words.

So passed my two springs and a fall on the prep team. During the springs while my friends in the dorm tossed Frisbees on the South Quad or escaped for an afternoon to the Michigan dunes to celebrate the end of a long, cold South Bend winter, I plodded off to practice to put in my time as cannon fodder for the varsity. Once I was particularly struck to see some of my fellow students—in cutoffs, T-shirts, and bare feet—tossing a football around, having fun! I had just survived another two hours of bone-crushing practice with no sign that I had improved my standing in the coaches' eyes—and here I saw people playing football as if it were enjoyable! A fleeting desire to quit passed through me, but only briefly. *That* kind of enjoyment clearly was not what I was after.

In the fall we on the prep team settled into a rhythm. There was no more day-to-day hope that today my true worth might be discovered, followed by frustration when it was not. Once the season started, major roster changes were made only in cases of injury or gross incompetence. What we on the prep team did seemed irrelevant. We could only settle in for the duration of the season, deriving whatever satisfaction we could in our own ways. The occasions for such pleasure came most often on Tuesdays and Wednesdays. For the varsity players the rhythm of the week was different. On Sunday, everyone was to report to the practice field sometime in the afternoon for loosening up, jogging a few laps, and working kinks from yesterday's game out of the body. On Monday, the first team did not wear pads, but came to practice only for the calisthenics, noncontact drills, and an introduction to that week's opponent. After the starters had departed for the locker room, those who had suited up for the game on Saturday but did not play much scrimmaged against the freshmen or the prep teams—in what we not so affectionately termed the "Toilet Bowl." The purpose was to guarantee that the varsity backups did not grow stale from lack of game activity. We preppers were to keep them sharp.

Tuesday and Wednesday were the workdays for the varsity. Having been introduced to the week's opponent and seen him for the first time on film on Monday night, the players now settled down to perfecting the game plan designed to exploit the opponent's weaknesses most effectively. After calisthenics and drills, the offensive units ran plays against our prep-team defense, aligned in the appropriate formations. One period would be devoted to passing, one to running; then practice would conclude with a short controlled but live scrimmage, whose purpose was to maintain the varsity player's competitive edge. On Thursday, practice lightened up: we preppers were to go three-quarters rather than full speed so that the offense could execute cleanly, and no live scrimmage took place. On Friday, we all reported without pads, the preppers offering passive resistance as the varsity ran crisply through plays for timing. After only forty-five minutes to an hour, Coach Parseghian called us together for some inspirational words, we led some cheers, and then we broke for the locker room. On Saturday was the game.

For the preppers, the week had a different rhythm. We required no easy buildup to midweek intensity, then a tapering off before the climactic game on Saturday. On Saturday I was sitting in the stands with my roommate and friends, watching the players I had practiced with all week playing before me as if I were just another spectator. I felt much more ambivalent as a Notre Dame fan during that 1967 season than I had the year before. As a Notre Dame student I wanted my alma mater to have the best football team in the land. But as a frustrated prepper, I resented the fact that I was in the stands watching sixty others who wore the blue and gold below. These were no longer my heroes on the field, but my teammates of a sort. They held no mystery for me; in some cases I was not even convinced that they were better players than I was. I also felt estranged from my fellow students sitting all around me. I could not cheer with

them as I had as a freshman, with untroubled enthusiasm and
admiration for the players. I was a more subdued fan in 1967 as
I watched the team compile an 8–2 record. Losses to Purdue's
Mike Phipps and Leroy Keyes, and to O. J. Simpson and Southern Cal, did hurt, but not as much as they would have the year
before. Victories over the remaining eight opponents were comparably not as sweet as last year's. I could not truly feel that I
had contributed to those successes. But neither could I just enjoy
them vicariously. I was neither fan nor player.

Our week on the prep team climaxed not on Saturday but on
Tuesday and Wednesday. Monday's Toilet Bowl scrimmage
offered us some opportunities to prove our abilities; in fact, this
was the only day on which we played before the varsity coaches
at our positions. The bellowing and raving of the coaches
reached a peak in those Monday scrimmages, as if they were trying to create gamelike intensity by the pitch of their voices. Joe
Yonto roamed behind our defensive line yelling at us, even com-
plimenting our good plays.

"C'mon, Oriard, show me something. Let's see you get to the
quarterback."

"Nice job, Wisne, let's see some more of that."

"What the hell do you call that? That was pathetic. Are you
going to let those guys run all over you?"

But after Monday, Yonto left us to return to his own players.
And none of us went with him. To us, the scrimmage meant little. It seemed an afterthought by the coaches, who suddenly realized that the first team was gone, and asked themselves, "Well,
what do we do with the rest of these clowns for the next hour?"
They seemed to work up an artificial frenzy to create the illusion
that the scrimmage was meaningful. The Toilet Bowl was a
whole lot of sound and fury, signifying nothing.

The contact on Monday did prepare us for Tuesday and
Wednesday, however. On the varsity workdays we preppers
were licensed to go as hard as we wished. There was never any
tackling before the final scrimmage, but we could unload on the
offensive players—from their perspective, benefiting them by the
hard work; from ours, giving us an opportunity to humble them
if we could. On Tuesdays and Wednesdays, we preppers could
be "bad-ass dudes" and revel in the role. We were the outlaws,

the misfits, the untouchables, the dirty dozen less one, with little to gain, it seemed, but nothing to lose. From my defensive end position I was most often matched against a tackle or fullback who had to block me. Although these individuals were supposedly my teammates, I did not feel that they were, and this attitude empowered me to handle them as roughly as I could. I felt alienated from them by my status on the prep team, but also as a walk-on I was doubly removed from the football mainstream. I never saw these people away from football; I did not know them at all—and it is much easier to batter anonymous figures than friends or even acquaintances.

On Tuesdays and Wednesdays I played with a quiet fury. I was never ostentatious or mouthy, but on play after play I rammed my shoulder and forearm into the shoulders and headgear of the man trying to block me, forcing him to recognize me, to acknowledge my existence. I wanted him to feel an ache at ten o'clock that night and think, "That sonuvabitch Oriard. . . ." We were not permitted to tackle, but my object on every play was to demonstrate clearly that I could have made the tackle had I been allowed. My deeper motive, however, was more direct—more brutal perhaps. I wanted physically to dominate the offensive players attempting to block me. I wanted to feel contempt for their inability to do so, and satisfaction in knowing I was tougher than they were. "Victory" for me could not come in the stadium on Saturday before 59,000 fans, but only in the private stadium of my mind in Tuesday and Wednesday practices.

The advantage was all mine. The offensive players were building up to Saturday's game; Tuesday and Wednesday were just practice days to them. To me they were the climax of the week; whatever satisfaction I was to derive from playing football had to come from these workouts. As the season wore on, a couple of the fullbacks, Ron Dushney and Ed Ziegler, began to take notice of me at training table. Passing through the cafeteria line, on more than one occasion one of them turned to me and said, "Hey, Oriard, how about taking it easy in practice tomorrow?" I mumbled something noncommittal, but made no changes next day. Had our personal contact been greater, I would have been forced to deal with these individuals in more human terms. I could not have continued to maul someone I had come to *know* —even if only a little. But I did not know them. They had not consciously avoided me or I them, but as a walk-on living on the other end of campus, with serious academic interests, I had lived in a different world except for the few hours we shared each day through football. They weren't even my teammates, because I did not suit up with them on Saturdays. Their requests for gentler treatment did not reach me on a personal level at all. They only fed my satisfaction that I was making my presence felt.

Only Rocky Bleier forced me to consider what I was doing. Rocky was the team captain in 1967, and a truly admirable one. At five eleven, 195, he was neither as big nor as fast as a great running back should be, but he accomplished more with his limited physical skills than countless supposedly more talented backs. He ran harder, with more determination, than anyone on our team or on any team we played all year. I recall numerous occasions when he ran through or over the top of tackler after tackler, turning a routine play into a fierce expression of human desire. His later career in the NFL, including his recovery from the crippling war wound and subsequent fine play with the Steelers, did not surprise me. This was simply the same Rocky playing the game the way he had at ND. I did not know Rocky any better than I knew Dushney or Ziegler, but one day in practice he forced me to recognize him. I had been butting the full-backs with my usual disdain, when a new formation or an unusal substitution sent Rocky out to block me. I drove into him and pushed him back as I had been doing, when suddenly he began throwing elbows at me, and continued long after the play ended. The exchange was not violent enough to require the coaches' interference, but I was shocked. I had only been doing what I was entitled to do—at the expense of my opponents on the offense—but here was one opponent who was not going to let himself be used in such a way. I was trying to force others to recognize *me;* Rocky instead forced me to recognize *him.* For the first time I was made to see an individual *person* across the line of scrimmage. Here was Rocky Bleier, a proud athlete who was not just going through the motions of practice, but who had his own hopes and angers and determinations just as I did. Instead of the abused prepper, depersonalized by an indifferent coaching staff and offensive unit, I saw myself suddenly as someone who had tried to prove I was *somebody* by ignoring the fact that those I played against were people, too. The fact that it was Rocky Bleier whom I had aroused particularly dismayed me. This was the Rocky who had opened his door to a timid freshman on his first day on the strange campus, and the same Rocky whom I genuinely admired and respected for both the kind of person he was and the way he played on Saturdays. I had managed to suppress all this during practices. The only way I could prove *myself* was at others' expense, and the less I thought of those others as people the easier it was. Rocky had just complicated my football life, and the result could have been paralyzing. But it had only been a fluke that had sent him out to block me. I went back to banging on Dushney, Ziegler, and the others, avoiding a fuller consideration of my brief glimpse that my dreams could only be built on a shaky foundation. But I began to feel periodically uneasy, and on those occasions when Rocky was assigned to block me, I played my prepper's role less aggressively.

The highlight of my Tuesday and Wednesday practices was the goal-line scrimmage at the end. Coach Parseghian did not believe in a lot of full contact between games; the risk of injury was too great, and the need to recover from minor hurts suffered in the last game took precedence over whatever benefit might be gained by increased head-banging during the week. But not to hit at all between games might dull the players' competitive instincts. In the final ten to twenty minutes of Tuesday and Wednesday practices, the first and second offensive units alternated trying to score from ten yards out in four plays against the prep team (on another field the prep offensive unit was attempting to do the same against the first- and second-team defenses). Only the quarterbacks were not live—we could not tackle them —but otherwise we played under game conditions.

This was game time for the preppers. Our performance showed up in no record books; our victories could only be "moral" ones. But if we kept the varsity offense out of our end zone, we gained for ourselves the sweetest triumph that was available to us. Again, we had the advantage in certain ways, for

the offensive players were simply looking forward to the end of
a hard practice in preparation for Saturday's game. For us this
was the Game of the Week.

By midseason, because it was dark when the scrimmage
began, we staged the scrimmage on one of the two lighted practice fields. As in my high school games in Joe Albi Stadium, the
enveloping darkness around the intense lights overhead made
the playing field seem the center of the universe. Goal-line offensive and defensive strategies further narrowed the focus. The
offense had fewer options than it did at midfield. Ten yards of
playing field plus ten yards of end zone left little room for
receivers to maneuver in, and the horror of costly mistakes, of
turnovers that surrendered scoring opportunities in games, reduced the number of possible running plays to a few basic ones.
In goal-line situations the two lines simply hunkered down, dug
in, tensed up, and prepared to explode into each other on the
snap of the ball. There was no thought of breaking off a long
run; each *yard* seemed a long one and had to be fought for more
tenaciously than was necessary for large chunks of yardage
upfield. To have the ball inside the opponent's ten and not score
was the greatest crime an offensive team could commit; to prevent an opponent from scoring from within its ten was a defensive unit's greatest triumph. The terms of combat on the goal
line were power and determination vs. power and determination.
It was winner take all.

By the time of the goal-line scrimmage we were well warmed
up, well grimed, well loosened up by the previous hour of limited contact. We defensive linemen filled all the gaps; the offensive linemen narrowed their splits from each other to cover us.
Nowhere else in football did I get such a feeling of primal combat, as I tensed in my stance ready to lunge low and hard at the
snap of the ball. The key was to be lower than my opponent,
without simply burying myself. If we on the defensive line could
get under our men, raise them up, and neutralize their momentum, we would plug every hole, giving the back no place to run.
The offensive linemen, on the other hand, had to get under us to
tie up our legs or turn us to the side. A gap of only a foot or two
is a gaping hole in a goal-line defense; 210-pound backs can
knife through such openings so easily that physical laws seem to

be suspended. The individual battles in the line are for the slightest of advantages, the narrowest bits of space. Footwork and fancy techniques give way to sheer force.

For the goal-line scrimmage, Parseghian came down from his observation tower to call the offensive plays himself. His presence on the field increased the intensity of all his coaches, each of whom wanted his own players to perform well.

On our side of the scrimmage line, only Brian Boulac was there to rally us. He wanted to prove something, too. Brian yelled encouragement: "C'mon, Oriard; c'mon, Wisne; let's go, Kiliany. Be tough." The offensive team broke the huddle for the first play. I lined up in a four-point rather than a three-point stance, my elbows cocked to keep myself lower than usual. I was on the offensive tackle's—George Kunz's—inside shoulder. He was higher in his stance than I, because he could not give away a clue whether the play was a run or a pass. Hanratty barked signals. Out of the corner of my eye I watched the ball. At its first movement, I lunged forward, driving my left shoulder under Kunz's left, throwing my right forearm to anticipate a block from Dick Swatland, the guard on my inside. Feeling no pressure from the inside, I drove off my right foot with all my force into George, then saw a ballcarrier nearly upon me. I thrust my head and shoulders into his stomach, felt bodies swarm all around me as we collapsed in a pile. A whistle blew; coaches began yelling. "Where was the hole on that play? Are you guys going to block that way against Southern Cal? You'll get run off the field." From our side of the line Brian boomed, "Great job, Oriard, Wisne, Reynolds. That's the way to shut it off." As we unpiled, I saw that the ball had not moved, second down, still ten yards to go.

The entire action had taken two to three seconds and from the sidelines would have looked simply like a collision of two thoughtless masses of bodies. To me on the field it was a series of instinctive actions and reactions determined by countless repetitions of similar plays, and charged by a fierce desire to keep Notre Dame's hotshot number one offense out of my end zone. Down the line to my right, my cohorts on the prep team had fought individual battles in a similar way—and we had come out on top. Once. It was too early to feel any elation, but we

shouted congratulations back and forth, and encouragement for
more of the same on the next play.

The offense broke the huddle again, and ran up to the line
with more obvious determination than on the last play. George
Kunz looked angry; I knew George did not like to be beaten and
he was furious with himself. Again I cocked my elbows in my
four-point stance; George cocked his lower this time, too; the
hell with disguising the play. Hanratty called signals, the ball
snapped, I lunged. This time our shoulder pads collided with a
resounding pop. No pressure from the inside again, but as I
drove into George I had no leverage: we were fighting on the
same plane. My legs churned, I lowered my head and slipped
under his pads. But George kept driving, too, and though I was
under him, my momentum was carrying me into the turf, while
George smothered me with his body. The whistle blew, the
coaches yelled their praise and disgust, and I saw Bleier had cut
off George's block to pick up four yards this time. *I* was angry
now. Brian yelled, "C'mon, Mike, don't let him do that to you."
My self-loathing increased. I kicked the turf, twisted my face
mask once or twice, hunched my shoulders into my helmet, tens-
ing my neck muscles, dropped into position before the offensive
huddle had even broken.

Third down. Six yards to go. Same formation. Same determination on both sides of the line. The darkness had thickened, but
the lights gleamed more brightly in contrast. Nothing existed
but six yards of chewed-up grass and twenty-two men fighting
for possession of it. As the offense broke the huddle, their
coaches growled and shouted as if this were the Cotton Bowl
and a national championship at stake. George and I squared off
again. The all-American tackle and the prep-team defensive end.
But this was my Cotton Bowl and only a Wednesday practice
for George. Cocked elbows, snapped ball, the lunge and collision. George had tried to knife inside to cut me off; I knew immediately that the play was up the middle. But I was low and
angry. I forgot about the ball and drove into George's outside
shoulder and rib cage, pushing him into the pile of bodies to the
inside. We had completely stuffed the hole, the ballcarrier absorbed in the mass like one more ant dropped onto a swarm. I
kept driving a couple seconds longer, just to let George know I

got him that time, to make him look bad in front of Ara Parseghian—pushed around by a lousy prepper. Take that and
shove it.

The offensive coaches—Parseghian, Jerry Wampfler, Tom
Pagna—were furious. Southern Cal was coming to South Bend
in three days, and Kunz & Co. couldn't budge their own third-
team defense. On our side, we were feeling like real football
players for the first time all week. Stop them one more down
and we would win the day, no matter what else happened. We
didn't say this to each other, but we shared an understanding.
Up and down the line we came together into a tight group,
proud of ourselves and each other. If only we didn't let up now.

The huddle broke. Fourth down. George wanted this one
badly, I knew, but I wanted it worse. On the snap of the ball we
lunged; George popped into me then set up in my face. It was a
pass. In my mind the thought flashed; we've won. When they
have to pass, they've conceded. They're still playing by football
rules, but not by preppers' rules. To beat the prep team, they
had to win it in the trenches where the real battles took place.
They couldn't take advantage of our secondary—trick us rather
than overpower us. The prep defensive backs were closed off
from the linemen and linebackers in certain ways. They didn't
have to knock heads, to go one on one on every play, putting
their bodies on the line. But as quickly as this thought flashed
through my mind, another followed it. Don't let them score.
Don't let them escape with even half a victory.

It was a quick pattern, as they all were at the goal line. No
chance to get to Hanratty. As the ball was relased into the left
flat, I followed its flight anxiously. Don't let it be caught. The
coverage was perfect. Brian Lewallen slapped his left arm in
front of the receiver and batted the ball to the ground. Four
downs and only four yards. We'd held.

Before we could get too carried away by our self-congratula-
tions, the second team was ready and the process started again.
Some afternoons the offense scored easily. George Kunz had his
days; he didn't save everything for Saturday afternoons. Sometimes we held them all but a couple of times. And sometimes
they did not score until, long after practice was supposed to
have ended, an unspoken signal passed among our secondary to

let the back score if he broke through the line. The troops are weary and hungry, the signal said. On our finest afternoons, neither unit ever did score. The screams of the offensive coaches increased in volume and frequency. Ara ignored the clock which said practice should have ended, until in disgust he called the team together, declared curtly, "You'd better play better than this on Saturday," and sent us in with a gesture of dismissal.

I never minded practicing beyond the scheduled limit on such occasions. Those days sustained me through my weeks of futility. Knowing in my own mind that I had taken on ND's best and not yielded gave me what little hope I had that I would not be relegated permanently to the prep team. Praise shouted by Brian Boulac, and even, on rare occasions, in an oblique way—"Are you going to let Oriard do that to you?"—from the offensive coaches, was the public recognition my efforts received for a full year. Yet such praise was important to me. At the end of a Tuesday or Wednesday practice when we had been particularly tough, Jerry Wampfler, the offensive line coach, would often holler over to us, after lambasting his own troops, "Good job, prep team." The offensive coaches, for all their railing against their own, were pleased when we offered such opposition. We were preparing their players well for Saturday. Ironically, the resentment and anger we preppers felt helped the very people against whom it was directed. We were being applauded for our rage. But I took Coach Wampfler's compliment seriously and *personally*. Praise did not come easily or often on the prep team.

Spring practice of my sophomore year began as a continuation of the previous fall, and of the spring before that. I had not suited up for a single game in the fall, and now in the spring my name was right in place near the bottom of the depth charts at defensive end. The starters from the fall were both returning, as were their backups; there were even newcomers from the freshmen team to contend with. A year before, in the same position, I had vainly hoped from day to day to be "discovered." Like Lana Turner in a tight sweater catching the producer's eye at a soda fountain, I would do something so stunning that Joe Yonto would come up to me and say, "Young man, I'm going to make you a star." This year I nourished no such fantasies. A year on the prep team had shown me some of the basic inertia within the system. Players did not very often move back and forth between prep team and varsity; what movement occurred was more often downward than up. What good plays I had made in fall practices had been witnessed by Brian Boulac and the offensive coaches; if I had shown any promise, Joe Yonto remained oblivious to it.

For the first time I had to seriously consider quitting. My participation in football was not hurting my studies, but during the season it consumed virtually all my waking hours outside the classroom and library. Even during the off season football made constant demands. It cut a little into work time and absorbed play time altogether; the question I had to ask myself was not so much, "Can I afford the time away from my studies?" but, "Is it really *fun* anymore?" I found some pleasures on the prep team—in those goal-line scrimmages when we whipped one of the best offenses in the country. But such pleasures seemed too private; they wanted confirmation from Ara Parseghian, Joe Yonto, and the student body. I felt close ties to a few of my fellow preppers, particularly to Brian Lewallen, a defensive back from near South Bend; and Jim Bergquist, a tight end from Fort Collins, Colorado, both walk-ons like myself, both dreaming my dreams, fighting my fights. But ours was a bond of mutual frustration. And my other pleasures came from noble futility rather than triumph. I longed for the satisfaction of success; it was only success that could transform the physical hardships into a positive experience.

The time had come for me to quit, but I did not know if I had the courage to quit. It was much easier to continue doing what I was doing than to face the consequences of conceding failure. I had had my successes in high school, but they seemed now to have come too easily (aches and pains were signs of gains, you know). Not so with making the football team at Notre Dame. When I imagined my life without football, I pictured a great void, a sense of failure. My reason told me that life would go on; I would make my mark in other fields. But in my guts I was less sure. To admit that I had failed at my first *real* challenge seemed more than my ego could bear. The football field was my testing ground, as it had been since my earliest experiences in the game. I felt that I had failed already, but until the public act confirmed the private reality, my failure was not irrevocable.

And then came Jerry Wampfler, the offensive line coach. I knew him as one of the coaches who marshaled the first- and second-team offenses against the prep team in our scrimmages. An intense man in his late thirties, taller that most of the other coaches, Wampfler had an uneasy laugh and a nose that turned up at the end as if he had gotten too excited one day and de-cided to show one of his linemen how to stick his head in there —but forgot to put on a helmet. But I did not really *know* Jerry Wampfler. I could not recall that he had ever spoken to me, ex-cept for that generalized "Good job, prep team," that included me in its sweep. But after a workout midway through spring practice, Coach Wampfler spoke to me some most astonishing words.

"Oriard, how'd you like to see if you can learn to play center?"

I didn't know what surprised me more—that he had noticed me at all, or that he was suggesting I might play center. Center? I had thought centers were short and squat. I had also thought of myself as a defensive end for many years now. I had played in the offensive line in grade school and high school, but after I discovered as a freshman how big collegiate guards and tackles were, I had dismissed the offense from my consideration. In pickup games the most inept player on the field was made cen-ter, because he would be the only ineligible receiver. Center? I had never considered such a possibility.

The rest of our conversation was even more astonishing.

"I watched you last fall on the prep team, Mike," he told me. "You gave a hundred percent all the time. You worked our players hard, and even worked some of them over pretty well. You responded to coaching, and I think you could learn to play this position. We're thin at center, and I'd like to give you a shot at it."

I *had* been noticed! All those days when I thought only I and maybe Brian Boulac knew I was even on the field, Jerry Wampfler had known, too. It appeared now that much of my rage at being overlooked had been unfair; yet my rage had also guaranteed that I would be noted.

I did not know how to respond. What do you say when a chance to realize your dream is laid at your feet? Hell, yes, I wanted to play center!

To Coach Wampfler I showed more restraint, but could not entirely contain my delight. Not wanting the magic moment of this conversation to end, I asked questions: how should I begin? when do I start? how about my size? Short, squatty centers were out, I was told. Height was an advantage, and my weight was fine for blocking most nose guards and middle linebackers. A few more pounds would not hurt, though. All of this was just conversation. The only thing that mattered was that I had a chance to play.

Coach Wampfler's announcement came at the end of the first phase of spring practice. An accident of the calendar broke up spring football into the two weeks preceding the university's Easter vacation, and the three weeks after. Wampfler had me report to him the morning before I left for break, so that he could teach me the basic techniques of snapping the ball to the quarterback while simultaneously charging out of my stance to block. With a football tucked under my arm, I went home with my roommate to his north Chicago suburb—to eat his mother's good cooking, and see his friends from high school, but more to practice my new art. In Bob Ryan's backyard in Wilmette, as I snapped the ball to Bob and his younger brothers who played my quarterbacks, I felt for the first time in a full year that my efforts had a clear object. I counted varsity centers—old habits do not die easily—but I was interested less in the total I arrived at than in the fact that I was in their company at all. How could I project my chances against theirs when I did not really know what it would take to be a good center anyway? I had to reorder my world view from the other side of the scrimmage line.

I returned to spring practice transformed. I was not only oblivious to the barefoot Frisbee throwers on campus, I relished coming to practice early to work on my new skills. I was one of two centers working with the second-team offense; my rivals of the previous fall were now my teammates. Our quarterback was a skinny freshman from New Jersey named Joe Theismann. I am sure that Joe bears to this day the physical reminders of our early teaming up together. The exchange between center and quarterback seems the simplest action in an otherwise complex game—until an unaccountably fumbled center snap costs the team a touchdown inside the opponent's five. Actually, like most other phases of the game, a clean exchange requires more coordination and precision than is apparent. The center snaps the ball *backward* at the same time he begins his charge *forward,* while the quarterback retreats into the backfield at the same time his hands must ride forward with the center's tail to receive the ball. Any quarterback and center who have not played together must practice long to accustom themselves to each other; most fumbled snaps in games occur when a new player enters at either position. With an entirely new center learning his role for the first time, the problems in timing are greatly increased. Joe Theismann gained some swollen knuckles and jammed fingers as we learned to work together.

The remaining three weeks of spring ball were a blur of new sensations. The qualities I did possess—toughness, intelligence, coachability, and willingness to work—were ideally suited to learning my new position. I was "coachable" because I was both willing to learn and capable of putting what I learned into practice. Many athletes, for a variety of reasons, are resistant to coaching. They cannot unlearn old techniques, they resent the interference, they react negatively to the coach's authority perhaps. I was a sponge both in the classroom and on the field, soaking up everything I could learn. Raw physical ability was less important than it had been on the defensive line. At the conclusion of spring practice, I was alternating with another center, Mike Holtzapfel, behind the starter, Tim Monty, and I went home to Spokane that summer feeling a part of Notre Dame football for the first time.

Other things were happening in America during the summer of 1968 which were of slightly greater import than my quest to make the Notre Dame football team. The assassination of Robert Kennedy following by just two months the murder of Martin Luther King; the Democratic convention in Chicago with all its demonstrations, arrests, and abuses of police power; racial disturbances and antiwar protests—all marked the summer of 1968 as a particularly cataclysmic one in recent American history.

Football received a great deal of hyperbolic praise and

vilification during this time. Right-wing ideologues trumpeted athletics, particularly football, as the last bastion against radicalism and moral decay. From the other side, football was attacked as the breeding ground of imperialism, and of the crypto-fascist state that America was said to have become. Football was neither.

The sport for me did not conflict with the antiwar movement. Football's meaning was personal, not political—a result of my political naïveté, perhaps, but also of the period in my life when I was playing. I "found myself" through playing football, as others of my generation were finding themselves through eastern religions, encounter groups, and even the antiwar movement. My quest to play football for Notre Dame remained divorced from my political consciousness. As a *citizen* I was greatly disturbed by my country's official actions; as a *person* I was still completing my adolescence, seeking through the attainment of a long-frustrated goal the confirmation of my own self-worth.

I reported to fall practice with my greatest enthusiasm in years. I had built myself up to 220 pounds over the summer, so that I finally weighed two pounds more than Hanratty, the starting quarterback. Progress of sorts. The novelty of my new position and the prospects of actually playing carried me through the weeks of training camp. By the opener against Oklahoma I was second-team to Monty, and virtually assured of playing time. In the locker room on September 21, 1968, for the first time I put on my dark-blue jersey with the large white "54" on front and back, and tucked it into my gold pants. I had learned only hours before that I, not Holtzapfel, was to be Monty's backup; now, as I checked the straps to all my pads and tested my face mask to make sure it was tight enough, I was about to venture for the first time as a varsity player into the same arena where Johnny Lujack, Leon Hart, Paul Hornung, Nick Buoniconti, and so many other Notre Dame all-Americans had played. I felt a fairly minor part of this 1968 team, but a part nonetheless. The 59,000 fans who roared when we took the field were cheering mostly for Hanratty, Seymour, Kunz, McCoy, and the other familiar stars, but they were cheering for me just a little bit, too. The campus newspaper in its pregame issue had not even listed me on the team roster. By number 54 was printed "Larry

Vuillemin," the center from my freshman team who had been assigned the number during our first spring practice. Chronic
shoulder separations had forced Vuillemin to give up football
long before, but his name remained on the school paper's roster
in place of mine for the entire 1968 season. My friends enjoyed
calling me "Larry" for a long time afterwards. I lived with the
official oversight for I knew who number 54 was.

Oklahoma had been ranked number three the year before and
came in highly regarded to begin this season. But a 14–7 first-
quarter lead was the last the Sooners held. Hanratty threw two
touchdowns to Seymour, and Bob Gladieux scored on three one-
yard plunges, as we rolled to a 21–14 half-time lead, 35–14 after
three quarters, and a 54–21 final margin. Playing the last half of
the fourth quarter with the second team, I discovered that I
could indeed play major-college football. Riding the momentum
that the starters had generated, we moved the ball against the
Sooner defense, I handling my man with little difficulty. It was
too early to make judgments, but I felt like an honest-to-God
football player for the first time in two years.

As a result of our convincing victory over Oklahoma, we were
ranked number one in the UPI poll and number two by the AP
going into the next game against Purdue. The Boilermakers held
the alternate one and two positions, setting up a nationally televised clash of the top two teams in the country. I watched
forlornly from the bench as Purdue, behind Mike Phipps and
Leroy Keyes, continued its surprising mastery of the Irish. The
teams combined for fifty-five first downs and 993 yards of total
offense, but the final score, 37–22, clearly indicated the frustrations we faced all afternoon. We moved the ball inside the
Boilermaker 30-yard line seven different times without scoring.
Hanratty completed twenty-four of forty-four passes for 307
yards in a brilliant individual performance, but Keyes ran for
two touchdowns and passed for one, and even defensed Jim
Seymour in crucial situations; and Phipps hit a substitute receiver named Bob Dillingham whenever key yardage was
needed. Two games into the season, we had already lost our shot
at the national championship.

Rebound victories over Iowa, 51–28, on the road, and Northwestern, 27–7, at home, came as expected, but the Northwestern

game produced an unforeseen turn in my own fortunes. After completing 60 percent of his passes in the first three games for nearly 250 yards per game, Hanratty had the worst half of his career in the first thirty minutes against Northwestern. At the end of the third quarter we held a slim 13–0 lead, when Parseghian began to substitute. I played the entire fourth quarter, against a couple of good 240-pound defensive tackles. Coach Wampfler told me afterward I had been sent in to provide stronger straight-ahead blocking—and had come through. After we scored twice more, once on a 47-yard run by Bob Gladieux, I read my name in the South Bend *Tribune* the next day for the first time, as one of five reserves who were "certainly prominent in the fourth period." I read that phrase over and over, savoring every syllable. More important, when I walked into the locker room for the following Monday's practice, I glanced at the depth chart that always hung on the wall, to find my name listed with the first offense.

First team! I did not want to gawk, but I found whatever opportunities I could to glance again and again at the board—perhaps to assure myself that no one had come to his senses and rearranged the names, but also for the simple pleasure of seeing those familiar letters—O-R-I-A-R-D—next to Kunz's and McKinley's and Dinardo's and Reilly's on the starting offensive line. I talked to no one, not wishing to call attention to myself in any way that might break the spell. Nothing was said to me at practice, but I simply began working with the first unit, snapping the ball to Terry Hanratty instead of Joe Theismann, opening holes for Bob Gladieux, Jeff Zimmerman, and Frank Criniti instead of my former mates on the second team. When I returned to the dorm that night, I said nothing to my roommate or other friends, knowing it was five days until Saturday and many changes could be made in that time. I finally told my roommate on Thursday, but swore him to secrecy lest my anxieties prove true and the lineup be reordered.

That week in practice was the longest of the season. I felt like an intruder in the new huddle in which I now took my place. The players on a football team share a bond, but other bonds within specific groups are stronger in some ways. The first-team offense had its own bond that separated it from the second team and the defense. The offensive linemen had yet a different bond. My replacement of Tim Monty had disrupted our starting line; I could not simply step in and become a part of it immediately. I was like the pin set into a broken bone that in time becomes part of the healed limb. But only in time. I was accepted without comment by Kunz, McKinley, Reilly, and the others. But I would remain a partial outsider until I had shared some common struggles with them. Forged in fire.

Each day my first act on walking into the locker room was to check the depth chart again. By Friday there had been no changes; the dream was actually becoming a reality. I was to be the starting center against Illinois the next day. With an 0–5 record at that point, Illinois hardly presented formidable opposition; our coaches were concerned chiefly that we would take the game too lightly, creating problems for ourselves by our own lack of incentive. Motivation was no problem for me. Had Illinois been Ohio State or her mediocre defensive players been all-American candidates, I could not have taken the game any more seriously than I did. I had studied Illinois's defensive guards and linebackers in their 6–2 alignment so carefully that I could visualize what they would likely do against each of our plays. I noted that Tony Clements, one of the linemen I would be facing, was 6–3, 225, and the other, Jim Whiteside, was 6–2½, 219. They were no bigger than I but I mentally transformed them into awesome monsters for whom I would have to be intensely prepared. To have the object of my quest within reach then let it escape by my own unpreparedness or incompetence was unthinkable. Come one-thirty Saturday afternoon, I would be ready.

Friday's practice was a typically light one, as we zipped through our plays, rehearsed our two-minute offense and our kicking game, and gathered for team cheers. The offense and defense competed with each other to create the wittiest cheer of the week—a bit of doggerel verse that lampooned each other or the next day's opponent. The defense went first:

> Hey, offense—
> Give us a break;
> Score some points
> For pity's sake.

Then we responded:

> Hey, defense—we've got a plan:
> Tomorrow let's get the job done;
> If you can hold 'em to 50 points,
> We'll score 51!

Coach Parseghian awarded our side the laurels for the week and sent us in.

I ate dinner and attended the pep rally as usual that night, sitting grimly in the balcony with my "game face" already on. Our routine for the evening would be the same as it had been for the three previous home games. We would watch a movie and spend the night at Moreau Seminary across the lakes on campus away from the noise and partying of the other students, then we would gather for pregame meal and final meetings in the North Dining Hall on Saturday morning, after which we would report to the stadium. On this vigil of my first start, every act, however familiar it had become, was charged with new significance. Walking to Moreau Hall, I stopped at the Grotto to meditate alone for a few minutes. The Grotto is a small cavernlike shrine to Notre Dame's patroness, the Virgin Mary, tucked away into the underside of a slight elevation on which the major portion of the university stands. For all its proximity to other campus activities, the Grotto radiates a quiet peacefulness that is particularly meditative at night, when the flickering glow of many dozen votive candles creates a cozy haven from the outside world. I sat on one of the chairs and stared into the hypnotic candlelight, no longer the simple Catholic boy who padded to the school chapel to pray before high school football games, but still unwilling to neglect one of my traditional pregame rituals.

From the Grotto I proceeded to Moreau Seminary for a very different kind of ritual. As on previous Friday nights before games, the entire team convened in the building's auditorium for a movie—a John Wayne movie. Usually the Duke himself was in the film, but even if he was not, it was still always a "John Wayne movie." Whether the choice of films was due to the personal taste of the assistant coach who selected them or some careful plan was followed—a decision to appeal to certain emotions in us rather than others—I don't know. But I do know that we invariably spent the nights before games watching good guys killing bad guys, saving the helpless from the wicked, and maintaining decorous relationships with adoring but modest females. What better psychic preparation for facing the hated Boilermakers—or even Illini—the next day?

After the movie, we dispersed to our assigned rooms, spartan twelve-by-eight singles with bed, desk, closet, washbowl. I felt rather monkish in my cloistral compartment—exactly how I wanted to feel on this solemn vigil. I mentally rehearsed yet again our offensive game plan against the defenses we expected to see, and against the specific opponents I would be facing. But I was not above using this most momentous of nights for non-football purposes as well. My girlfriend, Julie, had broken up with me the year before, but we maintained a friendship which I still hoped could be translated into passion. I had accordingly brought paper and pen to write a letter that night before going to bed—knowing well that my emotional state would likely produce a particularly soulful one, and even hoping that my promotion to the first team would impress her as much as it did me.

After this bit of calculated romance, I returned one more time to the playbook, then tried to sleep. Images of tomorrow's game, possible scenarios of my glorious success or appalling failure, would not leave my consciousness. I took a sleeping pill and tried once again to clear my overactive mind. Eventually sleep did come.

Adrenaline began flowing almost before I awoke. Outwardly I was calm, but inside I was churning. I had looked forward to this day so long and so intensely that its arrival brought with it almost a sadness. Play well or badly, I would perceive my life differently after today. The frustrations of what-seems-so-unlikely would disappear, but so would the pleasures of what-might-be. After today I would have either experienced a rite of passage to a new level of self-regard, or failed to seize the opportunity that had been given me by a fortuitous chain of events extending over many months. Mass was offered in the seminary chapel. Afterward, we walked in small groups to the North Dining Hall for the pregame meal of steak and baked potato. I had little desire to eat, but told myself that three hours from now I did not want to feel weak from so foolish a cause as hunger. After the meal, we met in groups, the offensive linemen with Coach Wampfler for a final review of blocking assignments. For the first time all week, public mention was made of my elevation to the first team.

"You were put in the game last Saturday, Mike," Coach Wampfler said quietly before the group at the end of our meeting, "for your run blocking. You did the job. Today just go out there and give it everything you've got on every play. Don't save anything. You haven't played for long periods this year, but if you get tired, we've got people who can come in for you. Put out a hundred percent on every play."

I kept my eyes on Wampfler's face all the time he was talking, nodded my head with slow determination, then looked down at my feet, clenching and unclenching my fists, telling myself, "Hell, yes, a hundred percent all the time. I'm going to *do* it." I did not look at Tim Monty; I had not really talked with Tim all week. I liked him. He had helped me on numerous occasions with advice and encouragement as I was learning my new position. I did not know him well, but he had been the friendliest of the seniors all fall. My gain now, of course, was at Tim's expense. I regretted that fact but could not afford to dwell on it; I had more or less avoided Tim during the week. As the meeting broke up and we went our separate ways for the hour or so before it would be necessary to report to the locker room, Tim came up behind me and put his hand on my back.

"You'll do a good job, Mike."

"Thanks, Tim," I mumbled, and wanted to say more, but I did not know what. He gave me a pat and walked on. Much more was felt on both sides than was said, but we understood each other.

I wandered about the campus for a while, both aware and unaware of the people streaming by, laughing, talking, enjoying the October sunshine and the anticipation of the game and the parties afterward. I tried to sit and relax a couple of times but could not remain still. I ran into a friend from home, Nick Scarpelli, a teammate at Gonzaga Prep who was at ND, too, and who eventually became captain of the baseball team. His girlfriend visiting from Spokane knew Julie; in fact, she brought a good-luck message from Julie—a collage made from *Sports Illustrated* clippings. I told them I was starting against Illinois and basked in their congratulations. The scenario for a reconciliation I had imagined last night was working out even better than I had hoped.

I felt a sudden need to tell my roommate that indeed I was starting. In the dormitory among friendly well-wishers I realized that I did not want to talk after all: I wanted nothing that distracted me from my inner thoughts. I found Bob alone in our room, gave him the news, accepted his handshake and congratulations, then left quickly.

It was still early, but I walked slowly toward the stadium, having conceded that I could not kill time. The brick oval looked no different from the way it had on all the other occasions I had seen it, but my own sense of drama made me study it more intently. This was it. Mike Oriard—number 54—starting for the Fighting Irish. I thought nothing beyond that simple fact. I did not rehearse the feelings and events of the past two years, but only that simple fact. I, Mike Oriard, was going to start for Notre Dame.

Around the locker-room entrance a few kids clustered, watching for their favorite players. I passed easily through them, and moved past a few teammates to my own locker. Each part of my uniform was familiar now, but *I* was different, and I devoted more care to each stage of my dressing than I normally took. Putting on the uniform was a significant part of the players' ritual preparations for the game. Like most of my teammates, I put on each article in the same order every week, practicing a superstition that I would not have admitted, but whose sequence I would not want to have altered. I watched my gradual transformation from a mere mortal to a mighty athlete. As I put on the various knee pads, thigh pads, and hip pads, then slipped the shiny gold pants over my blue nylon knee-high socks, I took on proportions and brilliance that made me feel larger than life. When I looked in the mirror, I was someone who impressed even me.

Shoulder pads and jersey were the last two articles to be put

on. I was ready for the game. At the proper moment Ara Parseghian called us together. On game day, the coach's normal intensity was heightened to a nearly uncontainable level. His dark,
deep-set eyes burned into me—not to sear or pain but to fan the
flames of my own inner fire. Parseghian wore what he always
wore: navy-blue pants and sweat shirt, with gold letters against
a white border spelling out N-o-t-r-e-D-a-m-e on his chest. He
paced nervously while the players from the back of the locker
room made their way to the front, but even when he stopped,
his nervous energy created the illusion that he was still moving.
As I watched him, waiting expectantly for whatever he would
say, to all my other motivations was added an overwhelming
desire to play well for this man. He was truly my coach now. No
more the distant figure who spoke once to an unknown freshman, or the slightly less distant man on the tower overhead
yelling instructions to my opponents across the line, he was now
my coach. There was no particular closeness between us. He was
more a detached all-powerful father figure before whom I
needed to prove myself. I felt deeply his presence in everything
I did with the football team. Parseghian did not very often deal
directly with his players, rather delegating responsibilities to his
assistants, but I knew that my playing today was not just Jerry
Wampfler's idea. Nothing happened that did not come from the
top. Ara did not get close to individual players, but he exuded a
care and commitment for the entire team. This fall, feeling at
last a member of the team, I finally sensed this.

Wampfler, Yonto, and the other assistants stationed themselves on the outside of the circle of players on the floor and
benches around Ara. A few cleats scraped against the concrete,
and shoulder pads crunched as players settled against the walls.

"Don't be tricked into complacency today," he told us. "Illinois
has not won a game, but they're a good enough football team to
beat you if you let them. On any given Saturday, any team in
the country can beat any other. You know by now that every
team plays its best against Notre Dame. If Illinois beats you
today, their season will be a success. You can bet that they know
it, but you know it, too. Be ready for anything—on-side kicks,
fake punts, trick plays. They've got nothing to lose and a lot to

gain if they beat you. Don't give them the chance. I want sixty
minutes of football out there today. Not thirty minutes, not
forty-five minutes, but sixty minutes. Now let's go!"

It was a much less emphatic pep talk than Ara had given before the Oklahoma or Purdue games, but his personal dynamism
charged the familiar phrases with new urgency. I hung on every
word as if Ara had directed it to me alone; as a starter now, I
seemed to be hearing these formulas for the first time. After one
of the priests from the university's administration led a team
prayer, we rose with shouts and growls to strap on our helmets
and clatter down the concrete stairs to the tunnel below and the
entrance to the field. As I crowned myself with my own Golden
Dome, all my ordinariness left me. The last thing I saw as I left
the locker room was the motto on the wall:

> What Tho The Odds
> Be Great or Small
> Notre Dame Men
> Will Win Over All!

This was no silly platitude, but the secret message I carried like
a holy vessel with me onto the field.

The crowd roared its greeting. Calisthenics. Brief blocking
and passing drills. Running our plays against no defense—
quickly, sharply, crisply. Cocaptains George Kunz and Bob
Olson representing us for the coin toss. A final word from Ara on
the sidelines. The whistle blowing. The ball sailing off the tee as
the game began.

On a day on which General Curtis LeMay publicly berated
the Johnson administration's restricted bombing policy in Vietnam, on which Bill Toomey won the Olympic decathlon in Mex-
ico City while teammates gathered three other gold medals,
Notre Dame's rout of overmatched Illinois was barely news-
worthy. For Notre Dame supporters, Terry Hanratty made the
game memorable by surpassing the immortal Gipp's school total
offense record, and the offense's 673 yards rushing and passing
established another school mark. The 58–8 final score was the
most lopsided defeat Illinois had suffered since 1906. But this
game had a significance for me that was retained in no record
book. The game itself was lost in the same blur through which

an offensive lineman sees most games. I spent the afternoon slapping the ball into Hanratty's hands, driving my helmet into the breastbones of defensive linemen, cutting off middle linebackers, and pulling away from the scrimmage line to pick up defensive ends or blitzing linebackers on pass plays. Having discovered on the first few downs that my anxieties about my opponents' possible superpowers were unfounded, I expanded confidently as the game progressed. I could not have handpicked a more ideal opponent for my initiation. I blocked on play after play as Bob Gladieux, Jeff Zimmerman, and Coley O'Brien consistently made solid gains, and as Hanratty picked out his receivers—usually Seymour—for 269 yards and three touchdowns. Ironically, I would have played almost as much on this day had I remained on the second team. The starters played only one series in the second half, leaving a 31–0 lead to the reserves, who scored the final 27 points. I watched the remainder of the game from a contented sprawl on the bench, arms draped over its back, feeling a little like a cattle baron surveying his acreage.

My private satisfactions far exceeded the true difficulty of the test I had undergone, but under the circumstances I was not inclined to qualify the significance of that afternoon. In the locker room afterward, I laughed and exchanged congratulations with my teammates—who seemed more truly teammates now—soaked luxuriantly under a hot shower, and returned to the dormitory. I chose not to leave the locker room through the main exit—where I would have to pass through swarms of autograph-seeking kids who would ask, "Who're you?" before thrusting their pencils and scraps of paper at me. I was in no mood to have to explain who I was. Feeling notable for the first time, I did not want to have to plead my case before a jury of twelve-year-olds. I slipped out a back door through the equipment room, passed through the sparse crowd under the stadium, and walked back to Dillon Hall, where my friends waited to share in my pleasure. As I walked across campus, I strode with a new self-importance. Glancing at the Golden Dome, I felt more a part of my Notre Dame world—felt that I had now imprinted my name in the records of Notre Dame football and become a permanent part of the institution's history. I reflected on the timidities, the uncertainties, the anxieties, the frustrations of the previous two years and could not help but marvel at my new status. I felt fine.

The remainder of the 1968 season completed my introduction to Notre Dame football. A frustrating loss to Michigan State, three easy wins over Navy, Pittsburgh, and Georgia Tech, and an initially exhilarating but finally unsatisfying tie with Southern Cal rounded out our season. The Michigan State game marked my first start on national TV; for the introductions before the cameras I maintained a properly grim demeanor to signify my recognition of the game's high seriousness and the frivolity of media intrusions. The game itself was pure frustration. We outgained the Spartans 454 to 247, Hanratty was superb in passing for 312 yards; but we moved the ball almost effortlessly between the 20-yard lines then failed to score. Down 21–17 with three minutes to play, we marched on Hanratty's seven-for-seven passing to first and goal on the MSU two. Two rushes failed to score, an obvious pass interference in the end zone against Seymour was missed when the backfield judge slipped on the turf, and Al Brenner nailed Hanratty short of the goal line on fourth down. My own opposition from linemen Charles Bailey and Ron Curl and middle linebacker Rich Saul was much tougher than the previous week's. I shared my teammates' self-disgust at not having moved them when we had to.

The Navy game next provided my first national recognition, in an article by Paul Zimmerman in the New York *Post*. "Junior Center Fighting to Be Irish," highlighting the fact that Notre Dame's starting center was without a scholarship, was a pleasant boost to my ego, though unimportant compared to the simple fact of playing. The game itself was a walkover. We scored on our first two possessions, Gladieux ran for 117 yards, and we turned the game over to the reserves with ten minutes to play and a 38–14 lead. One more touchdown made the final 45–14. My opponent for the day was Navy's top defenseman, a middle guard named Emerson Carr whose quickness had concerned me during the week. My handling him restored some of the self-esteem lost the week before.

Pitt and Georgia Tech offered little resistance to the number two-ranked offense in the nation. Whatever concern we had before the Pittsburgh game was due to a freak injury to Hanratty's knee in a midweek goal-line scrimmage that sent Terry to surgery and Joe Theismann to quarterback. Joe had thrown eleven passes all year, but against Pitt he quickly took charge, guiding the offense to touchdowns the first six times we touched the ball. The starters sat down on the bench before the end of the second quarter while the reserves made it 49–0 at the half. Ara agreed to run the clock continuously in the second half, and instructed Bob Belden, Theismann's backup, not to pass at all. The result was 56–7, with Pitt scoring after recovering a fumbled kickoff— the only time it possessed the ball across midfield.

The Georgia Tech game was remarkable only for the heavy rain and resulting mud through which we sloshed to a 34–6 victory.

The season ended before 85,000 spectators in the L.A. Coliseum and a national TV audience, in one of the more memorable games in the ND–USC series. The Trojans, undefeated and ranked number' one coming into the game, were led by O. J. Simpson, having a spectacular Heisman Trophy senior season. At 7–2 we were the underdogs for the first time in fifty games, and a 21-yard interception for a touchdown forty seconds into the game seemed to foretell our doom. But we rebounded for an 86-yard drive in eighteen plays—the kind that tells the defense, "We are going to run right at you; see if you can stop us"—and followed minutes later with the single play from that season that I recall most vividly. The call was a simple running play for Gladieux. I made a solid block on Trojan middle linebacker Jim Snow, driving him seven or eight yards off the line of scrimmage. As I looked up I saw out of the left corner of my eye number 20 cutting off my block and turning upfield. The result was a 57-yard touchdown run, the longest of the season, and I felt I had made a key contribution to it. The look of helpless frustration on Snow's face after the play—the kind of mute testimony a lineman craves but rarely receives—completed my satisfaction.

The score read 21–7 at half time, after Theismann caught a razzle-dazzle 13-yard touchdown pass from Coley O'Brien, to whom Joe had just handed off the ball. The Irish were rolling. Unfortunately, we stopped rolling at half time, while USC put two second-half scores on the board. The tie was sealed with 33 seconds left when Scott Hempel missed a 33-yard field goal attempt. Southern Cal had narrowly escaped; outgained 422–239, the Trojans managed to avoid defeat. For our part, we had the satisfaction of holding O.J. to 55 yards in twenty-one carries— the lowest output of his career—and the moral victory of tying the number one team. But it should have been a real victory, not a moral one.

With no bowl game possible, the USC game capped a 7–2–1 season and a number five-ranking in the writers' poll. Ara later observed, "This team deserves a better fate than seven–two–one." A single play here or there could have made us 9–1; 10–0 had even been possible. Hanratty, Seymour, Gladieux, Kunz, Kuechenberg, and their fellow seniors had been a particularly talented group; 7–2–1 could not accurately reflect their excellence.

But for me there could be no disappointment. From an obscure walk-on I had become a starter, realizing a dream that had directly or indirectly enticed me for a decade. In my adolescent groping for self-esteem I had achieved an unambiguous goal whose aura could support me through many self-doubts. On those occasions when I would wonder, who am I and what am I doing with my life? I could answer, "I'm Mike Oriard, starting center for Notre Dame." That was a very temporary role, and a trivial one from some perspectives, but it sustained me while I was evolving a more mature sense of myself. I left my adolescence behind me after that football game with the University of Illinois on October 19, 1968. From that point onward, football began to mean other things to me.

FIVE

My Notre Dame

FOR MY ACCOMPLISHMENTS during that 1968 season, I was not crowned with a laurel wreath, but I did receive a scholarship and a monogram jacket. The jacket was of navy-blue wool with dark-blue leather sleeves and a gold "ND" over the left breast. When as a freshman I had first seen students wearing these jackets, I did not find them very attractive. Until I learned what they stood for. No one could buy them; only lettermen in varsity sports could wear them. Over the next three years that jacket became the symbol of my quest, the holy grail, or rather the holy robe which I had to prove myself worthy to wear. When I picked mine up in December after the season, I slipped my arms through the sleeves as solemnly as if I were donning a sacred vestment. It fit perfectly. No jacket I had ever worn felt so much as if it had been tailored for me alone. I looked in the mirror and seemed to expand. The heavy material made me feel substantial; I looked broader in the shoulders, more powerful in the chest. I couldn't just walk in such a jacket; I had to swagger a little. I felt conspicuous in it—not awkwardly conspicuous as I had felt at high school dances, but more notable and impressive. The interlocking gold "ND" over the left breast signified to the world that I was part of the finest football program in the land. To most of the world, anyway. In Spokane over Christmas vaca-

tion I bought a hamburger at a drive-in one evening. The girl
counting my change looked at my jacket and asked, "Do you go
to North Dakota?"

In my new role as returning starter I felt surprisingly comfortable that winter and spring. Only one other senior-to-be remained from the 1968 offensive team. Left tackle Jim Reilly had
started for two full seasons and would be back to anchor our
line in 1969. Junior-to-be Larry DiNardo had started every game
at left guard until a knee injury felled him late in the season.
The three of us would provide most of the maturity on the
offense the following fall. Having started the last three games at
quarterback after Hanratty's injury, Theismann would be the
most seasoned backfield returnee; for the most part we would be
young and inexperienced. Accustomed to feeling largely unno-
ticed by players from my own class and classes ahead of me, I
found the respect and even deference of the underclassmen
warming. In the weight room of the new Athletic and Convoca-
tion Center to which we had graduated that year, I met many of
the freshmen who would be competing for positions on next
year's team, and who looked to me as a leader. Even the
coaches, when they stopped by the weight room to check the go-
ings-on, paused to chat with me about our prospects for the season, as if I were to be part of the nucleus around which that
team would be built. Jerry Wampfler, my line coach, was particularly friendly. Jerry had virtually created me, transforming a
defensive end to a center, then overseeing my improvement
through the season. He had understood me well, realizing I responded better to encouragement than to abuse, and that I was
extremely coachable. What he taught me to do, I did. He took
pride in his handiwork and we were mutually grateful: I had
made him look good as a coach; he had made me into a player.

Spring football opened on an altogether new note for me,
compared to my previous springs. From day one I was a fixture
in the middle of the offensive line; *others* would have to scramble and claw for the right to play. I was not susceptible to complacency because I was still new enough at my position that I
was no casual master of all its skills, yet I felt neither anxious
nor threatened. I was in the ideal position of being established
but having room to improve; neither frustration nor stagnancy

was a danger. By the very nature of my position as an offensive
lineman I had to work hard. To a center each play was more a
struggle for survival than a demonstration of technique.

Spring football was physically as demanding as ever, but emotionally and psychologically supportive. The physical pressures
had changed. I was now on the other side of the scrimmage line
from my former prep teammates. No bond remained between us.
My feeling of unity with them had merely supported my desire
to escape their fate. A bond of necessity and of the moment. I
harbored none of the animosity toward the prep team that I had
felt against the offensive players when our roles had been
reversed. Now, when we drilled, I was in no way driven to
prove myself *against them.* Rather, my motives were more inner-
directed. To overpower a prep-team opponent was not to prove
my superiority over him but to demonstrate my growing mastery
of a difficult position. Not until the games in the fall would my
opponents be truly "opponents" again.

The major tests that spring came in "the cage," a metal-mesh
contraption with five compartments, each about four feet high,
four feet wide, and six feet long. Five offensive linemen lined up
in their stances at the entrances to the sections of the cage.
Straddling a foot-wide plank, we had to drive prep-team opponents through the cage and out the other end—remaining low
because of the ceiling overhead, and maintaining a wide stance
because of the plank between our feet. The year before as a
prepper I had gloried in stuffing linemen in the cage, refusing to
be driven out. Now, having to assume the other role, I was
thankful to discover that there were few players on the prep
team as ornery or determined as I had been.

Spring football progressed with conditioning and contact
drills, countless repetitions of running and passing plays, and
filmed scrimmages on Wednesdays and Saturdays. My seniority
wore better and better, until a week before the culminating intrasquad game, when my perspective on the coming season
suffered a jolt in one of those Saturday scrimmages. Having
marched through the second-team defense to score, we lined up
for the extra point. Crouched over the ball I sighted Joe Theismann's hands waiting to receive the ball to spot it for the placement. Looking up again to check the defense and be certain my

teammates were set, I noted that the middle linebacker, a freshman eager to make the team, was lined up seven yards deep for a run at the line, hoping to break through on his momentum and block the kick. I knew such efforts were futile, but I prepared myself mentally for his onslaught. Looking back between my legs again, I sent Joe the ball on a low arc, then raised my head and braced my neck for what I knew was coming—I *thought* I knew what was coming. The freshman backer exploded into me, sending the most extraordinary pain I had ever experienced searing through my neck, shoulder, and arm. He never got beyond the line of scrimmage and the kick was successful, but my left arm hung limp from the shoulder, feeling as if someone had attached a vise to the chunk of muscle and nerves above my collarbone and was cranking it tight.

The pain was excruciating. I hunched my shoulder to my left ear and grunted a long, low "Unhhhh . . ." as I jogged awkwardly from the field. Coach Wampfler and the trainer, Gene Paszkiet, met me on the sidelines, where Gene attempted to reduce the pressure on the pinched nerve. Wampfler told me to sit out the rest of the scrimmage, and as I slumped on the bench unable to relieve the deadening ache, I flashed back to the first game of my senior year in high school. I knew enough about pinched nerves to realize it would haunt my senior season as torn cartilage had done four years before. I had no clear expectations yet, but doom hung over me in my own private cloud. I did not know the degree to which I would be hampered, but I realized that the anticipated pleasures of my senior season had just been complicated.

A pinched nerve is like a criminal record: once you've had one it's yours forever. My own problems were compounded by a most unsuitably long neck. Football players, linemen and linebackers anyway, should have no necks at all—perhaps a steel pin on which their heads can swivel, like turrets on a tank. Playing football is not a natural thing for the human body to do, but no surgeon has ever discovered how to remove ankles, knees, shoulders, and necks, yet leave the athlete enough parts to play the game. During practices before the final intrasquad game, I jammed my pinched nerve at least half a dozen times a day. My left arm would temporarily go numb, and I would lean over in the huddle, dangling my arm and scrunching my head and shoulder trying to relieve the pain and restore feeling before the next play. A worse result was that for the first time I became conscious of my neck before I made contact. I could no longer recklessly use my head as a battering ram. I had to hit my man hard enough to block him effectively, but not so hard that I jammed my pinched nerve again. I felt as the laboratory rat must, who cringes during that split second between hearing the bell and receiving the expected electric shock. Away from the field my injury stayed with me. At lunch I found myself reaching for the saltshaker with my left hand only to realize I had to pull my left arm to me with my right. Sleeping was complicated by a dull continuous ache.

At the conclusion of spring ball I met with a representative of one of the equipment companies and discussed ways in which a pair of shoulder pads might be built that would stabilize my long neck sufficiently to prevent further aggravation of the injury, without preventing me from swiveling my head back and forth to check defensive alignments, and from looking back between my legs for long punt and extra-point snaps. I left for summer vacation with the hope that I would return in the fall to find the miracle pads awaiting me.

During the summer other matters intervened. My major project was to increase my bulk and to report in the fall in the best physical condition of my life. The coaches had instituted a new program: on our return at the end of summer we would be tested on our conditioning in one of three events. I planned to run the quarter mile. Backs were expected to do it in sixty seconds or less, linemen in sixty-five. After work all summer, I ran miles, sprints, and starts, and worked on my various techniques with another Notre Damer from Spokane, Bill Etter, a sophomore quarterback. I lifted weights three days a week, noticeably increasing my strength and bulk. And I took protein supplements. Determined to come back to South Bend a physical brute, I drank every day at least two cans of a liquid protein called Nutrament. For one four-week period at midsummer I made my big push—six cans a day, in addition to my regular three substantial meals and an occasional snack when I could squeeze one down. At 375 calories per can, I was consuming

2250 calories each day in Nutrament alone. I got up at seven, fixed myself toast and eggs and juice, then choked down three cans of the chalky, vanilla-flavored stuff. Feeling mildly bloated, I went off to load trucks for eight hours, breaking for a large lunch at noon, then reported to the weight room or track for a workout at the end of the day. Dinner at home and a few hours of recreation set the stage for the final attack on my digestive system. Three twelve-ounce cans of thick, creamy Nutrament waited to be drunk. At bedtime I chugged them down as quickly as possible. To savor something so unpleasant was impossible, but I also needed to get them down before I could realize how full I was becoming. Thoroughly gorged, my stomach bloated near to bursting, I went groaning to bed. I slept on my back that summer.

The results of my efforts were satisfying at first. I arrived on campus at 237 pounds, bigger and stronger than I had ever been, and I ran my quarter mile in 59.1 seconds. Two-a-day workouts in South Bend's heat and humidity exacted their toll, however. By the opening game I weighed 225, by the end of the season I had slipped to 218. What I didn't realize was that protein supplements were useless for putting on extra muscle, and were even potentially dangerous to the kidneys. Coaches and trainers were not nutritionists, and the common wisdom of the time was wrong. The average adult American utilizes only a third of the protein he takes in daily. What I was getting from my normal diet was sufficient to convert all my weight-lifting into extra muscle. The additional protein was simply extra calories—which meant body fat. Once I started training camp, the fat came off, and I weighed what I should have weighed anyway—225.

The team that emerged through spring practice and summer training camp to start the 1969 season was a very different group from the one that played the year before. Most of last year's high-powered offense that averaged over 500 yards per game had been lost to graduation. The preseason football guide for 1969 said in bold type, "If the Offense Is Only Adequate, Then the Defense Will Have to Be Superb." The superb defense was led by Mike McCoy and Bob Olson. McCoy, known as "Man Mountain," was just that; listed at six five, 274, he looked even bigger, his massive chest and trunk providing a nearly immovable barrier at left tackle.

Bob Olson at inside linebacker was the defensive leader. At six feet, 226, Bobo was built like a very large fireplug, yet he ranged from sideline to sideline blotting out ballcarriers. After he introduced himself to a running back at the line of scrimmage, the running back remembered him the rest of the afternoon. Strong and built low to the ground, Olson could not be driven backward. On more than one occasion that season, I saw a halfback lower his shoulder to drive into Bobo's chest, only to be bounced onto his back as if an invisible hook had reached out and yanked him by the collar, ending a bad act on amateur night. Olson and McCoy were surrounded on the defense by a collection of junior and senior returning starters at linebacker and in the backfield, and a trio of sophomore defensive linemen, two of whom—Walt Patulski and Mike Kadish—were future all-Americans and number one pro draft picks. Before the season was over, three more members of a very talented sophomore class had won starting assignments at linebacker and deep back.

The offense was to be the "adequate" part of the team that year. Halfbacks Denny Allen, Andy Huff, and Ed Ziegler were strong, capable runners, but none had exceptional speed, nor even Bob Gladieux's uncanny instincts. Gladieux had been neither big nor fast, but I never saw him knocked backward. He had the ability to slice through the narrowest opening, and to twist at the moment of contact to prevent a solid hit and gain another yard or two by lunging forward. Our backs in 1969 were more workmanlike, less elusive. At fullback Jeff Zimmerman was returning as a two-year starter, but his injury problems reached a climax early in the 1969 season when he was discovered to have a congenitally defective kidney and would have to give up football. His replacement, Bill Barz, was another big, strong, competent, but slow back. We had no aristocrats carrying the ball in 1969, only solid yeomen.

At quarterback, Joe Theismann proved to be the catalyst we needed. He was a very different athlete and personality from Hanratty. Terry had been known as "the Rat" to his teammates. He, Gladieux, and Ron Dushney were the well-liked free spirits who charmed even Coach Parseghian, because their playfulness stopped when the serious play had to begin. Once when Parseghian in exasperation exploded at Dushney, "What am I going to do with you?" Dushney instantly responded, "Why, Coach, I think you ought to kick my butt." With mock exaggeration Ara did just that, the rest of us burst into laughter, and practice continued with lighter spirit and more efficiency. The number two offense in the country could afford to joke on occasion. Hanratty was also known at other times as "Powerful Pierre," after a Bluto-like cartoon character who harassed the Mounties in a current TV program. At six two, 220, and heavily bearded, when Hanratty put on a stocking cap he truly looked like a north woods lumberjack. As a quarterback, too, he was powerful, dropping straight back into the pocket to rifle the ball with his strong arm 50 or 60 yards when required.

Theismann was his opposite in every way. At six feet, 170, he looked more like Road Runner than Powerful Pierre. Much faster and quicker than Hanratty, he was a better runner and scrambler, but his slight build made him appear much more fragile than he in fact was. He had not come to Notre Dame with a reputation as a passer, but he proved that year that as well as being more durable than he seemed, he could throw. Like smart coaches everywhere, Ara adapted his system to his personnel. Because Joe's threat to the defense lay in his scrambling ability, Ara had him sprinting out to pass rather than dropping back into the pocket. Joe was also brash, even cocky, but in an engaging manner that exuded confidence rather than conceit, and provided the kind of leadership we needed at quarterback. Throwing to Dewey Poskon, a senior tight end without much previous playing time, and split end Tom Gatewood, a sophomore who would become one of Notre Dame's greatest receivers, Joe gave us a sound passing game.

The offensive line was slightly more experienced than the backfield and receivers. Senior Terry Brennan was a returning letterman at right tackle, but the guard on that side, junior Gary Kos, had seen little action the year before. On the left side, Jim Reilly was a first-rate tackle and Larry DiNardo a fine guard, giving us a tandem with both experience and excellence. Reilly in particular was superb. At six two, 247, he was big without seeming mammoth, but he blocked as if he weighed five hundred pounds.

At center, I brought six games of experience to our line, but as a whole, despite individual excellences, we were a yeoman group, as our backs were. Last year's line, with the same Reilly and DiNardo on the left side, but also George Kunz and a solid guard, Tom McKinley, on the right, had been more uniformly talented. The offensive line in 1969, and the offensive unit as a whole, was distinguished by fewer individual stars, but over the course of the year we became a fine *team*. Perhaps what was most remarkable about that 1969 season was the absence of friction among the players. No one begrudged another's recognition in the press or blamed another for failing to block or to run through the right hole. Sharp words were rare. More often, if we were playing badly, we became collectively angry at ourselves. No one could be accused of loafing. We played teams with more physical talent than we had in 1969, but none that worked any harder.

A week before the season opener my rise from walk-on to starter was capped by an even greater miracle: I was elected offensive cocaptain. My Horatio Alger story was complete, or so my career was interpreted in most of the press coverage I received that year. "Walk-on to Captain, That's Story of Oriard," read the headline to an article in the South Bend *Tribune*. "Oriard Beats the Odds, He's the Walk-on Captain," said the Chicago *Sun-Times*. Mere Algerism did not explain what had happened. My good fortune in having men such as Brian Boulac and Jerry Wampfler to believe in me, the complex of circumstances by which a center was needed and I was given a chance to play, even the fact that I was six five, not five eleven—all of these factors fell into a neat pattern. But I had worked hard. I had struggled and clawed and persevered—paid my dues many times over. Even if everyone who worked as hard was not so fortunate, I felt that I had earned my honors. I had been driven to prove my ability to unbelievers and now I had received the ultimate endorsement from my teammates. I would be able to tell my grandchildren in the next century that I had been captain of the 1969 Notre Dame football team. I felt I had just been visited by my fairy godmother, but I also felt immensely satisfied by what *I* had accomplished.

In college football's centennial year, we opened at home with Northwestern. I had returned to South Bend at the end of the summer to find no miracle pads awaiting me, but only an ordinary pair of shoulder pads with an overly thick sponge "horse collar" that did not protect my pinched nerve at all. Gene Paszkiet, the trainer, proved more inventive, securing a leather collar from a harness shop that he adapted to fit me. It locked my head so rigidly that I decided to wear it only during practices; for the games I would simply have to stick my neck out, so to speak. The Northwestern game established the pattern for the ten games that followed. I could do the job, but without the recklessness that could overwhelm opponents and be so satisfying to me. Having to be conscious of self-protection as well as attack—drawing in at the same time I was driving out—I felt less liberated than hardworking all year. No caution could prevent the five or six occasions on which I jammed my neck each game, returning to the huddle with dangling arm and agonized expression, grateful for the moment between plays. I never missed a down due to the pinched nerve, but I missed much of the pleasure that unrestrained play would have given me. Sometimes aches and pains are simply signs of injury.

We started slowly against Northwestern, as if to prove that anxieties about our offense were justified. The Wildcats put ten points on the board before we ran our second play; the first had been a pass intercepted by Rick Telander and run back to our 14-yard line. Before the first period had ended, we put together two long touchdown drives to regain the lead, but as the fourth quarter opened the score remained 14–10. Then occurred a sweet moment that I perhaps above all others on the field could appreciate. Brian Lewallen, my fellow walk-on from South Bend, broke open the close game with a 44-yard punt return for a touchdown. Brian and I and Jim Bergquist had been prep-team buddies, and now Brian, too, had emerged from obscurity. Jim, unfortunately, never got a chance. When Brian came off the field after his return, I ran to embrace him. We exchanged a look whose meaning was clear: we did it—by God, we both did it!

The offense followed up Brian's game-breaker for two more scores for a respectable 35–10 final.

The following week's game against Purdue provided the key to our entire season. The Boilermakers under Coach Jack Mollenkopf were an enigma. Always a physically dominating team and usually very talented besides, Purdue was capable of beating the best team in the country one week and losing to the Little Sisters of Charity the next. Unfortunately, their best game year after year seemed to be reserved for Notre Dame. The Irish under Ara had beaten our instate rivals in 1964 and 1966, our national-championship and near-national-championship years, but lost in every other. Purdue was also the only team to beat Ara in back-to-back seasons. In 1969, Leroy Keyes had departed, but Mike Phipps returned with two straight victories and we desperately wanted to deny him a third. Perhaps that was our problem. The coaches did everything possible to get us psychologically and emotionally ready. Assistant Coach Tom Pagna read us a letter he had received that week from Rocky Bleier—recuperating in a Tokyo hospital from the leg wound received in Vietnam. Many of us remembered Rocky with a special regard, and were moved that he would think of us under such circumstances. But on the bus to Lafayette I suspect we thought more about not being beaten than we did about winning. I had no fear of the Boilermakers, but I felt the peculiar hold they had on us. They clearly came out expecting to win; we came out fighting not to lose.

Phipps was brilliant that day, particularly on third down. Purdue scored its first touchdown on third-and-14 from our 37-yard line. Phipps spotted a blitz, called an audible at the line, and hit his receiver for the score. The second touchdown came at the end of a 63-yard drive in eleven plays, including two more third-down conversions. For the day Phipps was 12–20 for 213 yards—not dazzling statistics—but he was six of nine on crucial third-down plays. Our defense continually put him in a hole, but he dug his team out again.

The keys to the game for me, however, were a single play in the third quarter and a long drive in the fourth. Down 14–7, we were moving the ball well, until on third-and-one on Purdue's 26

we were called for illegal motion. After a running play gained
nothing, we faced fourth-and-six from the 31. Theismann called
a rollout; with the snap of the ball I set up to check for an inside linebacker blitz—my first responsibility—then turned to
pick up any rush coming from the backside. Too late, I saw Purdue's speedy Billy McKoy sprinting in from the right. I never
got to him as he trapped Joe for a 17-yard loss. Neither then nor
afterward did any coach blame me for costing us the game. One
play may not be the sum of a game perhaps, but that was a particularly crucial one. Ara believed, though, that *teams* won and
lost, not individuals. He would not tolerate mistakes due to insufficient effort, but he never blamed anyone—either publicly or
privately—for being humanly fallible. Ara demanded perfection
of only one person: himself. I shared his view. I was disgusted
for missing McKoy, but I only had to deal with that failure privately, without having to defend myself against others' criticism.

Football taught me that I can demand perfection of myself
but I cannot expect it, and that I had better be able to accept
myself as less than perfect. That Purdue game more than any
other contributed importantly to my education. Late in the
fourth quarter, down 28–7 now with virtually no chance to win,
we began a drive on our own two-yard line. Eleven plays later,
with only three minutes left on the clock, Theismann hit Tom
Gatewood for 20 yards and the touchdown that made the final
score 28–14.

Of the seventeen games I started for Notre Dame we won
twelve, lost three, and tied two. We set offensive records in two
of the games and outscored our opponents by huge margins in
many others. From all those seventeen games, that futile but
noble drive marks my proudest moment on the field. We were
already defeated but we were not beaten. On play after play I
forgot about the score and played for pride—determined that no
Purdue players would even touch Joe Theismann while he
picked out his receivers. If no linebacker blitzed or rusher came
from the outside, I picked out one of my teammates who appeared to be having trouble and buried my head and shoulders
in his man—to let him know that we were still here and would
be until the final gun sounded. All we could gain was the inner
satisfaction of playing well in the few remaining minutes and of

hanging another touchdown on the scoreboard for our own sake. The papers would say our final touchdown was too little too late, but the reporters were not down on the field playing the game. Ara talked frequently to us about "breaking points"— about pounding and pounding our opponents until they broke, after which our complete mastery of them would become easy. I saw and felt it happen many times. An opponent played us tough, grudgingly giving up yardage, until a decisive touchdown sapped his spirit and we rolled effortlessly the rest of the afternoon. Ara liked particularly on our first possession in the second half to march the length of the field without once throwing a pass—just pounding, driving, pushing the ball down the field, matching our strength against theirs and proving ours superior. In game after game the opposing defense noticeably sagged after a successful drive of this kind. When we came to the line of scrimmage I could see in the eyes of the man across from me that he was whipped. He didn't want to be there; he felt that resistance was hopeless. The man who cracked a head-ringing forearm against my helmet in the first quarter, and gave up every inch of turf as grudgingly as if it were his family homestead, now merely absorbed my block, accepting it as inevitable. He no longer cared. Having battled but lost, he no longer believed he could win on this day.

To those who knew what to listen for, the break echoed loudly through the stadium. A sudden fumble or interception that turned a scoring opportunity into a touchdown for the other team could cause it. Once or twice while I played, our opponents were broken before they took the field—simply by the idea of playing Notre Dame. But often it happened in a long drive, when we rammed the ball down their throats time after time until they gagged on it. We heard the snap and saw the white flag go up. But there are no truces on a football field.

Ara also told us that *we* were *not* to have a breaking point, and our final touchdown drive against Purdue told me that, indeed, we had not given up. The emphasis on winning in American society offers few opportunities to discover the positive lessons of failure. Perhaps little can be learned from losing consistently, but to lose when victory is customary can be a valuable experience. Failure need not be permanent. We recognize

our own fallibility, but we can also discover our inner resources
to come back and try again. A loss on Saturday does not prevent
a victory the following week. In the locker room after the Purdue game I truly felt my captaincy for the first time. In victories
we laughed and joked and shouted, but in defeat we pulled
closer together as a team. I circulated among my teammates on
the offense, putting an arm around someone's shoulders, mumbling words of support to another.

"Hey, we've got nothing to be ashamed of."

"That last drive was beautiful."

"We'll come back next week. Let's keep our heads up."

I picked out Joe Theismann. He had not passed the ball especially well against Northwestern or Purdue—until that final
drive, when he was matchless. I told Joe that I wanted to thank
him for that last touchdown, that it made me proud and was important to me.

I don't know if that 98-yard drive and my encouragement afterward were as important to my teammates as they were to me,
but I began to feel a new determination and bond with the
other individuals on the team. The pain of losing lingered on,
and the memory of Billy McKoy slipping by untouched to smack
Theismann for a big loss caused me to cringe in self-disgust. The
bus ride back to South Bend was a quiet one. In the darkened
interior each of us was alone with his own thoughts, and my
thoughts were not altogether pleasant ones. I realized that our
possibilities for an undefeated season had ended. Without conference affiliation, we were eligible for only one championship,
the national one, and that was beyond reach now. On our arrival
back on campus, I sat down under a tree outside Dillon Hall
and cried, my emotions finally overcoming me. We cry for many
reasons. The disappointment of a third straight loss to Purdue
was one of mine now, but mine was also a liberating cry, a final
release of game-day adrenaline and the emotional turmoil of re-
constructing something positive from defeat. From that dark
night of despair we came back to create a successful season. We
did not become the best football team in the country, but we
were as good as we could be. Even in America that should be
enough.

Our resurgence started the following week with a win over

another traditional rival, Michigan State, and continued to the end of the season with one partial hitch. Another up-and-down team that always played us tough, Michigan State fell this time 42–28; then we toppled a series of lesser opponents. Army caved in 45–0. Two weeks later the defense recorded its second shutout, this one over Tulane by a 37–0 score, and a week later picked up its third, 47–0 over Navy. Pittsburgh scored, but only once to our seven times for a 49–7 final. Georgia Tech offered more resistance, dropping a 38–20 decision, and the Air Force made us struggle to a 13–6 win in the last week of the season. Only Southern Cal refused to fall into line. In our fifth game of the year, at home in Notre Dame stadium, we battled with the Trojans to our second tie in two years. The year before we had deserved to win but hadn't. This year we deserved to tie. Both teams gained barely over 200 yards in total offense, both teams gave up a score on a crucial turnover, both teams were aided by a controversial call by the referee, both teams missed a field goal that could have supplied the winning margin. We had the last chance to break the tie, but Scott Hempel's attempt from 48 yards away struck the crossbar squarely in the middle and bounced back onto the field, as sixty players in blue and gold and 59,000 breathless fans in the stands sagged with resignation. The game was my toughest in two years. Against six-foot-one, 237-pound nose-guard Willard Scott, and six-five, 237-pound middle linebacker Greg Slough, I slammed my helmet and shoulders into them on play after play struggling to a stalemate. Ties are like kissing your grandmother, I had always been told, but last year's had been worse than this one. This year we earned it.

The highlights of that 1969 Notre Dame season for the statistician were varied. The 42 points against Michigan State were the most scored in Duffy Daugherty's fifteen years coaching there. Our 720 yards of total offense against Navy produced a new school record, surpassing the mark set in my first start the year before against Illinois. We also ran up 617 yards against Army and 384 yards rushing against Tulane. But for me my senior year of football at Notre Dame is recorded in no statistician's record book but in a kaleidoscope of memories—most of them unrelated to touchdowns or rushing yardage.

There was the travel. As a provincial northwesterner I saw for the first time such cities as New York, Atlanta, New Orleans, and Pittsburgh—as well as West Lafayette, Indiana. American geography became more real to me, even if all I knew about these places was what I could see on a bus ride from the airport to the hotel and from the hotel to the stadium. I felt a little like a kid playing "dress up," when we stayed at elegant hotels—the Hilton in Pittsburgh, the Waldorf in New York. Any room with a firm, large bed and a television set would have satisfied me, but to stay in posh surroundings added a small bit to my pleasure in football. What I most remember about the rooms is watching TV in them—*Star Trek* on Friday nights after a movie and before bed, and a cartoon program called *George of the Jungle* Saturday mornings before the games. I have had a hard time in recent years finding people my age who even remember *George of the Jungle*, let alone remember it fondly, but for me that show will always be a favorite. It was a key part of my ritual of game-day preparation.

While staying at swank hotels I became no gourmet, but I did develop a critical appreciation of two different meals. On Friday nights we always ate prime rib, baked potato, soup, and salad; on game days it was steak, potato, soup, and dry toast with honey. (This was before football coaches learned that carbohydrates, not protein, are what athletes need before a game.) I remember marveling at the tomato soup on Friday night at the Waldorf, which actually tasted like tomatoes, not Campbell's, as I had marveled at the fresh-squeezed orange juice at the Ambassador in Los Angeles the year before. I rated the steaks and prime ribs of the various establishments against each other—and complained about none. Compared to Notre Dame's dining-hall food, the worst meal on the road was an exquisite delight.

The trips to New York and the South were the most memorable from my senior year. In New York, I felt like a hayseed gawking at the tall buildings and dazzled by the fact that we were staying at the famous Waldorf-Astoria. Fortunately, I did not get hungry at night, as four of my teammates did, and order hamburgers from room service. The hamburgers I was used to eating cost thirty-five cents; I would have felt rather sheepish when I told the bellhop I did not have enough money to pay him. At Yankee Stadium the next day I felt more like a pilgrim than a bumpkin. The House That Ruth Built rivaled the House the Rock Built in its sacred associations. It turned out to be a lousy place to play football—with the sidelines set askew on a field intended for baseball, not football, and the bare dirt of the pitcher's mound and base paths choking me when it was kicked up on running plays. But such quibbles were overwhelmed by the honor of playing on the same field where Ruth, Gehrig, DiMaggio, and other great Yankees created their legends years ago. The great football Giants—Huff, Tittle, Gifford, Robustelli —added luster, too, but I did not associate them with Yankee Stadium to the degree I did the baseball players. The stadium's distinctive structure, its plaques and pennants, recalled images that had stayed with me since childhood: the Babe's stiff-legged waddle around the bases after stroking a home run, Gerhig's tearful goodbye to his fans at the end of his long career, DiMaggio's effortless lope after a long fly. I had seen none of these events, but had read about them or seen film clips. They were part of the mythology of heroes I grew up with. To play football on the same field where these events took place was a rare privilege.

We forayed into the South twice in 1969—to New Orleans to play Tulane and to Atlanta for Georgia Tech—and were afforded the kind of welcome that we Yankee Catholics ought to have expected in Dixie. Tulane's Green Wave played with the same style that Faulkner attributed to Confederate cavalrymen in the Civil War—gallant but futile. They yelled and danced and flung themselves desperately into every play—and never gave up—but our lines outweighed theirs by thirty to forty pounds per man, and the result was a 37-0 drubbing. At Georgia Tech, good ole boys with names like Smylie Gebhart, Bubba Hoat, and Joe Bill Faith were no more fond of us Yankees than their Tulane cousins had been, but it was the fans who were truly rabid in Atlanta. They hurled full cans of Coke, whiskey bottles, cups of ice, and dead fish (it was not even Friday) at our coaches and players on the sidelines. The message was clear —Tech fans were unreconstructed—but the South did not rise again that night.

The most significant part of my first venture into the South took place off the field. We played Tulane on Saturday night and were to return to South Bend Sunday morning rather than right after the game. Ara released us from curfew—which meant, of course, turning us loose on Bourbon Street. Through eight years of high school and college football I had not had a single drink during the season. How I came to take the Frank Merriwell code against drinking and smoking so seriously is something of a mystery—I suspect Coach Frazier was the major cause—but I faced a moral crisis as I walked down Bourbon Street with my teammates. Despite what reason told me, in my guts I felt that my good fortune and success were a reward for the purity of my dedication. Would demon rum (mixed with fruit juices and called a "Hurricane" at Pat O'Brien's) bring down the wrath of the gods upon my no longer worthy self? The lure of good times overcame superstition, and the following week I played well and injury-free against Navy. Retribution does not always follow the fall.

Back in South Bend, the football season played itself out in a rhythmic pattern that structured everything I did. My entire collegiate career was governed by such patterns—its seasons not so much fall, winter, spring, and summer as football season, off season, spring football, and summer training. The rhythm of a year in football was governed for me not by equinoxes, temperatures, and the life cycle of plants but by playing the game, building up my speed and strength, and then playing again—I hoped with clear signs of improvement. During the season, the rhythm fell into weekly cycles. Sunday meant light running around the practice field and films of yesterday's game at night. Monday through Thursday meant workouts of varying intensity, followed by films of our upcoming opponent. Friday was a light day. Before a home game, we practiced without pads, attended the pep rally in the field house after dinner, then retired to Moreau Seminary for a movie and undisturbed sleep. Before a road game, Friday meant traveling in the early afternoon after a light morning workout, checking into a hotel, then sharing dinner and a movie at a local theater. All of these days pointed to the game on Saturday, which had its own rituals, then the emotional release and a resumption of a new week the next day. Around this unwavering pattern I fit my studies, my friends, my social life, and whatever else filled my week. If there was tedium in the routine at times, there was also comfort. When I was actually playing, not just struggling to play, the regularity of my life suited me well. Meaningful order was difficult to find in the world around me; to find it in my own life created a satisfying sense of stability.

The games themselves gave me pleasures, too. Although I was now a veteran starting center and captain besides, something of the grim struggle of my prep-team days remained as a constant in my approach to the game. My opponents on Saturday were anonymous enemies I wished to overpower. But my attitude was less insistently personal. I wanted to prove my superiority, if possible, and earn the respect of my opponents, but I also gloried in my *team's* dominance of the opposition. A long drive consisting entirely of running plays, on which we whacked the ball into the line on play after play, scoring finally several minutes and many downs later over our physically and mentally beaten opponents, was immensely satisfying. Other, more aesthetic, pleasures were possible for me now as well. Even for a center, different plays required different techniques and skills that demanded excellence and gave satisfaction when done well. On a running play up the middle, I had to stick my face mask into a nose guard's or middle linebacker's chest and simply root him out of the hole—strength against strength with the better man prevailing. I particularly liked plays on which the back read my block, cutting off my tail for a good gain into the secondary. On an outside running play, I would have to rely on quickness more than strength to cut off a fast-moving linebacker flowing toward the hole. If I could get my head and shoulders in front of him, I could drive him back or at least run him by the hole for the back to cut off my block again. On pass plays, intelligence counted most. I had to set up, quickly read the defense for any of the possible combinations of blitzes, then, if left free, respond to a number of options: pick up a backside rush, help my guards inside or the tackles outside. If I had a man on my nose, I had to be a barrier between him and the quarterback, obstructing my opponent in whatever way I could. As a center, I rarely had the simple task of a straight-ahead block, but most often had to scramble to cut off a defenseman at a difficult angle. But every play, no matter how chaotic or random it may have looked to spectators, was a carefully designed complex of coordinated actions that demanded sound execution by eleven players. One major difference between high school and college football, I soon discovered after arriving at Notre Dame, was that *each* individual on the offense, no matter how far from the hole he was lined up, had to make his block for the play to succeed. To be a part of that coordinated effort, and to perform my own role in it flawlessly, was to create something beautiful.

On rare occasions I felt transformed from mere toiler to artist. Those moments of perfect clarity, that I first glimpsed in grade school when a pass floated over my shoulder to nestle into my outstretched arms, came infrequently but often enough now to be a longed-for part of any game. Time would seem to wind down. The longest play in a football game rarely takes over four or five seconds, but on occasion I would be transported into a state in which I could watch my actions unfold as slowly and beautifully as a blooming lily. Instead of a chaotic collision of bodies in which I instinctively drove for position against my opponent's resistance, pads popping, legs churning, arms punching, and voices grunting, I would see my man transfixed like a bird mesmerized by a striking snake. I would see a distinct target, into whose center I would drive my head and shoulders, feeling complete control rather than scrambling desperately to make contact only to see him slide off and make the tackle. Such moments came infrequently, but when they did, they provided the supreme physical pleasure of the game—a unity of mind and body and will so complete that for an instant I seemed to transcend my human limitations.

The anxieties and frustrations of my first two years had not disappeared entirely by my senior season. Missed blocks dampened the pleasure of good plays; periodic feelings that I was still an outsider interfered with the bonds of camaraderie that grew from my shared experiences with my teammates. Both my personal fortunes and the fortunes of the team were a mixture of the positives and negatives that football offered. The loss to Purdue and the tie with Southern Cal kept our official success at a less than spectacular level. My career at Notre Dame educated me to expect success only after a great deal of hard work, and then to find it complicated by periodic setbacks. My most obvious mixture of pleasure and pain in my senior year came from the hurt and frustration of the pinched nerve in my neck, which tempered the satisfactions of my improved ability and my leadership role. I felt that I played well, but not as well as I might have played had I not been physically vulnerable. In other ways, too, my pleasure was not unmixed. My rise from a walk-on provided my supreme satisfaction, but it also left me feeling still different from my teammates, particularly from the members of my own class. I was both a leader and an outsider during my senior year—a paradoxical combination that sums up the essence of my Notre Dame career. My senior year had the feel of a culmination. During that season I watched myself emerge from obscurity to become a public figure of a minor sort. My election to captain at the start of the fall was headline news in the South Bend and Chicago papers, and it earned mention back in my hometown. Later in the season emerged my second media image, after the walk-on who made captain: I was presented as a scholar-athlete. Bill Gleason, a columnist for the Chicago *Sun-Times*, described in admiring terms my schedule on Mondays, Wednesdays, and Fridays during the season: up at 8:30 for history of the English language at 9:05; then government of the Soviet Union at 10:10, metaphysics at 11:15, and lunch; after lunch came tragedy at 1:15 and satire at 2:20, then on to the locker room at 3:10; practice, dinner at 6:30, and an hour meeting at 7:30 left three hours at the library until 11:45 closing time. The schedule seemed heroic to at least one reader, who sent me a very touching letter in response.

People wrote for other reasons, too. Grade school children in Van Nuys, California, sent streams of fan letters to me and many of my teammates. And a man in Pittsburgh sent me a postcard before every game. A few excerpts:

SEPTEMBER 22, 1969:

Congratulatons on being elected co-captain. I don't know where you came from, last year. I'm happy that you got here, wherever you came from. You men made a great comeback last Saturday [against Northwestern]. I know that most of your offensive team are a little green yet. If they can only play over their heads for a few weeks they can get experienced against Navy. You men have played like champions and I hope that's what you will be, at the end of the season. Win or lose, I'll still be for you. I'm mighty proud of you.

SEPTEMBER 27, 1969:

You men never quit [against Purdue] and gave it all you had. No fair man could ask for more than that. I'm still *mighty* proud of you and your teammates.

OCTOBER 19, 1969:

That [USC] game was a humdinger, one of the great ones in Notre Dame history. . . . The courage, determination and effort, displayed by you men, will not soon be forgotten, certainly never by me.

Such cards and letters were a potent reminder that the role I played was larger than myself. Playing football at Notre Dame was a private quest that enabled me to struggle through adolescence to a tentative sense of my own worth, but it also involved me in a symbolic activity that was meaningful to thousands of people outside my own narrow world. The public significance placed on what I did enabled my playing to have the private potency it held for me. Everywhere I looked I found confirmation that to play for Notre Dame was a great honor.

I shared that honor with people close to me in 1969, as I had not been able to in previous seasons. My parents and my younger brother, David, flew to South Bend for the Southern Cal game, as did aunts, uncles, and cousins from Minneapolis and Springfield, Missouri. To have nine people who were important to me in the stands watching me play intensified my experience. In what other activities can we feel ourselves so clearly to be representing others, to be acting out the vicarious hopes and fears of individuals about whom we care deeply? The Southern Cal game made real a vague feeling I had had since my first varsity game, that my actions on the field somehow had larger implications than their personal importance to me. I gave my family pleasure, but the relationship was reciprocal. For whatever pleasure I gave them by performing on the field while they watched from the stands, they gave me in return their warmth and consolation after the frustrating tie. I discovered the ideal relationship between player and fans.

My girlfriend, Julie, was in the stands for the Air Force game. Playing football had always been a more ascetic experience for me than that associated with the popular image of the football player. We can't all be Joe Namaths. After football games in high school I had not been carried off the field on the shoulders of my teammates into the clutching arms of doe-eyed beauties, and at Notre Dame I did not walk away from the stadium to wild parties where luscious nymphs rewarded me for my heroic acts on the field. But for one game, the last of the regular season of my senior year, a special girl, not just my buddies in the dorm, waited for me after the game.

With the conclusion of our regular season, that 13–6 squeaker over the Air Force, public recognition was added to the private pleasures and satisfactions of my senior year. Together with Jim Reilly, I was named to the *Sporting News* All-American squad on the second team; Mike McCoy was on the first, as he was on every first-team all-American list in 1969. I was also selected by the National Football Foundation and Hall of Fame as one of eleven recipients of the organization's scholar-athlete award. The honor brought me and my rented tuxedo to New York for two days of lunch at Toots Shor's, tickets to the Broadway musical *Hair,* and a culminating banquet at the Waldorf. The National Collegiate Athletic Association also chose me with thirty-two other senior football players to receive a one-thousand-dollar postgraduate fellowship. I had actually come to hope for some major all-American recognition. I had been receiving various signals since the previous spring that I was rated among the top centers in the country, by the pro scouts at least. Each time a new all-American team was announced, I hurried to the campus newsstand to buy a copy and anxiously run my eye over the picks, hoping to find my name. I understood already that all-Americans, particularly linemen, were created by sports information directors, and I knew that Notre Dame had more likely candidates than me for our SID to promote that fall. But I hoped against reason that I could have somehow caught the eye of some particularly independent voters. My ego was not above lusting for a little fame. My failure to be so honored was only a minor disappointment. The awards I did receive may have had a secondary importance compared to selection on the major all-American teams, but to me they were exhilarating.

The emotional high point of the season—or low point (it is hard to know which)—took place on the field. A few days before the Air Force game, the university's administration announced that for only the second time in college football's one hundred years, Notre Dame would be going to a bowl game. In 1925 Knute Rockne and the Four Horsemen had beaten Ernie Nevers' Stanford Indians 27–10 in the Rose Bowl. Now, forty-five years later, I was to be a part of only the second Notre Dame team to have such an opportunity—this time against number one-ranked Texas in the Cotton Bowl. The Cotton Bowl was a fitting climax to my Notre Dame career in many different ways. Hopes, dreams, and frustrations, glamorous spectacle and day-to-day toil, public hype and private contemplation—all went into that final game. Rumors about a possible bowl bid had popped up periodically for weeks before the university actually reversed its forty-five-year-old policy to entertain the offer from the Cotton Bowl committee. Then the team had to vote. I was surprised to discover that enthusiasm for the game was not unanimous. The aches and weariness of a long season made many desire an end to football and a Christmas vacation such as normal college students would enjoy. To pass up an opportunity to play the top-ranked team in a major bowl was unthinkable to me, but not everyone had quite the storybook perspective on Notre Dame football that I had. The vote was not very close, the outcome had never been truly in doubt, but one team member—Jim Reilly, our best offensive lineman—announced his refusal to play. No persuading could sway him. Jim's absence tarnished the game a little for me: I was dismayed to realize that his excellence, which I so admired, had not been accompanied by equal pleasure.

Ara was the least autocratic of coaches throughout the voting and preparations for the game. We took off a couple of weeks after beating Air Force, then resumed practice indoors, without contact, until a week before Christmas (I was even allowed to miss two days of practice to fly to Seattle for an unsuccessful interview for a Rhodes Scholarship). We then went home for a week, to reconvene in Dallas on December 26 for a final week of preparation. Brisk workouts, with a little hitting for sharpness and timing, were bracketed by a variety of social activities planned for the team, and tableaux planned for the media. I found myself in Cotton Bowl Stetson posing with fellow captain Bob Olson and two Texas coeds, who flashed the hook-'em-horns gesture at us while we indicated our disapproval. A couple of nights later the singer in the Fairmont Hotel's lounge picked me from a ringside table, where I sat with several teammates, to accompany her in a duet. She should have chosen better: I had been one of those kids in grade school whom the singing teacher asked just to mouth the words. Press conferences, an official pregame luncheon for both teams, and other festivities rounded out the week before the game.

The game itself, on January 1, 1970, was the last I played with the full, uncomplicated emotional intensity of youth. I played for self-respect, for the realization of dreams, for my school and team, and for my coach—a fine and good and charismatic man for whom I could have played my heart out had I no other motivation. I took with unambivalent seriousness the charge of my captaincy and my role as representative of Notre Dame's traditions and of the university's followers throughout the country. For the last time I played a football game as if it were a holy crusade.

Texas was favored by 7½ points. In fact, rumors had trickled back to South Bend from the moment the pairing was announced that the undefeated Longhorns did not feel we, with an 8-1-1 record, were a worthy opponent. We had more to prove than they did, but this emotional edge was countered by a tragedy for one of their players. The Longhorns had their own "Gipper" in Freddie Steinmark, a junior defensive back whose cancerous left leg had been amputated following a season-ending victory over Arkansas. Even we were affected by the sight of the fellow on crutches along the sideline, with one pant leg pinned to his back pocket and flapping forlornly when the wind gusted. He died a few months later.

The largest TV audience for a sporting event to that time, plus 73,000 in the stadium—including the three living members of the Four Horsemen and ex-president Lyndon Johnson, as well as my parents—watched what was called afterward "the most magnificent game in the history of the thirty-four-year-old Cotton Bowl Classic." With the fourth-best defense in the nation we shut down the Longhorns' vaunted wishbone offense early, while Scott Hempel kicked a field goal and Theismann hit Tom Gatewood for 54 yards and a 10–0 lead. The ease with which we moved the ball confirmed my contempt for that Southwest Conference brand of football which I felt was inferior to the game we played. We missed a second first-half touchdown on an interception at the Texas 13, but I felt no anxiety. The Longhorn defensive linemen and linebackers were offering little of the resistance we had struggled against with Southern Cal.

But the Texas offense, particularly fullback Steve Worster, was not convinced of our superiority. Despite Bob Olson's extraordinary play, and by running consistently away from Mike McCoy, Worster and his teammates put together a 74-yard drive to cut our lead to 10–7 at half time. At the same time *our* offense suddenly went dead, and we had a real fight on our hands. Someone had forgotten to tell those Texas defensemen to roll over for us.

I was both a player and a spectator in that game. When we had the ball I was conscious of nothing but my own responsibility. In the huddle we ringed Joe Theismann with intensity as he called the play. As soon as I knew it was a run or pass, a play over me or away, I anticipated my moves. Over the ball, I surveyed the defense quickly, called out the blocking codes to Gary Kos and Larry DiNardo, the guards on either side of me, and awaited Theismann's signal. I gripped the ball with my right hand, the knuckles of my left resting on the ball with the same pressure on every play—not to tip off the defense whether a run or pass was coming. As Joe stationed himself behind me, I inwardly tensed in expectation of his signal. I was programmed to explode on the first sound, or the second or third. With the call, I reacted rather than thought: right arm slapping the ball into Theismann's hands as I sprinted the few yards necessary to cut off the middle linebacker, or drove into one of the defensive tackles. My view of the game was limited to the few yards on all sides of me, my sensations to the sweat and indistinguishable noises that enveloped me, and to the impact of collisions on my body.

When the defense took the field, I rediscovered the panorama of the game. I became aware of the crowd, of the Texas bench across the field, of two teams—a full twenty-two players—contending on the field. I noticed the sun again, the bright January day so unlike the snow and cold of South Bend; the brilliant colors in the stands, the friendly cheers from our section, and the abrasive ones from theirs. I also felt helpless as I watched others playing for me. If we had just punted after not moving the ball, I mentally kicked myself and hoped that the defense would get it back for us quickly, so that we could do it right. The third period passed like this—me jogging onto the field after our defense had held to run a few plays, then have to punt and become a spectator again. I watched our 10–7 lead disappear to become a 14–10 deficit, and became angrier at our inability to put more points on the board. I did not know why we weren't moving the ball. I had no fear of Texas' players and felt I was getting my own job done, but we were breaking down somewhere. From my limited perspective on the field I couldn't diagnose the problem. I had jammed my pinched nerve only once—a temporary hurt I was able to shrug off. But I couldn't shrug off our offensive lethargy.

We finally came untracked as the fourth period opened. After Theismann hit Jim Yoder for a 24-yard touchdown to cap a long drive, I trotted off the field to slap hands and swap yells of elation with my teammates on the bench, particularly the defensive players who had gotten little help from us for a full quarter. But then I had to watch again, as the defense took the field and Texas chewed up six precious minutes on the clock in seventeen excruciating plays. Twice I thought our defense had held, and snapped my chin strap, ready to take the field and protect our 17–14 lead. But each time I watched helplessly as the Longhorns squeezed out fourth-down gains from our 20 and then our 10 to keep their drive going. The second one came on a diving catch by Cotton Speyrer at our two—a bad, wobbly pass that Speyrer turned into a game breaker. Three plays later, Texas scored for a 21–17 lead, leaving 1:08 to play.

As I took the field for our last offensive effort, I felt the fiercest determination of my football career. This final minute was the culmination of thirteen years of working, struggling, and dreaming. Texas knew we would pass; we knew they would forget about everything else to get to Theismann. And everyone in the stadium knew all of this as well. I had no sense of the crowd as individuals, but as an enveloping force that charged our actions with greater intensity and confirmed the significance of what we were about to attempt. To play without such an audience would have produced an effect something like the tree falling in the empty forest that the philosophers talk about. But 73,000 screaming fans, and tens of millions at home, assured me of the importance of that last drive. They all knew that after fifty-nine minutes of football everything depended on the next few plays. While Chuck Kennedy (replacing the injured Terry Brennan), Gary Kos, Larry DiNardo, Dan Novakov (substituting for the absent Jim Reilly), and I flung ourselves into the Texas defensemen, Theismann connected on passes of 16 and 27 yards to move us from our own 23 to the Texas 39 With 38 seconds left, tight end Dewey Poskon worked open at the 18; Joe's pass soared just over Dewey's fingertips by a few inches, to be intercepted at the 14. Our season ended with a whimper, not a bang.

In the locker room I felt devastated. Unlike after the Purdue game, there was no next week to regroup for. We had proven our worthiness as an opponent to the number one-rated team in the country. We knew in our hearts that Texas' players had not been hit so hard or so often all year. The game had been an aesthetic masterpiece, particularly the fourth quarter when it seemed that only the clock could stop either offense. But once again we wanted a real victory, not a moral one. I tried to fight back tears but lost, and when Lyndon Johnson entered the locker room to offer condolences and congratulations, I escaped to the farthest end of the room. I had been disgusted with Richard Nixon's well-publicized telephone call to the Texas locker room after the Arkansas game, bolstering his own public image while he continued to prosecute the war in Southeast Asia. I needed no consolation from another politician. I would console myself and place things in perspective in the weeks to come. For now, I only felt defeat—and it hurt.

The public record of my two years of starting at Notre Dame was moderately impressive. With a 7–2–1 record in 1968 and

8–2–1 in 1969 we finished number five in the final AP poll both years. Although not overwhelmingly successful, our football team kept Notre Dame before the public eye, sustaining the tradition of excellence that dated back nearly to the turn of the century. The private impact on me was incalculable. Playing football at Notre Dame organized my life for four years. It did not obliterate all my other interests and aspirations—academic, social, political, personal—but it provided the most distinct, unambiguous focus for my efforts and desires. From the day I arrived on campus I had both long-range and short-term goals to work for in at least one important part of my life. In order to realize my dream of making the Notre Dame team, I had to commit myself virtually every day to that cause. In season and out I had a clear purpose.

Playing football complemented my other interests, particularly my studies. A disciplined football player can be a disciplined student, and the reverse is true as well. Contrary to the popular stereotype, there are few dumb football players: the game itself is too complicated to accommodate stupidity. But contrary also to the opposing image of the scholar-athlete which football organizations like to promote, not all college football players in America are dedicated students. Notre Dame's academic record has been impressive. All of the seniors in my class graduated in four years—as remarkable an accomplishment then as it would be now. When I took over as center during my junior year, our offensive line from tackle to tackle had a 3.4 grade point average. In 1981 it was revealed that over 97 percent of all Notre Dame athletes graduate—as opposed to figures usually half that or much less among major athletic powers. Of the thirty-five former Notre Damers in the National Football League in 1980, only one had not graduated, and he was finishing his degree in the off season. The emphasis on academics at Notre Dame begins with the president, Father Hesburgh, who tells his coaches that losing is permissible but cheating is not. Athletes who are unlikely to survive academically are just not recruited. When Ara Parseghian left as coach in 1975, his proudest boast to Father Hesburgh was not that he had won two national championships but that he could say, "I'm not leaving any dirt under the carpet."

Father Hesburgh established the policy for the entire univer-

sity, but Ara Parseghian set the tone for the football program—
valuing academics as highly as athletics, believing in football as
a part of the player's total education. Even when I became captain in my senior year, I never felt especially close to Ara. He
never sought me out to chat, or invited me to seek him out. Our
exchanges were brief ones on the practice field or in the dining
hall. Ara did not play the role of buddy to his players at all.

But Ara Parseghian impressed his personality upon me. He
was a charismatic coach: intense, dynamic, competitive, darkly
handsome—a hard taskmaster who drove himself harder than he
drove us. I never felt I was one of Ara's boys, but he never had
"boys." During my junior year he seemed to find particular pleasure in the shenanigans of Hanratty, Gladieux, and Dushney,
but essentially he treated us all the same. If he was not close to
us, he was consistent and fair. He did not clap us on the back
one week after a win, then vilify us the next after a tough loss.
He never set himself apart from us, saying in effect, "I gave you
this wonderful game plan and look at the way you screwed it
up." He never blamed anyone for a loss, either publicly or privately. He demanded good performances from us but tolerated
honest mistakes as inevitable. We won together and we lost together. He truly believed in the "team." As a walk-on given the
chance to play, I knew better than anyone about his fairness.
After I graduated, I heard of programs in which walk-ons were
not even allowed to try out. Ara strove to field his twenty-two
best players; he did not care if they were the ones he had been
clever enough to recruit. If he was not close to us, he was always
available—to talk about football or about personal matters. If he
was not close to us, he always made me feel we mattered to him.

His job was the toughest in college coaching. The thousands
of Notre Dame supporters around the country who enabled me
to feel a special sense of destiny and purpose demanded that
Ara produce victories, and not just victories sometimes but victories by wide margins. He was unfairly blamed for not winning
the big ones—a familiar charge against good teams that are less
than perfect. He was hounded for years afterward for settling
for the tie with Michigan State in 1966, a decision he made for
good reasons at the time but which he probably later wished he
could undo. The press was particularly hard on Ara for that

game. In fact, I never thought that the press felt very kindly toward him at all. On the other hand, I knew of at least one former major-college coach who was the darling of the media, popping one-liners and witty quips on all occasions. But one of his players, a friend of mine in Kansas City who had been a consensus all-American, would pass his coach on the campus and not even be acknowledged. My friend was also blamed by his coach for a big loss, because of missing a single block—much as I had missed Billy McKoy in the Purdue game my senior year. I have more respect for a coach who treats his players well and is indifferent toward the press than for one who inverts those priorities.

A single event in the spring of my senior year epitomized for me the kind of man Ara was. In May he invited all of the graduating seniors to his home for a picnic. None of us had any eligibility remaining. We would never play another down for Ara or benefit him in any major way, but he gave us a party to thank us for our years of service under him. We played whiffle softball in a park across the street from his house, then gathered on his patio for barbecued hamburgers, potato salad, and beer. Someone had learned that the next day was his birthday, and to my astonishment, as we sang "Happy Birthday" to him, a handful of my fellow seniors poured cans of beer over his head. It was an anarchic act that was perhaps a liberating reversal of roles for the ones who did the pouring, but most astonishing of all, Ara laughed and accepted the blasphemy with perfect grace. At Miami of Ohio, Northwestern, and now Notre Dame Ara had been a coach whose success was matched by few, but he was also a fine man who allowed himself to be human.

When I read in the fall of 1974 that Ara was giving up the pressure of the Notre Dame job to give more time to his family, I wrote the only letter I had sent him since graduation. I knew he had a daughter with multiple sclerosis who was very dear to him—I had seen her helped into pep rallies on her father's arm when I was playing—and I knew he had always been devoted to his wife and other children as well. Now, more than ever, I was filled with admiration for the man who could give up the most prestigious coaching job in college football—a man who was intensely competitive and obsessively committed to his job—be-

cause the job conflicted with more important human consider-
ations. Ara was among the best at what he did in football, but
he was also able to decide that other things were important. I
was fortunate in many things at Notre Dame, not the least of
which was the man I played for.

Playing football at Notre Dame was a private experience, but
it also forced me to see beyond the narrow boundaries of my
own world. Football at Notre Dame was both more intensely
personal and more intensely public than it could have been anywhere else. During my weeks of preparation for each game, I
viewed the coming contest as *my* challenge, but then Saturday
exploded my self-absorption, bringing football back into the
public arena. The pageantry, the crowds, the chanting and
cheering and booing and singing reminded me that playing football at Notre Dame was not only my private communion with
the past but also a public celebration in the present that engaged thousands, even millions, of people.

Playing big-time college football is not an ideal experience for
everyone. We have become too aware of the low graduation
rate, of fixed transcripts and misused players and the high cost—
both financial and at times moral—of running many successful
athletic programs, to fool ourselves into believing that football is
the ideal preparation for manly adulthood. But the potential for
valuable experiences is still there, as it always has been.

One of my most vivid experiences during my senior year at
Notre Dame came on walks back to the dorm from the library
late at night. Muffled and gloved against the piercingly cold
wind in the dead of winter, I strolled along the cleared walks
between tall banks of glazed snow. I liked my feeling of
aloneness on the deserted campus, illuminated by lampposts and
a three-quarter moon under the dark vault of the sky. I strode
along with a distinct feeling of proprietorship. This was *my* campus, *my* university. I had become a part of it and made it a part
of me through my achievements on the football field. When I
had first arrived on the campus three and a half years before, I
had felt myself an insignificant intruder. Now, I felt that I
belonged—not just belonged but was one of the builders of
Notre Dame's history. In subsequent years I would marvel at the
pretentiousness of that feeling, but even as my name began to

die from Notre Damers' memories, the impact of my special experience remained a permanent part of me.

When my four years at Notre Dame came to an end, I did not
regret their passing. In the next few years I occasionally became
nostalgic for what seemed the simpler life of my college days,
but I had new challenges. I had been drafted by the Kansas City
Chiefs, the current world champions, and throughout my final
semester I wondered what professional football would bring.
From the inquiries I had received, I had expected to be drafted
by Dallas or Pittsburgh. The only contact from the Chiefs had
been a phone call the night before the draft asking if I was six
feet three as the program said, or really six five. I also had been
led to believe I would be drafted in the first three rounds, despite my intention of going to graduate school. After the Chiefs
did call, I phoned Julie in Spokane, to impress my future bride.
I told her that I had gone in the fifth round. Mike McCoy had
been the second player taken overall, Jim Reilly had been
picked in the third round, and Bob Olson was taken in the fifth
as I was.

"Fifth?" Julie sounded puzzled. "I thought you told me that
Olson was good."

That spring I also won a Danforth Fellowship for graduate
study in English Literature leading to a teaching career. I wondered how those two lives would mix. Should there be any
conflict, graduate school would come first. I might play football
for a few years, but teaching would be my lifelong profession. I
wanted to get in those few years, though. I was no longer desperate to prove something to myself on the football field, but
professional football offered the supreme challenge any player
can face. Would I be good enough? As a kid I had dreamed of
playing for the Los Angeles Rams. At twenty-two, I was less in-
toxicated by fantasies than I had been at eighteen, but I was
fired by the realization that yet another dream might become a
reality. According to my draft board and my liquor control
board, I was no longer a minor. But a football player in certain
ways is always a kid. Now I had a new league, a new world to
play in.

PART THREE

Playing for Pay

SIX

Rookies and Veterans

IF PLAYING PROFESSIONAL FOOTBALL was the fulfillment of another childhood dream, training camp was its nightmarish underside. My first professional training camp was not with the Kansas City Chiefs, but with the 1970 College All-Stars, preparing for the midsummer charity game against the current world-champion Chiefs. When I arrived in Evanston, Illinois, to join my fellow All-Stars, I was deeply impressed. This was my first such game. I had been selected for the East-West Shrine Game in December, and the Coaches' All-American Game at the end of June, but I had missed the first due to Notre Dame's bid to the Cotton Bowl, and the second by begging out. In Evanston, then, I found myself for the first time in the company of the best collegiate football players in the land. Terry Bradshaw, the first pick in the draft, remained in camp only a few days before returning to Pittsburgh with an injury. But Steve Owens, the Heisman Trophy winner from Oklahoma, was there, as were Mike Reid from Penn State, who won the Outland Trophy; old rivals Mike Phipps of Purdue, Al Cowlings of Southern Cal, and Bob McKay of Texas; plus a number of small-college stars who were destined for great pro careers, including Mel Blount, Kenny Burrough, Rich Caster, Raymond Chester, and Duane Thomas. Two Notre Dame teammates, Mike McCoy and Jim Reilly, joined me; and two other Kansas City draftees, Sid Smith from Southern Cal and Clyde Werner from Washington, were also on the team. The All-Stars were a collection of a few familiar and a lot of unfamiliar faces. What was most strange after my collegiate career was to be starting a new experience in football on equal footing with all of them.

The longer I stayed in All-Star camp, the less impressed I became. Collectively we lacked the seriousness and clear purpose that I had come to expect at the beginning of a new season. The game for which we were preparing had little meaning to any of us. It was but a minor preliminary to our real task, which for each of us was to make the NFL team that had drafted us. Our playing in the All-Star game was, if anything, a hindrance. While our fellow rookies were in their own teams' training camps, learning the new system, proving themselves before the coaches whom they would have to impress in order to make the team, we were frittering away three weeks with a group of coaches we would never see again, learning a system we would never use again. We bided our time, hoped to avoid injury, and waited for the end of the game, when we would depart from Evanston to join our real teams.

Our engagement in this particular All-Star game was further complicated by a players' strike that summer. NFL veterans were boycotting training camps in a dispute over their pension plan and other matters. As we went through our practice sessions at Northwestern University, we were aware that the game might never be played. Representatives of the Players' Association spoke to us about joining the strike, but we were in an awkward position. The National Football League had an agreement with the sponsors of the All-Star game that any individual selected for the game who refused to play would be banned from participation in any preseason games. To join the veterans' strike would risk our chances of making our clubs, but not to join the strike risked earning the veterans' disfavor before we had a chance to become their teammates. We felt that we were in a no-win situation.

Our dilemma was resolved for us. The Players' Association agreed that the Chiefs' veterans should go to camp a week before the game; to cause the cancellation of a major charity event would only undermine public sympathy for the strikers. The move signaled that support of the strike within the union had weakened. The association, feeling pressure to settle, signed an agreement—largely favorable to the owners—in time for veterans to report to training camps immediately after the game in Chicago. The players' union was not yet ready for the major confrontation with management that would be necessary in 1974.

The All-Star game itself was as uneventful as those games usually were before the event's cancellation after the 1975 contest. The Chiefs' veterans, even with only a week of preparation, easily outclassed and outmuscled us. I played but a few minutes toward the end of the game—a fact that added to my displeasure over the entire affair. By the time I entered the game, my opposition was Chief rookies; the veterans had already taken their seats on the bench to watch the conclusion of their uninspiring 24–3 victory. I did not even have the chance to discover if I could hold my own against real NFL competition. My three weeks as a College All-Star, for all the supposed honor that selection conferred on me, was a very minor interlude between real football seasons.

My true introduction to the NFL came not in Evanston but in Liberty, Missouri, the home of William Jewell College and the site of the Kansas City Chiefs' training camp. A town of 20,000 inhabitants located fifteen miles north of Kansas City, Liberty in the mid-nineteenth century had been a frontier outpost, one of the last civilized towns at the jumping-off point to Oregon, Santa Fe, and California. Now, it was to be my own "jumping-off point" into a different unknown territory. Liberty's tie with its frontier past had been maintained by a memorial marking the first bank that Jesse James ever robbed. Anyone interested in seeing this historic building met no difficulty finding it. Anything of note in Liberty lay within a four-block radius of the center of town. On the west end, a block off the main thoroughfare, sat the Dairy Queen drive-in restaurant where weary players from camp bought milk shakes, sundaes, and sodas in the evenings after meetings. Nearer the center of town were the two bars where we drank—one a pizza joint where I first tasted the Kansas City specialty called a mau-mau (malt liquor and fresh

lime), the other a classic corner bar with shuffleboard and pick-
led sausages to go with the beer. Rookies and younger players
tended to frequent the Dairy Queen and pizza place; veterans
gravitated more to the corner bar.

The first time I saw Liberty, on August 1, 1970, I was unaware
any of these places existed. Driving through town on the bus
with my fellow rookies, I saw the main street of a typical small
midwestern town, like many I had passed through in Nebraska
and Iowa when driving the southern route between Spokane and
South Bend during my college years. Drugstore, bank, town hall,
hardware store—all were strung out in a familiar pattern. Continuing east through town, we wound upward and around a
tree-lined drive to the campus of 121-year-old William Jewell
College, a Baptist school of 1400 students whose athletic budget
was heavily subsidized by the fees the Chiefs paid for training
camp facilities. The campus had an attractive small-liberal-arts-
college appearance. One road wandered around the quadrangle
of six red-brick colonial buildings that comprised the nucleus of
the campus. Seeing the college for the first time from the bus
window, I mused that in the prevailing flatness of the midwestern plains, William Jewell's situation on a small hill enclosed by
wooded areas must have created an appealing sense of isolation
for students eager to explore 2500 years of Western culture away
from the intrusions of the fast-paced modern world.

For six weeks that summer and every summer, three buildings
became the headquarters of eighty men less interested in 2500
years of Western culture than in a few seasons of professional
football. Our bus stopped before the red-brick dormitory that
housed all of the players, two to a room. As I climbed off the
bus, I *felt* Liberty for the first time, and the sensation was far
more powerful than any sight I had of the town on our passage
through. Earlier at the Kansas City airport, I had stood briefly in
the Gulf Stream humidity, walking from the plane to the waiting
bus, but other sensations had distracted me from fully noticing
the heat. Now, arrived at my temporary home for the next few
weeks, I felt positively assaulted by the dense, moist air. My return to South Bend at the end of each of the past four summers
from the temperate dry heat of eastern Washington had always
been something of a shock, but what I felt now was more an

electrocution. My first end-of-August walk across Notre Dame's campus had routinely left me sweating uncomfortably. Here, I didn't even have to walk; every pore of my body seemed spontaneously to gasp and pour out moisture in an impossible attempt to keep me cool. The temperature gauge outside the bank had registered 94 degrees; I had experienced much hotter, but I was discovering for the first time what such heat coupled with 90 percent humidity felt like. The high overcast sky continuing uninterruptedly to the flat horizon, which four years of college in the Midwest had not yet accustomed me to, seemed an opaque foil dome radiating all the rising heat back to earth again, endlessly recycling it. The air felt heavy, moist, and *used*. It seemed dense enough to pack into balls. I thought I could actually *see* it, as a substance that dulled the colors and blurred the sharp outlines of the objects I looked at, flattening everything into a sort of Impressionist painting.

With the unpleasant thought of actually putting on pads and uniform to practice in this humid heat, I carried my suitcase into the dormitory to find a typical dorm room, a ten-by-fifteen rectangle with two twin beds, chests, desks, and a single closet. This room had one other furnishing that I was not accustomed to: an air conditioner that I leaped on as if I were dying of thirst and had happened upon a desert stream. I turned the temperature gauge as low as it would go and the fan as high—and there they stayed for the remainder of training camp. Every year I was in Liberty, I contracted a summer cold because of the extreme transitions from air-conditioned room to outdoor heat to chilly room again. But I would no sooner have turned down the air conditioning than that thirsting desert refugee would have settled for a shot glass of water. Often during my five training camps, my body felt like butchered meat after long two-a-day practices; a chilled locker was the only place to store it.

My roommate was Sid Smith, my former opponent at USC and teammate with the College All-Stars. At six four, 255, Sid was a big teddy bear of a man rather than a granite Charles Atlas, but he had also been a consensus all-American at offensive tackle and was the Chiefs' number one draft choice in 1970. We had become competitors in All-Star camp, when Sid had been moved to center ahead of me. He had never played the po-

sition before, but, with E. J. Holub starting at center on badly
battered knees, the Chiefs were particularly seeking help at that
position and were looking to their first draft pick as well as their
fifth for a possible replacement. Although I had resented Sid's
playing ahead of me—he was a much better tackle than I, but I
knew I was a better center—I had quickly discovered that Sid
was so likable and that we had so much in common that my resentment could not be personal. I was beginning to experience a
dilemma that would confront me as long as I remained with
Kansas City. In earning starting positions at Gonzaga Prep and
Notre Dame I had not had to compete with close friends, or
even with other players who seemed truly my teammates. Particularly in college I had felt myself an outsider, with an impersonal rage against all those on the inside where I wanted to be.
In Kansas City, on the other hand, I was a high draft choice
from a prestigious university, accepted on equal footing with the
other rookies from the beginning, and with other veterans once I
made the team. I could not derive power from the wrath of a
lonely crusade, could not direct resentment against competitors
for my position. First Sid, then Jack Rudnay, who became starting center midway through my rookie season and remained
there for a decade afterward, were my *friends*. I could not compete against friends with the same single-minded intensity that
drove me against strangers. I was to discover that professional
football as a *business* was a very different game from the one I
was used to, but I also, surprisingly, discovered that, despite
what one might expect in a business, the other players on the
team, particularly the other offensive linemen, seemed more
truly my teammates.

Sid and I talked a little of the coming weeks, not mentioning
the fact that we might be competing for the same position, then
left our room to walk to the dining hall for lunch. As I walked
through the doorway, the hot, humid air slammed into my face
once again. No matter how long I came to live in Kansas City
and Liberty, each reentry into that sweltering climate came as a
shock. With thirty other rookies I walked over to the dining
room in Yates College Union. The Chiefs' veterans had scattered
from the airport to their homes, not having to report at Liberty
until dinnertime. A few out-of-towners with no better place to

go had come back with us rookies, however, and I was eager to see what they looked like. The Chiefs had not been a part of my consciousness before I was drafted by them. I was familiar with a few names—Lenny Dawson, Otis Taylor, Mike Garrett, Buck Buchanan, Jim Lynch—but from my youth of watching the Rams and 49ers on television I had remained a hard-core NFL fan, ignoring the upstart AFL. Joe Namath and the Jets' upset of Baltimore in the 1969 Super Bowl had seemed a fluke, but the Chiefs' repeat in 1970 over the Minnesota Vikings had forced a little reconsideration. When I was drafted by the Chiefs a few weeks later, I decided I had better find out a little more about my new team.

What my research uncovered was an impressive group of athletes. Len Dawson was one of the smartest quarterbacks around, a thirteen-year veteran who had grown with the new league into a top performer. Mike Garrett and Robert Holmes were solid running backs. Both were extremely short, but Garrett, a Heisman Trophy winner at USC, was amazingly quick and elusive, and Holmes far more powerful than his size promised. Gloster Richardson, Frank Pitts, and Otis Taylor were a fine group of wide receivers, Otis probably the best in the game; and Fred Arbanas was the best tight end in the AFL despite having sight in only one eye. The offensive line was even stronger, with Jim Tyrer and Ed Budde consistent All-Stars on the left side, Dave Hill a steady right tackle, Mo Moorman one of the better young guards in the league, and E. J. Holub, formerly an all-league outside linebacker, in the middle. The defensive line was better yet. Jerry Mays and Aaron Brown at ends and Buck Buchanan and Curley Culp at tackles comprised one of the fine defensive fronts in football. The linebacking trio of Bobby Bell, Willie Lanier, and Jim Lynch was the best without question, and the backfield of Emmitt Thomas and James Marsalis at the corners, and Johnny Robinson and Jim Kearney as the safeties completed an outstanding defensive unit. On the entire team, the major weakness was at center, where E. J. Holub's nine major knee surgeries made his status precarious. But at the outset of my pro career, I was less concerned with taking E.J.'s position than with discovering if I was even good enough to make the team.

The veterans I saw this first afternoon were not the starters.

Although they had to be fine players simply to be members of the current world champions, their names did not electrify me as the starters' would have. The athletes walking in small groups to the union seemed as ordinary as me, not unlike the players with whom I had been associated in college. The rookies who had already been in camp for three weeks exuded a sense of belonging, and of liberation from the routine of double practices. In the absence of the veterans we were the lords of the campus—its only inhabitants besides the few employees who served us in the cafeteria and an occasional administrative-looking individual who wandered by. As we trooped into the two-story dining hall, I experienced the pleasure I would always feel here on entering any building—the sudden change from oppressive heat to air-conditioned coolness. Inside, gorging myself on sandwiches, fruit, and milk with other hearty eaters was the same experience I had had in college preseason sessions. The setting was strange, but everything else so far was familiar.

At lunch I met a few more of my fellow rookies. Bob Hews, a defensive tackle from Princeton; Charlie Evans, an offensive lineman from Texas Tech; and Troy Patridge, a defensive end from Texas-Arlington, described what they had undergone with the Chiefs' coaches during practices, and told tales of the coming of the veterans during the past week. Charlie described how E. J. Holub was still a legend at Texas Tech, where he had been a great all-American linebacker a decade before. Bob and Troy commented on the players who had most impressed them. The size of the linemen had been the greatest shock to my fellow rookies. Buck Buchanan at six seven, 285, and Jim Tyrer at six six, 280, were the biggest, but every one of the guards and tackles on offense was at least six four and 255 pounds, and the defensive linemen were just as big. Curley Culp was only six one, but he weighed 275 and was the quickest lineman on the team. Most of the veterans, I was told, had been friendly the past week. There had been almost no hazing of the rookies, except to make them sing their school fight songs during mealtimes. As we talked, I felt more and more as if we were children talking about a gang of older toughs who had just moved into the neighborhood, and who we had discovered, with relief, were not ogres after all.

After an afternoon of explorations, dinnertime brought the real Kansas City Chiefs back to William Jewell. I played the rookie, trying to be as quiet and inconspicuous as possible, but watching and hearing everything I could. What struck me most as I watched the veterans file through the cafeteria line and into the dining room, was that these were grown men, not kids like myself. I saw thinning hair, weathered faces, bodies heavy with maturity. Len Dawson was in his fourteenth year in pro football; Johnny Robinson and Jacky Lee in their eleventh; Jim Tyrer, Tom Flores, E. J. Holub, and Jerry Mays in their tenth; Fred Arbanas and Curtis McClinton in their ninth; Bobby Bell, Ed Budde, Buck Buchanan, Reg Carolan, Bert Coan, Jerrel Wilson, and Dave Hill in their eighth. In football years these were *old* men, though the oldest, Dawson, was thirty-five and the others thirty-three or less. They seemed truly old to me. I was used to playing football with kids; these were men—with wives, families, responsibilities. Len Dawson was said to have a nineteen-year-old daughter; Ed Budde's son, Brad, was twelve. These were men more like my father than like me in certain ways. They probably worried about mortgages, life insurance, retirement pensions, and tax shelters. I was used to playing with athletes who worried about getting a date on Saturday night.

They also seemed incredibly *big*—big as big men grow bigger through the years. I saw no wedge-shaped Mr. Universe torsos, no youthful godlike physical beauty. Rather, I saw bulky, massive men who looked like the villains at professional wrestling bouts. Dave Hill's nickname was Butter Bean, someone had told me, and he indeed had a body that looked like one. But he was hardly alone. I was shocked at first; I had expected something more Adonislike. Then I was struck by how substantial, how solid, how capable and self-assured they all looked. I began to glimpse the differences between the emotional boys' game I had played for the past thirteen years and the game I would discover that these grown men played.

The dining room became filled with large bodies carrying trays of food, loud voices bantering with each other, large appetites devouring mounds of meat and potatoes. The arrangement of the room assumed a distinct organization: most of the blacks at one set of tables, the whites at another, apparently not by any

conscious segregation but by affinity. We rookies huddled together at our own end of a long row of tables, like incompetent
spies in an enemy's camp, trying to act natural and look as if we
belonged. We talked more quietly than we had at lunch, instinctively deferring to the seniority around us. Paradoxically, while
we in our youth were restrained, mildly serious even, the older
veterans were acting more childlike, yelling back and forth from
table to table, playfully sabotaging each other's trays of food.

E. J. Holub, the loudest of the celebrants with his strident
West Texas bray, suddenly hollered down to our group.

"Hey, rookies, let's have a little music. Let's hear a song from
our big number one draft pick."

Sid Smith stood up tentatively and began to sing the "Trojan
Fight Song."

"'Fight on, for old SC—'"

Shouts and growls from all over the room stopped him.

"Up on the chair, rookie," hollered E.J.

Sid stood on his chair and began again.

"'Fight on, for old SC—'"

Shouts again interrupted him.

"Grab your heart, rookie," yelled E.J.

Sid placed his right hand over his heart and began a third
time.

"'Fight on, for old SC—'"

Shouts yet again drowned him out.

"Grab your other heart, rookie," came from E.J.

"Heart" sounded more like "hard" this time, but Sid only
looked puzzled. One of the rookies who had been in camp and
been through this routine before whispered up to him. Sid nodded, resumed his upright position on the chair, placed his right
hand over his heart and his left over the crotch of his shorts, and
began one more time.

"'Fight on, for old SC, I say, fight on for victory . . .'" And to
the end.

"That's better, rookie," E.J. finally approved when Sid was
finished. "You're gonna have to learn to listen better from now
on."

As Sid took his seat again, someone called for Clyde Werner
to perform next. Having witnessed Sid's treatment, Clyde as-

sumed the proper position and rendered the Husky fight song. I
knew my turn would follow.

Jim Lynch called, "Let's hear from the Golden Domer."

With embarrassment and no pleasure, I stood on my chair,
placed my hands in their proper positions, and delivered my
off-key version of "Cheer, cheer for old Notre Dame." Boos and
hisses greeted me, but I continued on to the end, then sat down
quickly.

"Is that the way they teach you guys to sing at that place?"
Buck Buchanan called over to Lynch.

"Hell, no," Lynch rejoined. Then to me, "That was pretty
lousy, rookie. Maybe you'd better practice for a while and we'll
hear from you again."

I groaned under my breath, but resumed eating. If that was
the worst hazing we were to undergo, I could make no com-
plaints. I had heard how veterans in other camps hassled rookies
continually, made them play the role of gofers, sent them out on
pro-football versions of snipe hunts, and in general made the
normal anxieties of trying to make the team doubly bad. Our
veterans now returned to their own interests, ignoring us completely again. So far, we had it easy.

After dinner we filed upstairs for a team meeting. The second
floor of the dining hall was a cluster of rooms where the
different units on the team—offensive linemen, backs, receivers,
defensive linemen, linebackers, and backs—could meet in separate groups. But for this official opening of training camp for the
entire team, we all gathered in one large room. I sat in one of
the knots of rookies that dotted the room, feeling like a timid
freshman at my first large lecture class. I continued to study the
veterans, both to recognize in them the signs of common humanity that would make me feel one of them and to discover evidence of their heroic superiority. Aaron Brown had the biggest,
longest legs I had ever seen; they seemed to start at his armpits
and swelled into gnarls of knotty muscles in the thighs and
calves. Watching the Chiefs on film in All-Star camp, we had decided that the best way to pass block Brown was to jump in his
face right at the line of scrimmage, rather than drop back and
allow him to build up momentum in his rush. Now I understood
why.

I picked out Fred Arbanas, the tight end with sight in only one eye—a remarkable handicap for a receiver. I had found it impossible in high school to catch a pass with one contact lens missing; here was someone who had been named the American Football League's all-time tight end after playing with one eye. Johnny Robinson, with his shiny black hair looped in one curl over his forehead, needed only a black vest with pearl buttons and garters around his upper arms to look like a riverboat gambler from the television series *Maverick*. E. J. Holub looked like a rawboned cowboy (which he was in the off season); Morris Stroud, at six ten, looked more like a basketball player than a football player; Buck Buchanan just looked huge.

Bill Walsh, my new line coach, interrupted my observations to give me my playbook, a ring binder thick with team rules and organizational matters, and with all the Chiefs' offensive plays. Before I had time even to skim its contents, the head coach entered to begin the meeting.

Hank Stram was a short man—perhaps five eight—and stocky, and he appeared now as I would always see him. He was deeply tanned and impeccably dressed—even if only in typical coach's attire. His outfit was perfectly color-coordinated, his white Chiefs warm-up jacket, with red and gold insignia and cuffs, matched by red shorts and white socks with red and gold stripes. His socks were pulled up taut and his jacket and shorts had the sheen of newness of them; he had the self-consciously dapper look of someone very much aware of the image he projected. His manner was relaxed but authoritative as he addressed his players, the smallest of whom would have towered over him.

"Now we go to work, men. Things have been up in the air for a while, but all that's over, and we can settle down to business. The Kansas City Chiefs are world champions. Think about what that means. The best football team in the world. Only one group of players can say that. Look at those Super Bowl rings on your fingers; it's a great feeling to wear that ring. Our goal this year is to win the Super Bowl again. To remain world champions. To be winners. To be the best.

"People talk about how much tougher it is to repeat as champions than to win the first time. Well, we can do it. All we have to do is make up our minds today—in this room, right now—

that we are willing to make the sacrifices necessary to be winners. You are an elite group. God gave you a talent and an ability that few people have. But it's up to you to use it. You have to be willing to work hard, to dedicate yourself, to give a hundred percent so that you can be the best. I don't know about the rest of you, but I've enjoyed the last six months having people treat me like the coach of the best football team in the world. I would think you've enjoyed it, too. If you want to keep that feeling, you have to earn it. You have to go out there every day—no matter how hot it is, how much it hurts, how tired you are—and make the sacrifices necessary to be champions. You have to pay the price.

"Everyone in the league is undefeated right now, everyone is in first place. But come next January there's only going to be one champion. And every one of us has to make up his mind today that we're going to be that one."

The coach was talking to his veterans; we rookies were not world champions of anything. But he was also talking to our own desires to become a part of that world championship team. And he said something else that I felt was directed right to me.

"Every one of you has the same opportunity to make this team. Everyone starts off the same at the beginning of training camp, and I have every confidence that the forty men who make this team will be able to beat anyone in football. But you can't just throw your jock strap onto the field and expect people to roll over. You have to go out there and prove it."

This was what I wanted to hear. The competition to make the Chiefs' roster would be the stiffest in the league. But the rewards for making the team would be the greatest as well: a chance at the Super Bowl. When Ara Parseghian had delivered similar speeches, I had burned with the need to prove myself good enough to be a part of a Notre Dame championship team. Now I felt no such consuming necessity, but I was fired by a calmer desire to become a Kansas City Chief and Super Bowl champion. I had seen one of the veterans' Super Bowl rings—a large and gaudy setting of diamonds against some kind of red stone, in a wide, gold-filigreed band. Given the opportunity, I would wear one of those with pride—and no scruples about bad taste.

Stram followed up his opening remarks with a review of some of the details of camp life. While two-a-days lasted we would be awakened at 6:30 for mandatory breakfast, then would be on the field by 8:30 for the first practice. Lunch at noon would be followed by a meeting, then the second practice at 3:30. After dinner at 6:30, a second meeting would last until 8:00 or 8:30, after which we were "free"—until 10:00 curfew. All of this sounded familiar from college days—except for the additional meeting after lunch—until my new coach went on to explain the fine system. Absence from any meeting, meal, or practice would mean an automatic $500 fine. Tardiness would be punished by a $250 fine, plus $10 for every minute the player was late. After twenty-five minutes he might as well miss it altogether. Fines for breaking curfew, for having women in the dorm, for having hair too long or any facial hair at all, for being overweight—all these were clearly outlined, notifying me that the game might still be the same, but many of the rules would be different from now on. At stake was no longer just personal satisfaction, school honor, or even a chance for glory; the bottom line would now be calculated in dollars and cents.

With new playbook under my arm, I filed out of the room at the meeting's close, exchanging exclamations with Sid and Clyde over the extraordinary fine system. While the rest of the country worried about Vietnam and unrest at home, my obsession that summer would be to keep my alarm clock wound.

Back in our room, Sid and I settled ourselves on our beds to examine our playbooks more closely. The Chiefs' offensive system, I discovered, was much more complicated than Notre Dame's had been. I looked at a typical play—one called "Red right X, 52 full pop G-O inside"—and tried to figure out what all the codes meant. "Red" was the formation, "right" the direction to which the strong side of the formation lined up, "X" an indication to one of the wide receivers to split out; "52" meant the fifty-series run through the two-hole (around right end); "full" signaled a switch in assignments between fullback and halfback; "pop" told a back to block the defensive end while the tight end hooked the outside linebacker; "G-O" indicated both guards pulled; and "inside" dictated that the wide receiver would block the inside man forcing the play from the secondary, while the lead puller blocked the outside man. What it amounted to, then, was a sweep to the right with the combination of blocks clearly specified. I studied the center's assignments on this play—against the half-dozen primary defenses we were likely to see—and discovered that I would have to be able to recognize the defense and make the proper calls to set the blocking for my fellow offensive linemen. If I called "even," I would reach out to tie up the defensive tackle lined up over my pulling right guard, while my own tackle came down to block the middle linebacker. If I called "odd" because the defensive man was lined up too wide, I would exchange assignments with my right tackle. If a defensive player lined up in the gap between myself and my left guard, I would have to make the proper call that would tell the guard either to pull as the play dictated or to stay at home and block the man in his gap. My eyeballs were rolling after looking at only one play.

A knock on the door interrupted my studying. Jerrel Wilson, a punter in cowboy boots and western shirt, stood in the doorway asking if I had any change. I reached into the pocket of my shorts jingling my dimes and quarters, until I looked up to see that he held a fifty-dollar bill in his right hand.

"No, I guess I don't," I mumbled, as Jerrel left to try next door.

I looked over to Sid, wanting to laugh but not wanting my laugh to be heard in the hallway. I looked out the door to see that Jerrel was returning to a room across the hall. I followed him through the open door to discover that it was the poker room, with a game in progress. On the table I was amazed to see what looked like $150 to $200 in cash, but another rookie onlooker whispered to me that this was only an average pot. Around the table Len Dawson, Jerrel Wilson, Mo Moorman, Mike Livingston, and the trainer, Bobby Yarborough, were playing some kind of seven-card, high-low stud poker, with a ten-dollar maximum bet. The high stakes were simply one more astonishment. I learned that the game continued throughout training camp whenever there was free time, players winning or losing several hundred dollars at a sitting. Super Bowl checks had made wallets fat. I returned to my room with my head still swimming from all the wonders I had witnessed as a Kansas City Chief—and practice had not even started.

A banging on my door and a bellowing in the hall sent me leaping from bed in total disorientation, groping for awareness of what emergency had roused me. As my senses cleared and I looked at my clock, I saw that it was six-twenty. We were not supposed to be awakened until six-thirty. Robbed of ten minutes of sleep! I opened my door to discover the source of the racket. Continuing farther down the hallway, Bobby Bell was still hollering, and banging on doors with his fist, obviously taking some kind of perverse delight in startling his teammates from their sleep. At six-twenty I was not impressed that this was an all-pro linebacker. "Obnoxious sonuvabitch," I mumbled to myself as I turned back into the room.

In the washroom, standing at a row of sinks before a large mirror, my teammates did not look as impressive as they had the day before. Bleary-eyed, disheveled, faces still creased with the imprint of pillows, they appeared not as athletic superstars but as aging laborers roused to another day of drudgery. After a perfunctory face-washing and teeth-brushing, Sid and I fell into the trickle of players shuffling sleepily to the union.

In the dining hall, I saw several veterans check in with the boy marking attendance, then leave to return to the dormitory, apparently back to bed. Others were passing through the cafeteria line, taking only a glass or two of fruit juice, or perhaps a roll. Sid did the same, then headed back to the room. I felt no more inclination to eat than they apparently did, but in my need to keep up my weight I took two large scoops of scrambled eggs, several slices of greasy bacon, three pieces of toast—plus the same two glasses of juice the others took. I ate mechanically, not satisfying a hunger but following a necessary habit of eating three large meals every day to minimize my inevitable weight loss during camp. My breakfast finished, I walked back alone to the dormitory.

As I looked forward to my first practice, part of me was anxious to do well—to impress Hank Stram and Bill Walsh; to earn the respect of Jim Tyrer, Ed Budde, Buck Buchanan, and the other Chiefs; to become a great professional football player myself. But another part wondered what I was doing there in Liberty, Missouri, in that heat and humidity, presuming to be good enough to become a member of the best football team in the National Football League. Why wasn't I back in Spokane with Julie, whom I had left over three weeks before and now missed terribly? Why wasn't I simply working through the summer and getting ready for graduate school in the fall? If I was not going to be good enough to make it, I wanted to find out soon. I did not want to go through an entire training camp—earning twelve dollars a day, preseason games included, sweating buckets, bruising my arms, mangling my hands, jamming my neck—only to be cut at the end of the summer. If I was not good enough, I could accept that fact, but I wanted to know *now*.

At a few minutes before eight I walked to the locker room. The air was noticeably warmer than an hour and a half before. My skin was prickling with moisture before I crossed the hundred yards from the dorm. Inside, my overwhelming impression of the locker room was of drab grayness—gray metal lockers, gray wooden benches, gray cement floors, gray walls. It was suffocatingly warm, despite the attempts of a large fan to move the sluggish air through the room. I wasted little time lingering over rituals of dressing. I weighed myself—237, pretty good for me—put on my half T-shirt, supporter, and socks, slipped on my pants and shoes, and grabbed my helmet, shoulder pads, and jersey to put on outside. The locker room was depressing as well as stifling; I just wanted to be out of it. I walked down a flight of stairs through a storage basement at the bottom level of the athletic building, and out into the sunlight. My shoulder pads and jersey put on, I carried my helmet across the road behind the locker room, through a gate, and down a bank to the football field. In college, the coaches had expected us to show our dedication by arriving at practice early, to work on our own skills individually before the workout officially began. Here, a number of rookies and a few veterans were jogging nervously in twenty-yard bursts, or tossing a football back and forth, but just as many were sprawled on the ground, trying to salvage every possible minute of inactivity before the ordeal began. Simply standing in pads and uniform in the early morning heat, I had already begun to sweat uncomfortably. I knew that much more would come.

Just moments before eight-thirty, Hank Stram appeared, trotting down the bank to the field, color-coordinated in an opposite scheme from the night before—red jacket and white shoes this time. At his signal, one of the ball boys sounded an air horn, and we lined up in the end zone for the beginning of practice. We ran in groups by position through a few jog-sprints, did ten minutes of calisthenics, then were introduced to something new that year: an "obstacle course." It sounded easy enough when it was explained. We would run to six stations where we would do a different exercise at each for one minute. No problem, I figured —until we started. The first station was the ropes: running with high knee lift through a grid of ropes raised a foot off the ground. In sixty seconds we were able to run through twice. I was starting to breathe rapidly but still felt fine. We jogged to the next station: grass drills. We ran in place for several seconds, then dove on our bellies at the coach's command, then sprang up to run some more. After a minute of this I was not so sure the obstacle course was going to be a snap. I was breathing hard and sweating profusely now. I wanted to lean over with my hands on my knees to rest, but we had to keep moving. The dummies were next. We stood to one side of a dummy lying lengthwise on the ground, to leap over it laterally, back and forth for twenty seconds. We had to take turns, but the extra rest helped very little. I was gasping for air now and each leg weighed about fifty pounds more than when I started. I wanted desperately to rest, but we had to keep moving. At the next station, we stepped up on a plain wooden bench, then back to the ground, repeated for thirty seconds until the other half of the group took over. It looked easier than the grass drills or dummy, but doing it proved to be as bad as climbing the last row of stadium stairs in college. By now I thought I would die. Even jogging to the fifth station was painful. My legs seemed out of control; I started them moving and stumbled after them, gasping for air, pouring sweat. Now we drove the seven-man sled, a familiar drill for offensive linemen, but excruciating after the four previous exercises. We lined up and lunged into the sled to start it moving. I was too tired to drive the thing, but when I tried to just hold on and let its momentum carry me along, I discovered my teammates were doing the same, bringing the sled gradually to a standstill. When the coach barked at us to drive it, we lunged again, then grunted and plodded until our time was up. Permanently, I feared. But just one more station remained. The sixth and last. I could always make it through the last one. But the last one was the cruncher this time. We crouched, straight-backed, under the goalpost crossbar, until our fingertips reached the ground, then sprang upward to touch the crossbar with both hands, repeating for thirty seconds until the second half of the group took over. There was no doubt now; I knew I was dying. My legs were so rubbery I could barely stand, but I had to try to leap ten times to touch that crossbar ten feet off the ground. I hit it the first time and scraped it with my fingertips the second, but with each additional leap I missed it by more each time, until I don't think my feet even left the ground. My skeleton might have moved inside me, but my flesh remained firmly planted. Each attempt, no matter how futile, hurt a little more than the last.

The conclusion of the obstacle course meant the end of only the first twenty minutes of practice. We were given a short breather, but even a long nap would not have fully restored me. Whatever we would do for the rest of practice was guaranteed to hurt after that brutal twenty minutes. We broke up now into groups for individual drills. The offensive linemen ran a few starts, drove the seven-man sled again, took turns butting the heavy bag hanging from a chain. We paired off to fire out from our stances into each other, then pass-blocked against the other's rush. We ran through blocking assignments against various defenses, first in slow motion, then at full speed. Everything I did, the veterans seemed to do more effortlessly. I looked at their bulky bodies and knew I was in better shape, yet they seemed to have recuperated from the obstacle course while I was still wobbly. My anxiety alone—due to my uncertainty over making the team, over not knowing what it took to play in the NFL, over not knowing if I was good enough—burned enough calories to exhaust me. The veterans seemed able to hold something in reserve, to practice with only a portion of their resources. I held nothing back. My career in the NFL might end tomorrow; there was nothing to save myself for. The veterans were pacing themselves for a season and a long career.

When the defensive linemen joined us, we worked on pass-blocking, one on one under Coach Walsh's close scrutiny. As I lined up for my turn, I realized how different this was from college. Opposite me was no prep-team player, but Curley Culp, former NCAA heavyweight wrestling champion and one of the quickest and strongest defensive tackles in the National Football League. On my move to snap into my stance, Curley lunged out directly into me, both hands grabbing for my shoulders. I attempted to punch him away from me with my fists, then yank them hard and quickly to the outside to break his grip. But I could not stop Curley's 275 pounds with just my arms. I tried to stay squarely in front of him, but he butted me in the face with his helmet, then as I tried to counter his move by butting him back, he suddenly pulled me toward him, released his right hand, and turned my right shoulder with his left while looping his right arm over me. He slid by my right side, leaving me spinning too late to regain contact. It was a masterful move, working strength, quickness, and technique into a combination I had not seen in college. He had simply toyed with me, impervious to my countermoves or actually using them against me. I gave way to the next blocker.

Between turns I observed that the other rookies were handled by the veterans as easily as I had been. The defense had the advantage in this drill, but I also noticed that the veteran offensive linemen were able to sustain their blocks much longer than the rest of us. Their large, bulky bodies, outweighing mine by thirty pounds or more, simply could not be moved as easily as mine could. They countered defensive strength with their own, and forced the rushers into different tactics. Dave Hill, for all his size, used finesse, inviting the rusher to the outside, then letting the defensive player's own momentum drive him beyond the quarterback. Mo Moorman relied more on strength, setting up close to the scrimmage line and staggering his man with his first thrust, keeping him off balance from the beginning. Ed Budde and Jim Tyrer combined both strength and finesse, setting up solidly, then battling the defensemen to a standoff. I had much to learn—and wondered if I ever would.

The ball boys who assisted at practice could not bring water bottles fast enough to replace the fluids we were sweating out. Squeezing a thin jet of water into my mouth only teased my thirst. I wanted to bury my head in a bucket of ice water and drink my way out of it. I fantasized lying facedown in a swimming pool, water lapping over, around, and in me as I opened my mouth and sucked it in. Instead, I had this trickle of water once every twenty minutes or so. I was not sure I would make it to the end of practice.

After the pass-blocking drill, we came together as a team, for the offense to run plays against the defense in dummy scrimmage. "Dummy" meant only that the backs would not be tackled; for the linemen "live" and "dummy" were not clearly distinguishable. Instead of prep-team players for opposition, we ran plays against veterans who were not about to let rookies push them around simply for the sake of offensive timing, or against other rookies trying to impress the coaches and make the team. This would be no light, crisp drill. I took my turns at center, unsure of the plays, unable to make the line calls, uncertain whether the defensive players would despise me for blocking as if the plays were live, or the coaches would dismiss me for coasting if I did not. Individual players against whom I lined up reacted in different ways. Willie Lanier, in his fourth year, had already established himself as the best middle linebacker in the National Football League, and felt no need to prove himself. He knew what he needed to do to get ready for the season, and it did not include playing every down in practice as a madman. When I blocked Willie, he accepted the block in an unspoken compromise: he would go through his movements toward the ball, I would go through mine to cut him off, neither of us would try to make the other look bad. Buck Buchanan in his eighth year was also well established, and as "professional" in his attitude as Willie. He would give one good initial hit, but allow the offensive player to set his block. But Buck was uncannily hard to hit squarely. For all his great size he presented a very small target. From a six-seven frame coiled into his stance he gave merely

a shoulder or an arm, absorbing the blow easily, rolling away
from it, but protecting his body from a full clean shot. I never
quite figured out how at six seven, 285, Buck could be so elusive.
Curley Culp was temperamentally the antithesis of Buck and
Willie. He was always ornery, always trying to make the offensive
linemen look bad. He relaxed for four plays in a row, allowing
himself to be blocked, then with no warning exploded on the
fifth into the unsuspecting blocker, darting by him as if untouched, making the offensive player feel foolish—and angry. I
should have simply decided that every play with Curley was live,
but I was afraid my pinched nerve could not absorb the constant
pounding that would result. In all-out war, I was afraid I would
be the loser. I allowed Curley to set the tempo—and paid for it
often.

Thirty minutes of dummy scrimmage brought the morning's
practice to a close—except for running and weights. What we
had done in practice seemed less strenuous than our two-a-day
sessions in college, yet I was more exhausted than I had ever
been at Notre Dame. And I was not finished yet. After removing
our helmets and shoulder pads, we moved onto the quarter-mile
cinder track for four laps around the field. Despite my weariness, I set off at a good pace, running through my tiredness into
a rhythm that would push me but that I could bear. As I
rounded the turn for the beginning of the second lap, I noticed
that we had fallen into well-defined groups. I was running with
mostly other rookies; the veterans were strung out behind us,
and several of them—Culp, Lanier, Hill, and others—were
barely jogging. I marveled that no coach screamed at them for
loafing, or demanded extra laps. I had never seen anyone move
so slowly on a football field, but once again I was viewing my
new world through old eyes. We rookies might have been in better shape, but we also foolishly thought we would impress the
coaches with our conditioning and desire. We had not been told
that no one ever made an NFL team by running fast laps after
practice.

After the mile, we moved through a series of exercises with
the weights. By now, I was thoroughly exhausted and feeling
slightly sick from dehydration. From observing everything about
me, I had gone to awareness of nothing but my own tiredness. I

was oblivious to players coming and going, even to coaches, of whom I was only vaguely aware as anonymous judging presences all around me. I felt leaden, mildly nauseated, unbearably hot. I approached each of the six exercises with the weights as if it were the last one, telling myself, "Just one more time. Just one more." As I gripped the bar for military presses, I blanked everything from my mind but the need to jerk the weight to my shoulders and thrust it quickly over my head six times before my arms rebelled. With a grunt and an intake of breath I drove myself through the six repetitions without exhaling, dropped the bar back to the ground, then went limp again as I moved off to rest a few minutes, hoping to recapture some little strength. "Just one more. Just one more." I had to do these weight-lifting exercises well, I told myself, because I needed to prove to the coaches that I was stronger than my body weight indicated. In fact, with the barbells I was one of the stronger players on the team, but real strength for a lineman was not measured by his ability to lift this or that weight; it was the total power he could generate in blocking. I might be able to press more pounds than one of our 265-pound guards or tackles, but I could not overpower Curley Culp.

When I dropped the bar after my sixth exercise, I felt liberated for the first time that morning. I moved off to the side, bent over at the waist with my hands on my knees, and hung my head for a few minutes, breathing deeply, blocking my mind to everything but the thought that all I needed to do now was gather up enough energy to collect my helmet and shoulder pads for the trudge up the bank to the locker room. As I finally moved off in the direction of my equipment, Coach Walsh hollered over to me.

"Take some long snaps before you go in."

I groaned. To do anything at all was too much. Instead of a shower and several cups of Gatorade, I must now spend fifteen more minutes in the punishing sun, snapping the ball to Jerrel Wilson and the rookie punters, who for the past two hours—while we had been drilling, banging heads, sweating—had been leisurely kicking the ball back and forth, working on their timing. I watched others who had finished with the weights plodding wearily up the bank to relief in the showers, while I walked over to the forty-yard line to the waiting kickers. The first ball I snapped reached the punter on one bounce; the next two, though they made it in the air, were so wobbly they could barely be handled; finally with the fourth one I settled into a rhythm and could zip the ball back fifteen yards in a tight spiral. Each snap was an explosion of energy. I tensed, coiled, whipped the ball; throwing hands, arms, head, shoulders, back through my legs toward the outstretched hands waiting fifteen yards upfield; then sagged again with numbing weariness. I thought I had reached my physical limits with the weights; I found now that I had a little bit more. I hoped I would not have to discover if I had more yet, when this was done.

After fifteen or twenty minutes of snapping for punts and field goals with the other centers—E. J. Holub, Jack Rudnay, and Remi Prudhomme—and with Bobby Bell, who snapped on punts as well as played linebacker, the coaches finally called an end to the drill and sent us in. Coach Walsh walked up the hill with me, chatting casually about Notre Dame. He had been an outstanding center for the Irish in the late forties, playing with Leon Hart, Johnny Lujack, Emil Sitko, and other great players under Frank Leahy. To be talked to personally made me feel a little less anonymous, but what I needed even more was to collapse somewhere, drink several quarts of water, and *rest*.

In the locker room, I wrapped my arms around the drinking fountain and hung on for life, drinking long and deep. I peeled off my saturated clothes and stepped on the scale—231, down six pounds, which I had to try to replace before the afternoon practice. I filled a cup with ice and drank five glasses of water before walking unsteadily to the shower. I hung my head and simply let the cool water run over me, feeling but a little relief from my weariness. I gradually made the water colder, almost expecting to see steam arise from me as it hit my burning skin and was instantly evaporated. After ten minutes I toweled off and dressed —then immediately began to sweat again. With less than thirty minutes until lunchtime, I saw no point in returning to my room, but walked instead to the union, where I sprawled in a large plush chair to wait for the dining room to open. All about me were rookies who appeared to be in the same state I was in. The only talk was in funereal whispers, as if we lacked the energy required for normal speech. There was little conversation of any kind; I suspected they were preoccupied with the same thoughts that troubled me: how many days of this would I have to go through before a ball boy knocked at the door to deliver a message:

"Coach Stram wants to see you. Bring your playbook."

This was known as a visit from "the Turk," and it was the chief dread of every rookie in camp. No cut was due for some days—because the league had a regular schedule of gradually reduced squad limits, we measured our survival from one major cut to the next. As a member of the All-Star team, I did not have to be counted in the squad size until nearly the end of summer, but I drew little comfort from that fact. I would not know if my surviving another cut was due to my good standing or simply to the fact that I did not have to be officially counted yet. My uncertainty would simply be prolonged.

When the doors to the dining room opened, I filled my tray with sandwiches, potato salad, fruit, and desserts. I had no appetite—all I wanted to do was drink liquids until I sloshed when I walked—but I knew that I had to eat lots, to replace those six pounds I had lost during the morning workout. I ate slowly and steadily, eating not to satisfy myself but to clear my plate, and I washed everything down with several more glasses of juices. The atmosphere was greatly subdued from last night's, but the veterans seemed much less stricken with weariness than the rookies. I did not understand yet that some of the veterans had their own very real anxieties; that we rookies, in threatening to replace them, were in fact the cause. But I could not conceive how the veterans felt; they seemed remote, impervious to the physical and emotional ordeal I was undergoing, and that I could assume my fellow rookies were experiencing.

The meeting after lunch was a new kind of torture. Simply having to be in a meeting room rather than back in the dormitory in bed was frustrating. My mind knew that the plays being introduced and diagrammed against the various defenses were particularly important to me, after having spent the last three weeks with the College All-Stars, but my body said that nothing could be as important as a couple hours of rest before the afternoon practice. I forced myself to pay attention for the hour, then headed directly back to the dorm and my bed. I was amazed to hear a poker game starting up across the hall; I could not imagine how anyone could want to do anything but sleep. I set my alarm for a few minutes before three and collapsed on my back in bed. I did not move; I did not know if I *could* have moved. My heavy limbs sank into the mattress. I felt as if all my body weight had shifted to my backside—that the part of me that touched the sheets was all lead while my front was inflated balloon. I did not fall asleep so much as surrender at last to my exhaustion.

When the ringing of the alarm finally registered on my consciousness, my body groaned a loud No! As I rolled from the bed to put on my sandals and moved slowly toward the door, I had a hard time believing that in a little more than thirty minutes I would actually be on the field, going through the motions of a football player again. I ached in my shoulders, neck, back, and hamstrings, and I felt as tired as when I had lain down an hour and a half ago. As I opened the door to the outside, I nearly staggered backward with the assault of the hot, humid air that engulfed me. I walked the hundred yards to the locker room with real dread: how could I possibly endure another session like this morning's in this heat? The scale registered 235; I would have extra weight to gain back tonight, in addition to whatever I lost during the next two hours. I dressed and took the field as I had in the morning—acting by rote, not ritual. The afternoon practice was much like the morning's: running, calisthenics, obstacle course, drills, and scrimmage. A five-on-five contact drill was new: one side of the offensive line, plus a back, running plays against half a defense. I felt nothing decisive from the drill—I was neither overwhelmed nor overwhelming—but I at least experienced my first real contact with professional football players, and began to sense that I could survive in this league. If I were given the chance. We also ran wind sprints at the end of practice, rather than the mile and weights. In my rookie anxiety, I pushed myself to be among the leaders of my lineman group in the sprints, while the more secure veterans comfortably lagged behind. The major difference between the two practices was that I started the afternoon session already wearied from the morning. No matter how much time I had between plays, between turns at drills, between sprints, I never had enough to catch my breath completely or regain my strength. For the last half hour of practice I wondered if I had enough stamina simply to get through the next play. Each time I did, I marveled that I was still going, but wondered about the next one. I became a robot, doing what I was told to do, going where I was told to go, thinking only in terms of the next play, the next turn, the next sprint. I did not know how long my automatic pilot could direct me, but suddenly practice was over and I was still standing.

As I walked off the field, I was surprised to feel through my exhaustion a peculiar sense of satisfaction. My body merely felt assaulted, but the realization that I had survived such a physical test, that I had pushed myself to my limits—and beyond what I had thought were my limits—never coasting, never letting up, never taking the easy way, filled me with a potent pleasure. There was nothing masochistic about it. I felt pleasure not in the pain or weariness itself, but in realizing that pain and weariness had not incapacitated me. As in the past, nothing else I did was capable of providing the intense experiences of football. When I looked around me at the other athletes dragging themselves to the showers, I felt for the first time a bond with them. Having gone through the same ordeal with these other men I felt a tie to them that had not been there before. I had now shared with eighty other men who had been strangers to me until two days earlier the sweat, pain, and exhaustion of an unimaginable double practice—giving us a common powerful experience. I felt a particular tie to the other rookies, because we shared the same fears and anxieties as well as the physical strain. If I should make the team, perhaps I would feel more truly one with the veterans, too. In time, pleasures as well as pains would become a part of the bond, but I suspect that a shared experience of extraordinary pleasure by itself would not create so potent a bond as a shared ordeal could—provided the ordeal ended satisfactorily.

No new feeling was acknowledged as we showered and dressed for dinner. Football players do not talk about such matters. I tried to recuperate as I had done in the morning. I stepped on the scale again—227! Eight pounds lost during practice, ten pounds for the day—I panicked at the thought of losing two or three pounds every day while doubles lasted. I gulped several cups of water and Gatorade, then walked to the union for the largest dinner I could stuff into myself. Another meeting with the offensive linemen and an evening visit to the Dairy Queen for more precious calories finished my first day of practice. The bank thermometer in downtown Liberty registered 88 degrees at nine-thirty; the humidity did not seem to have abated, either. I was no longer surprised, but could not become accustomed to such torturous heat. I looked forward eagerly to my air-conditioned room and bed, but there was a catch. If I went to bed early, morning would come that much sooner, bringing with it the same agonies again—perhaps even worse, because I would carry over my aches and weariness from today. But exhaustion won out. When the assistant coach came to my door for curfew check, I was already well settled in bed. I had gotten an ice pack from one of the ball boys, claiming a slightly sprained wrist. With the air conditioner chilling the room at maximum power, I dropped gratefully onto my back, placed the ice pack in the middle of my bare chest, and drifted into senselessness.

Lives changed in training camp. One morning I would come to breakfast to find that a half dozen rookies who normally sat at my table were not there. The roommate of one of them would pass the word in muted tones: the Turk got 'em. Where had they gone? What had they returned to? I never knew, but at times in my loneliness and uncertainty I almost envied the fact that at least they knew their fate.

The Turk did not visit only rookies. In my first summer I watched four-, seven-, and ten-year veterans cut as abruptly as the greenest rookie. I began to realize that veterans came to training camp with different anxieties from the rookies, but equally painful ones. For every rookie who made the team, a veteran had to retire or be released. For every rookie or veteran cut, a life was profoundly changed.

That first summer I made the taxi squad (a sort of reserve unit of seven to replace injured players), when Remi Prudhomme, a four-year veteran, was cut. I made the forty-man squad in my second summer when E. J. Holub was pressured into retirement. E.J. did not leave football easily. I did not know him well, but I understood from the first time I saw him that he would play for the rest of his life if he could—or until they dragged him off the field when he could not. I never saw the side of E.J. that felt the pain of knees operated on nine times and of the anxieties that age and crippled legs had to have brought on. I saw the side that hollered and crowed when the rest of us were dragging, that thrived on camaraderie and love of playing the game. From the day I arrived in Liberty in 1970, I was a threat to E.J.'s career, but he betrayed no resentment. He paid little attention to me, but on several occasions when I was having difficulty mastering some skill, E.J. pulled me aside.

"Here, rookie. Try it this way." And he proceeded to demonstrate how I might do whatever it was I was trying to do a little bit better—helping me to take his job.

E.J. was a cowboy and a good ole boy before such figures became fashionable in urban settings. He was tough as the leather of his boots and as loudmouthed as the frontier roarers that preceded him by more than a century in West Texas. When he was forced to retire, it hurt him, I know, to be told that he could no longer play the game. The team, too, was diminished by his absence, by the loss of an authentic "character" and a part of its history. I gained a spot on the team because of it.

In just two years I became a wise old veteran, consoling other rookies who struggled with the same anxieties that had tortured me. A guard named Ed Fisher slumped despondently in a chair in my room one day, moaning about his loneliness for the new bride he had left behind in Arizona. I liked Ed and knew he had talent, but I knew that there was no room for him on the roster. I wanted to tell him to go home to her now. But each rookie had to discover his own fate for himself. Ed was in fact cut, but he signed with Houston the next season and became a starter there for several years.

A rookie offensive tackle from Wisconsin named Elbert Walker showed up in camp one year so overweight that he was driven to lose thirty pounds in addition to surviving the normal agonies of training camp. He lost weight quickly, but passed out

twice on the field from heat prostration, and suffered as I had
never seen anyone suffer on a football field. The skin of his reduced waistline hung slack in front of him—leading someone to
joke that when Elbert went to bed at night, he could pull his
skin up to his chin for a blanket. But his constant exhaustion was
not funny. I wanted to take him aside, talk to him.

"Elbert, go home. Don't do this to yourself for fourteen dollars a day [our per diem had been handsomely increased from
twelve]. You could make more money checking groceries back
home in an air-conditioned store. And you have no chance of
making the team."

But each rookie must discover his own fate.

Through five summers as I aged and matured in the game,
training camp retained its distinctive rhythm. It began in seemingly endless two-a-day practices, when mere physical survival
seemed an extraordinary accomplishment. The players existed at
the most minimal level, our lives centered on simple physical
needs for food, drink, and rest. Thinking was an unwanted burden; it was easier to stumble from bed to practice field, to meal,
to meeting, without much reflection. But two-a-days eventually
gave way to preseason games. Actually to play football—rather
than to drill, run, and lift—was liberating and astonishingly
easy. Once the games started, double workouts remained only at
the beginning of the week, then disappeared altogether. We
were like felons pardoned from a life sentence at hard labor; we
began to *live* again.

When we left William Jewell two weeks before the regular
season opened, the real release occurred. The last night of camp
usually was the occasion for an official celebration. Cases of beer
were smuggled into rooms; perhaps the coaches even knew what
we were up to, but recognized its importance. The realization
that we were breaking rules—a token act of rebellion against the
authority of the coaching staff—was essential to our pleasure.
Invitations from a central gathering place went out. Rookies
found themselves drinking for the first time with veterans who
had begun their NFL careers when the rookies were in grade
school. Old and young, white and black, star and marginal
player, drank together in tacit recognition that all had survived
the same ordeal and were teammates now. An unexpressed senti-

mentality lingered heavily in the room. The aloof veteran became one of the boys, the antagonists from many on-the-field fights became drinking buddies, the mutually despising strangers toasted each other across the room with raised Schlitz cans. The redneck temporarily forgot his prejudice, the superstar his image. Many of the players may not have liked each other any better, but there was something in the atmosphere that temporarily dissolved animosities.

The ritual hoisting of beers at the end of training camp was an important event. Professional football players are, above all, physical creatures. Their lives center around performing extraordinarily difficult physical feats better than anyone else could do them. But professional football players are human, too. They have their fears, their hopes, their frustrations, and their satisfactions as anyone does—although they are less likely to talk about them. Perhaps their muteness distinguishes football players most of all. The aging veteran does not talk about his fears of growing old, the rookie does not speak aloud his deepest longings for fame or his dread of failure. Everyone bitches and moans about grueling practices and suffocating heat and unfeeling coaches, but no one confesses to more personal anguish, to physical fear of other players or to anxieties about his own ability. Maybe best friends do. In the privacy of their own room, perhaps with the lights off as they lie in bed at the end of a long training-camp day—speaking to each other in the dark as to an unseen father confessor, because they must speak to someone and their best friend would understand most clearly and judge least harshly.

Neither do football players express their deepest feelings for each other. Football players may be the least demonstrative American males of all in showing each other affection. They hug each other after touchdowns and victories, and slap each other on the butt without self-consciousness, but these are superficial acts. The powerful feelings that teammates generate for each other are never expressed. But they are deeply felt. The bond among football players is one of the most potent all-male emotions in our culture, even if words are never spoken or acknowledgment made in any way. In our end-of-training-camp parties in the dormitory at William Jewell College, the Kansas City

Chiefs enacted a sort of sacred ceremony that celebrated our renewed closeness.

To pack our bags and drive into Kansas City the next day was to be fully reborn. We became husbands, neighbors, citizens, and consumers once again, after nearly two months of being simply football players at the most elemental level. The "pleasure" of training camp was much like the pleasure the man in the old joke got from banging his head against a brick wall: it felt so good when we stopped. Training camp served a function. It conditioned us physically for a long season of extraordinarily demanding play, and enabled us to prove to ourselves that, however spent we might think we were, we could dig down a little deeper to find what was necessary for one more play. And another, and another, if required. The fourth quarters of September games in Indian summer heat, and of December games at the end of nearly six months of steady pounding on weary bodies, would demand such resources. But to a great extent training camp also created through its most abusive aspects the bond that brought forty or forty-seven grown men with widely different personalities and interests into a team. It was a peculiar sort of bond—rooted in shared pain and frustration, awareness of the many who had fallen to the Turk's sword, and relief that we were not among those unfortunate ones. It was a bond that aggressively excluded outsiders, that could interfere with players' other personal relationships, and that dissolved when football ended. A strange bond—but a potent one nonetheless, and a central experience of professional football players. Through it, rookies and veterans found their common ground and became a team.

SEVEN

The End of Toughness

THE TURK ACTUALLY DID GET ME during my first year with the Chiefs—but the swipe of his sword was not fatal. On the Monday before the regular season opened, a week after we had left Liberty, I returned after practice to the apartment I shared with my grandfather. My being drafted by the Chiefs had brought me to my mother's hometown; my grandmother's death in early 1970 brought me to live with my grandfather that first year. On that Monday, as I sat in the living room reading the newspaper, I caught my name mentioned on the television newscast. I crumpled the paper in my lap, jerking to alertness, as I heard other names rattled off, then the newsman continuing.

"This is the final cut of the preseason, and brings the team roster to thirty-nine, one below the league's limit. Hank Stram will be making his final decisions this week to determine the forty-man squad that will open the season Sunday against Minnesota."

I waited to hear a repeat of the list of names, to be certain I had actually heard my own, but the focus shifted to other news. I stared at the screen waiting for more commentary, but that was it. A brief report slipped in between baseball scores and an account of the previous day's preseason football games. The sportscaster's voice betrayed as much emotion in naming the released players as it did when reporting on the results at the

dog track. But I had just heard a decision that could drastically
affect the course of my life. *Overheard,* really. I felt like an in-
dicted felon who chances to hears his attorney and the rival
prosecutor in the next room, casually discussing his probable
conviction. All over the city, viewers had heard the same news
and were probably so concerned that they were now calling to
their wives, "Is dinner about ready?"

I felt instantly disoriented, as if not just cut from the team but
cut off from my moorings altogether. Then I began to grow
angry that Hank Stram had not even had the decency to notify
me in person of this decision. The next morning I turned immediately to a part of the sports page that I had paid little attention to before that summer. On one of the back pages, in a
"scorecard" section among the standings of the various professional leagues, the results of local horse racing, and the scores
from bowling tournaments in New Jersey and Colorado, were
the few inches of space devoted to "Transactions." Here the
reader could discover who had just been hired at North Texas
State University as assistant basketball coach, who had been
placed on the twenty-one-day disabled list by the New York
Yankees, and who had been injured, waived, or traded by the
twenty-six NFL clubs. That summer I had begun to read pathos
and tragedy into those brief items, instead of seeing merely a list
of inconsequential names which I had formerly slipped over. On
this September morning in 1970, I immediately found what I
was looking for.

TRANSACTIONS

MIAMI DOLPHINS—Cut rookie Bob Kuechenberg, guard, and
veteran John Boynton, offensive tackle, Jesse Powell, linebacker,
Barry Pryor, running back; placed on injured waivers veterans Tom
Goode, center and Jim Cox, tight end.

KANSAS CITY CHIEFS—Announced the retirement of Curtis
McClinton, running back; cut veterans Tom Flores, quarterback,
and Richard Armstrong, running back; waived rookies Bob Liggett,
defensive tackle, Mike Oriard, center, Jack Rudnay, center, and
Robert Hews, defensive tackle; placed on injured waivers Clyde
Werner, linebacker.

And so on through the remaining teams. Most of the names were
unknown to me, but several were not. Bob Kuechenberg had

been a teammate at Notre Dame, and I found the names of Bob
Gladieux, Paul Seiler, and Tom Schoen—all domers from my
era—among the cuts from other teams. Ken Mendenhall and
Lynn Larson, teammates from the All-Star game, were also
listed. I saw the names of veterans, whose careers had now
ended abruptly. Curtis McClinton had played eight years, one as
Rookie of the Year in the AFL, three as all-league, two as Super
Bowl participant. I did not know Curtis McClinton except as a
face on the team, but I did know that no one retired at the *end*
of training camp unless he was forced to do so. I discovered that
the Chicago Bears had cut Elijah Pitts, the fine running back
from Green Bay's championship years; Philadelphia had cut
George Mira, a former great college quarterback I remembered
from my youth; the Washington Redskins had released Gary
Beban, a Heisman Trophy winner at UCLA. How many of these
men had wives and families dependent on their salaries? How
many had legitimate careers outside football to fall back on?
How many felt the end of football to be the end of everything?
I didn't know the answers, but during that first summer in the
NFL I had come to realize that a life lay behind each of those
cryptic items: "Cut Elijah Pitts, running back."

The majority of the names on that September list were of
rookies in positions similar to mine. Their cases were less poignant than those of the veterans, but each of their names, too,
represented a destiny fundamentally altered. I was beginning to
realize that much of the real human drama reported in the
sports page lay in those lists of "Transactions" and in the four- or
five-line fillers at the ends of long stories about the big games of
the day—those brief obituaries of long-forgotten ballplayers who
batted .297 for the Chicago Cubs from 1917 to 1928, and had
now died in the nursing homes to which they had moved several
years before, after retiring as the custodians of high schools in
Little Rock or Philadelphia. As I read my own name in the
"Transactions" of September 15, 1970, I did not feel tragedy, but
I saw an unalterable finality to my brief professional career.

I arrived at the Chiefs' practice facility in Swope Park, to find
a very subdued locker room compared to the mood of previous
days. Players in jock straps and T-shirts, in workout shorts or
sweat pants, sat in front of their lockers as on any practice day,

but dotted among them and clustered at the end of the row where the rookies dressed were the five other players who had been placed on waivers—still in street clothes, talking quietly among themselves or simply staring at their shoes. Waiting. Waiting for what, they didn't know. The "what" turned out to be a message from Hank Stram that he wanted to see each of us. In his office Hank told me that I had cleared waivers—that no other team in the league had claimed me.

"I still want you to be a part of this team, Mike," he told me in his most compassionate but still businesslike manner. "I think you have a fine future with the Kansas City Chiefs. What I want to do is place you on the taxi squad. But it's up to you."

Having listened for many years to fatherly coaches whose every word and decision were to be trusted as for the best, I was moved to hear that Hank Stram felt positively about my future. We discussed the consequences of playing on the taxi squad. He told me the pay would be three hundred dollars a week—a respectable salary, I thought, until I considered later that it was three hundred dollars a week for only fourteen weeks. I felt that my only alternative to accepting the offer was giving up football and returning home. I said okay.

That may have been a fateful decision on my part. Jack Rudnay had also been waived, leaving E. J. Holub as the only center on the roster, but I did not realize that the coaches would never start a season with just one center. When Jack met Hank in his office for their little chat, Jack told him he would not taxi under any circumstances, and that he had been on the phone to a number of teams around the league that had expressed interest in him. One of the results of Hank's wheeling and dealing on that day was that Jack was restored to the forty-man team while I was placed on the taxi squad. I wondered for many months afterward what would have happened had I told Hank I was not willing to taxi. But I had been incapable of doing so. I had not yet fully realized that Hank Stram was my employer, not a surrogate father.

I remained on the taxi squad for thirteen games, before being activated for the season finale against San Diego. For my three hundred dollars I practiced with the team all week, but did not suit up for the games on Sundays; I shared in all the drudgery but none of the pleasure. I took a part-time job in a sporting goods store, lived quietly with my grandfather, and felt little connection to the team. I was given two tickets to all of the home games, but gave them away to people I met. Hank invited me to travel with the team, but I declined, claiming I had to work Saturdays at the store. I was too proud to sit in the stands and watch my quasi-teammates on the field, or to stand on the sidelines during road games in coat and tie rather than helmet and jersey. Too many associations with old prep-team days lingered on. An injury to a regular enabled me to suit up for the last game of the season, an anticlimactic loss to San Diego after we had been knocked out of the Western Division title race by Oakland the week before. My rookie season began and ended with that game.

My real initiation into NFL football began with the 1971 season. During the off season I had started graduate school and built myself up to a solid 242 pounds, and that summer I took E. J. Holub's place on the roster behind Jack Rudnay. One career ends as another begins. In my first full season as a Kansas City Chief, I discovered the range of experiences that make up professional football.

There were the places.

There was the Astrodome in Houston—the huge glass, steel, and concrete bubble that transformed professional sport in 1965. In future histories of American pastimes, the opening of the Astrodome will be seen as a landmark event, initiating a new era of sport as mass spectacle rather than as expression of an intimate bond between players and fans. To play in the Astrodome felt *unnatural*. I had never played on artificial turf before; when we arrived at the Astrodome the afternoon before our game, I could not dispel a certain uneasiness—as if I should be wiping my feet on a doormat or removing my spiked shoes before stepping onto the carpet. The surface felt hard, with none of the springiness of dirt and grass, and it had seams that had separated, leaving two- and three-inch gaps, and others that had overlapped, forming ridges high enough to trip over. But my eeriest feeling came from being *indoors*. When I looked up, I did not see sun and clouds and blue sky, but an enormous spider web of steel girders with patches of opaque glass behind the webbing. The air was nearly still; no wind rippled the sleeves of my jersey or disarranged my hair. Instead of natural sounds, I heard the mechanical hum and muffled clatter of huge air conditioners. Weather was one of the variables to which I expected to adjust during a football game. The weather may have been unbearably hot in September or paralyzingly cold in December, but it was an expected factor for which I learned to compensate. And sometimes —on crisp sunny days in October—the weather provided one of the most intense sensuous pleasures of playing football. As I loosened up in the Astrodome, I became instantly aware of the dull sameness the climate would always have. I knew it would feel exactly the same tomorrow at game time as it felt now while I was warming up. And would feel the same no matter how many times I played there in years to come.

The artificial surface had certain practical advantages. When I snapped the ball for punts out of the long grass in some stadiums, the grass actually produced a drag on the ball when I uncoiled, sometimes affecting its speed and accuracy. Snapping the ball off the fuzzy nap of the Astrodome's carpet provided no such complications. But I preferred the complications. In the Astrodome I felt surrounded by *deadness,* which clashed harshly with the vitality of the game I played. As a football player my body was a barometer that registered all the sensations created by my surrounding environment. I was acutely aware of sun, rain, stiff winds, light breezes, dryness, humidity, grass, mud, the dirt of skinned infields, when we played in baseball stadiums— even snow and sleet on rare occasions. All of it *alive.* All of it making *me* feel more intensely alive. Even the near-total exhaustion of training camp two-a-days—which made us moan, "I'm dying," or "I feel dead"—was actually an intense feeling of life. I was never more aware of my body as a living organism than when it hurt so terribly in every part. In the Astrodome I was surrounded by synthetic grass, synthetic air, synthetic light, synthetic sky—all dead.

Actually playing the game was a strange experience. I played well—so well, in fact, that I won my first game ball for special-teams play. I sprinted downfield under punts and kickoffs as I always did, making several tackles; blocked on punt and kickoff returns with more than usual success. But I never could dispel the feeling of unnaturalness—the feeling that I was playing an outdoor sport indoors. The presence of live fans could not overwhelm the artificiality of the turf, the lighting, and the dome overhead. After this game, I began to have a recurring dream in which I was playing a football game in a gymnasium, or sometimes even in a living room, with sofa and chairs pushed to the side but still obstructing play. This dream was not nightmarish, but in it I always felt frustrated and constricted. Football in the Astrodome verged on the claustrophobic; in more natural surroundings I felt expansive. Stadiums such as the Astrodome represent the future of professional football—virtual Hollywood sound stages for beaming the games to millions of television viewers. But the game played in such places is different from the one played on grass under blue or gray sky.

In contrast to the Astrodome, the stadiums in Denver and San Diego were organic paradises—grass fields played on in sunshine or rain, in genuine cold or heat. Each stadium around the league made its own imprint on my experience. Kansas City's Muncipal Stadium in its last year of existence was the most memorable of all. The opening of Arrowhead Stadium the following year meant an increase from 50,000 to nearly 80,000 fans per game, and a gain in comfort for players and fans alike. But it also meant an altered relationship between players and fans. Municipal Stadium was an intimate park; behind the players' bench the bleachers nearly encroached on the field, bringing the "Wolfpack"—the name by which the rabid bleacherites were known—more personally into the game. There were few distractions at the old ballpark to draw attention away from the contest on the field. I felt that we players were the focal point of all our fans' attention. I sensed the fans' presence, felt bound to them by a common passion. When we moved into Arrowhead Stadium the following year, much of this intimacy was lost. The spacious regularity of the perfect oval was very different from the asymmetrical arrangement of the stands in Municipal Stadium around a field that had been laid out for baseball. Arrowhead Stadium was one of the classiest athletic showplaces in the country, but in it I felt remote from the spectators; they seemed less fans than spectators now, having paid ten dollars apiece to be entertained for three hours. The huge electronic scoreboard

behind one end zone, with all its showy displays, competed with
the players for the spectators' attention. The bright colors—particularly red and gold—that I saw wherever I looked seemed
more appropriate for a circus than a football game. When I
looked up to the level of glassed-in suites below the upper deck,
I knew that behind the glass the social elite of Kansas City were
sipping cocktails, nibbling on hors d'oeuvre, and following the
game on closed-circuit television sets when it was not convenient
to look down on the field—if they followed the play at all.

In Municipal Stadium the game was simpler. It was football
without accompanying and competing spectacle. The fans came
to see the football, not to spend three hours in the stadium. Playing in Municipal Stadium, I felt the attachment to both the
game and the fans that I had grown accustomed to in college. In
Municipal Stadium I was less conscious than I would continually be at Arrowhead that professional football was big business and mass entertainment. In Municipal Stadium it still
seemed the heroic game I had discovered in my youth.

The places in the NFL that I discovered in 1971 were the sites
of games, of course, and in the events surrounding those games I
learned what it meant to be a "professional."

On Thanksgiving Day we lost a game to Detroit that Hank
Stram saw as the pivotal one in our season. Our record stood at
7–3–1, and as usual we were battling Oakland for the divisional
championship. We should have beaten the Lions easily, but our
offense failed to move the ball when necessary, the defense gave
up 32 points, and, worst of all, the special teams allowed a punt
and a field goal to be blocked. The final score of 32–21 was an
embarrassment to a team that had its sights set on a championship. Hank decided we needed a shaking up. When we reported for practice on Saturday after the Thursday game, we
discovered a change in our routine. Instead of watching the
game films in individuals groups, we viewed them together—
with uncharacteristically little comment from any of the assistant
coaches, and none at all from the players. Hank, who never attended film sessions, was present for this one, occasionally inject-
ing his disgust when a particularly bad play was run. We were
as solemn as mourners at a relative's funeral, made so less by our

own depression than by our awareness that the coaches were strangely, melodramatically grim.

After the last frame disappeared from the screen and the whirr of the projector was clicked off, Hank flipped on the light switch and marched to the front of the room.

"Well, what do you think? Does anyone have any comments to make? What about you, Lenny?"

"Not a very impressive performance," Dawson answered.

"Not very impressive at all." Hank nodded grimly. "How about you, Jim?"

"We played lousy," said Tyrer. "We should have won easily, but we gave the game away."

"Yes, we gave it away. Buck, what do you think?"

"Pretty bad, Coach. Pretty bad."

"Do you want to know what *I* think?" Hank now asked, his voice rising in pitch and intensity. "I think what I just watched was a *disgrace*. A goddamned disgrace! You are supposed to be professional athletes. You are supposed to be the best football players in the world, and you played like *that!*" He poked a finger at the screen as if he were pointing to a dog mess in the middle of the living-room rug.

"But I'll tell you this, gentlemen. That disgraceful performance is not going to happen again. The coaching staff put together the best game plan possible to beat Detroit. The offense and defense were certainly not great, but they played well enough to win. But the special teams were pathetic. Two blocked kicks! *Two!* How can that happen?"

No answer this time. We on the special teams were not Len Dawson, Jim Tyrer, or Buck Buchanan—team captains and all-pro veterans. We were rookies and young marginal players. We remained silent.

"Well, I don't know how it can happen either. But I told you it wouldn't happen again. You're professionals and I'm going to treat you as professionals. I'm going to hit you where it hurts so that you'll remember this well. Just to make sure that this disgrace doesn't happen again, I'm fining each member of the special teams two hundred and fifty dollars."

I was stunned. Then outraged. The amount of the fine hurt,

but the idea of it infuriated me more. I felt personally insulted, but even more irritatingly the act violated one of the fundamental assumptions by which I played the game. In grade school, in high school, in college, I had been taught that the players were not just individuals, but were a *team*. Anyone who had acted selfishly, contrary to the team's best interests, would have been put on the bench and left there if necessary, no matter how good he was. Ara Parseghian had told us repeatedly that we won together and lost together—as a team. Now I was being told that the coaching staff had done its part, the offense and defense had done theirs, but the special teams had failed, and had cost the rest of the team the game. As a matter of fact, in this particular case the defeat was indeed a team loss. The offense and defense had played badly, but Hank Stram could not fine Len Dawson, Jim Tyrer, Otis Taylor, Buck Buchanan, Willie Lanier, and the others without risking rebellion. We on the special teams were not secure enough in our positions to do anything but pay the fine.

The justification for the fine, apart from its real purpose to intimidate the entire team into playing better in our final crucial contests, was based on our grades for the game. Every player was graded by his assistant coach in every game—assigned a percentage based on a one for every play on which he did his job, and a zero if he did not. Coach Stram announced the grades of the special-teams players—all in the 50 to 60 percent range— as ample reason for the fines. Such incompetence by professional athletes was unforgivable. I was astounded. I had been more emotionally involved, worked harder, and felt the outcome of the game more intensely than in any other professional game I could recall. I had not just been doubled, but triple-teamed on kickoffs, and had fought through all three blocks. I had not made many tackles, but surely in occupying three opponents I had done my job. I did not feel I had had a spectacular game, but I had not made any mistakes, and I had performed my assignment nearly every time. Now here was the coach telling me I had graded out at less than 60 percent.

I seethed through practice, then, able to contain my rage no longer, I went to Coach Stram.

"I can't believe I played that badly," I told him. "I could understand a fine for loafing or for incompetence, but I have never played a football game at less than a hundred percent in my life."

Stram was compassionate but firm. He told me that he had never doubted my commitment or intensity, but I had graded out extremely low; the films could not lie. I could look at them myself if I wished.

I wished. I found the assistant coaches in the large meeting room and told them I wanted to see the special-teams film. The projector was threaded, the lights turned off, and the epic begun. I saw a kickoff: one blocker attacked me low immediately, did not knock me down, but tied me up briefly; as I continued downfield, a second blocker crossed into my path and tried to take me high; I was fighting him off with my hands when a third hit me; I kept my feet, but arrived much too late to help on the tackle.

"There's a zero," one of the coaches said. "You didn't even come close to making the tackle."

"You've got to be kidding. I fought off three blockers and you're giving me a zero for not making the tackle?!"

"That's right; keep watching."

We proceded through several more plays in this manner. My own recollections were confirmed: I saw an unimpressive but workmanlike performance that could not reveal the intensity with which I played, but which surely was a competent job. I continued to object to the coaches' grading until Pete Brewster, the receiver coach, became angry and flipped on the lights.

"Look, you either do the job or you don't. And you didn't do it!"

I exploded. I could not recall having ever been so frustrated. The fine had been gnawing away at me for two hours. I felt overwhelmingly what it meant to be *owned*. I was in the second year of a three-year contract—the one-sided standard player's contract that bound me to the club for three years plus an option year and indefinitely beyond that for all practical purposes, but which did not bind the club at all. I could be cut at any time, without compensation. In this instance I had two choices: I could either pay the fine and continue playing for the Kansas City Chiefs, or I could leave pro football. There was no third option. When Brewster started his harangue, I nearly leaped on him. I was so furious I was fighting back both tears and a desire to punch him out. I shouted a few incoherencies, and stormed out of the room.

Something snapped in me. Some psychic ligament deep inside that had bound me to my football coaches since the fourth grade and had made me feel that my own fortunes were truly less important than the welfare of the entire team snapped cleanly. Football had always had deeply personal importance to me. In college, my own struggles to make the team were more important to me than the team's efforts to win games. But I had never felt the two goals were in conflict, had never had to confront myself with a choice in which I rationally weighed my own interest against the team's. After I finally made the team, I would have had a hard time deciding if I preferred to play badly in a victory or well in a loss. For the first time the difference was clear. I understood now that Hank Stram was my employer and that my own performance was more important than the team's record. If we should lose but I play well, I would feel no pain. My security with the team was dependent on my own performance, not the team's success. Because I was a "professional." Hank had just defined the term.

Vince Lombardi is credited with having said one time that winning wasn't everything, it was the *only* thing—and ever since we have thought of that win-at-all-costs attitude as the sign of the "professionalism" that filters down into college, high school, and even grade school programs. Actually, Lombardi said something very different: "Winning isn't everything, but wanting to win is." And even if many coaches believe winning is the only thing, most professional football players learn at some point that winning is not even the most important thing in their careers. It is important to a degree, and every football player hungers for the Super Bowl—not just for the money but for pride. But ironically, NFL players learn that playing well actually is more important than winning. Simply notice how many veteran starters are cut from Super Bowl champions every year, because the clubs cannot continue to stand pat but must build for the future. Playing well in the NFL is important not for the personal satisfactions it brings but for survival. Winning is the only thing that matters to *coaches;* wins and losses indicate how well they do their job. But the situation of the players is different. Their value to the team is measured not by victories but by individual performance. This difference in primary goal between players and coaches can lead to an uneasy relationship.

If the Detroit game was the "bitter" of the 1971 season, the second Oakland game was the "sweet"—or, more truly, the bittersweet. The stake was clear: the Western Division championship and a shot at the Super Bowl. And I almost blew the whole thing.

With a precarious 13–7 lead at the beginning of the fourth quarter, I lined up on the punting team as I had done all day. My job was to block the man in front of me, Gerald Irons, long enough to stop his momentum, then release downfield to tackle the returner. On the snap of the ball, as Irons came across the line, I jolted him once but released too soon. I was already beginning to look back with uneasiness when I heard the rapid-fire thump-thump of a ball kicked, then blocked. There is no sicker feeling for a special-teams player than to be the cause of such a costly turnover—particularly at such a crucial point of an important game. I watched with anguish from the sidelines as Oakland moved in from our 26-yard line for the touchdown and a 14–13 lead.

I was desperate to atone. When I took the field for the ensuing kickoff, and for punts and punt returns afterward, I ached to make a decisive block to spring our man loose for a touchdown, or to block a punt and rectify that ugly seven points I had helped put on the board. But no opportunity arose. Jan Stenerud saved me. With 1:34 left on the clock, Jan kicked a ten-yard field goal, capping a 93-yard drive, to give us the 16–14 victory, the Western Division championship, and my own immense relief. I was a professional now, and wins and losses meant less to me. But championships were still championships and, above all else, I had my pride. We celebrated that night with a team party at a club partly owned by Johnny Robinson in North Kansas City. Virtually everyone got uproariously drunk. Dave Hill stood up from his chair at one point late in the evening, and collapsed flat on his back, all 265 pounds of him toppling as impressively as a giant redwood crashing in a California forest. But no one celebrated more joyfully than I did.

The most memorable game of 1971 was also the most memorable of my career—and one of the most memorable in NFL history. The date was December 25; the opponent was the Miami Dolphins; the situation was the AFC playoffs.

Santa Claus spent Christmas Eve in the Glenwood Manor that year. Hank required that the players spend the nights before home games at a motel in suburban Overland Park, well away from the temptations of bars and nightclubs. We may have been grown men, many with families, but Hank apparently assumed that at least some of us would stay out late, get irresponsibly drunk, and play badly the next day because of it. On the evening before the Miami game, we reported as usual, in time for ten o'clock bed check. Julie spent the first Christmas Eve and morning of our marriage alone in our apartment, while I spent it with Sid Smith at the motel, but I felt sorrier for the players with children. Pete Rozelle was criticized in the press for allowing football games to be played on Christmas Day, but since he did not deem it appropriate to rearrange the schedule after President Kennedy's assassination in 1963, Rozelle was not liable to worry much about anything so trivial as Christmas.

Very un-Christmaslike weather greeted us in the morning. Had there been snow on the ground rather than sunshine and fall temperatures, the incongruity of playing football on Christmas would have struck me more directly. Instead, the surprising autumnal crispness helped me feel nothing but eager anticipation for the game.

The day started with mass at eight o'clock in Hank Stram's room at the motel. In high school I had prayed fervently in the school chapel and in college at the Grotto for divine assistance in my passionate quest. But professional football was a different game. To pray in more than just a ritualistic way—a quick team prayer before the game—seemed slightly blasphemous now, like executives from General Motors praying before a board meeting for larger profits. To pray for victory seemed silly or hypocritical. What kind of god would be concerned with anything so trivial as a football game? In my youthful self-absorption I had made playing football a holy crusade, but I now understood it to be something very different. The priest who said mass was sometimes Monsignor Mackey, a sixtyish cleric from Boston who had become acquainted with Hank Stram in the nineteen sixties and soon became a sort of team chaplain. Monsignor Mackey showed a misplaced enthusiasm, I thought, by spending some of his vacations in the humidity of Liberty, Missouri, with the team. He was a kindly, sincere man whose good intentions were also misplaced. When he was with us on game days, he led the pregame prayer in the locker room; after consulting with Coach Stram, he usually presented us a pep talk in prayer form.

"O Lord," he would intone, drawing the "r" out solemnly. "Protect these young men today, defend them from injury and bless their efforts with success. They have worked hard and sacrificed much in their drive for a championship. Denver will offer difficult opposition today; let these men be alert on defense and intelligent on offense. And grant them the victory they desire, we pray to you, O Lord."

I didn't dare look in certain teammates' eyes after such a performance.

Monsignor Mackey was not with us on this Christmas Day, however. A routine mass was followed by breakfast at nine—the typical steak and baked potato I had become accustomed to in college. After breakfast, I drove with Sid to the stadium, arriving at ten forty-five for the one-o'clock game. Some of my teammates liked to arrive very early—three hours before game time in some cases—others, not liking to wait around endlessly, arrived as much as an hour and a half later. As I entered the locker room, a large rectangle ringed by wooden stalls, I saw a now-familiar scene. The early arrivals padded about in socks, jocks, and T-shirts with their ankles taped. Each of us had his own private ritual for pregame preparation. Some players insisted that their ankles be taped by the same person each week —by Wayne Rudy, the trainer; Bobby Yarborough, the equipment manager; or perhaps a young assistant from medical school who helped out in training camp and on game days. Some demanded that only a fresh roll of tape be used; everyone had a particular method of taping he preferred.

Different players acted differently. The younger players, in-

cluding me, were obviously more tense. We had played in no
Super Bowls, nor in any other game on which so much was riding. The veterans were more relaxed, casual. Next to my locker
Jim Lynch smoked, as others did around the room. I was no
longer shocked by this, but still could not entirely accustom myself to it. Many players padded to the urinals or toilets to empty
nervous bladders. The calmest players of all were the oldest. In
some, only a tightness about the mouth or hardness in the eyes
revealed that anything eventful was about to take place. Johnny
Robinson, a twelve-year veteran and the last of the original
Dallas Texans—who we all knew was playing his last season, his
last game if we lost—seemed as unconcerned as he would have
been at home, opening Christmas presents with his family.

The Chiefs had no wild men, no one who paced the locker
room snarling and grunting and banging lockers with his forearms. If pills were popped, I never saw any. Many players
talked or even joked. None of the self-conscious solemnity of the
high school or college locker room here. These were grown men
preparing to do something they had done dozens, even hundreds, of times. However important the game, no one envisioned
it as a holy quest.

But beneath the surface calm there was an unmistakable
seriousness. These *were* men after all, not boys. Johnny Robinson may have appeared unconcerned, but he spent longer on the
training table than anyone else, rubbed down by the trainer,
tired muscles and aching joints readied for one more assault.
Three or four players took turns standing on another table while
their damaged knees were wrapped. As a high school senior I
had felt that my playing hurt was an extraordinary event. My
teammates now oversaw the wrapping of their knees as routine
preparation; they were experts in the science and directed the
trainer to wrap them just so, for maximum protection. Others
throughout the room attended to their own injuries. Deep, ugly
bruises were covered by special pads, swollen fingers splinted
and taped to sound ones, tender ribs and not yet healed hip
pointers encased in protective wraps. No melodramatics; these
were men who knew well what to expect when they took the
field, and they quietly prepared themselves for it.

As the time approached when we would take the field for

warm-ups, players began putting on pants and shoes and taping their hands and forearms. Shoes were unimportant to the linemen, but many of the backs, receivers, and defensive backs took particular care with them. Loose shoelaces at an inopportune time could cost a touchdown. Many taped their laces securely after tying them. Many also, caring how their shoes looked, created "spats" with a coil of tape around the middle of the shoe, while others taped the entire shoe and even up the ankle, leaving continuous tape from shin to toe. The linemen and linebackers took equal care with their hands. Here, the object was not appearance but protection. The offensive linemen in particular had their hands taped like boxers'—gauze and tape wound between and around the fingers and over the back of the hand, continuing up the wrists. Pads were worked into the wraps, in an effort to protect hands and knuckles that would be punching defensive opponents. I always felt stronger, less vulnerable, when my hands were taped. I tried them against the walls and felt confident when a hard blow was absorbed comfortably by the padding. The defensive linemen paid more attention to their forearms, wrapping hard pads around them for protection, but also to create clubs to bang on the heads of opposing linemen. Many of the defensive linemen revealed solid tape from elbow to fingertips when they finished. The process prepared them mentally as well as physically for the game.

The level of intensity in the locker room increased. Talk continued, but it was more earnest, and exclusively focused on the game. Players confirmed assignments and signals. Ed Budde sought out Jim Tyrer: "When I call 'odd' on the sweep, I'm staying; otherwise I pull and you fill for me"; Willie Lanier and Jim Lynch double-checked their pass coverage against a "trips" offensive set. Jack Rudnay and I discussed Nick Buonaconti's quickness, and how best to counteract it. In one corner the quarterbacks huddled with one of the coaches, in another the defensive backs confirmed their coverages. No one growled a challenge to his teammates to stick it to Larry Csonka, or boasted what he would do when he got a shot at Bob Griese. These men had been world champions. They knew what had to be done.

The noise level and intensity increased as shoulder pads and jerseys were put on. Players began stretching muscles, bending and pacing nervously, making more stops at the urinals. An hour before game time, everyone involved in the kicking game grabbed his helmet and filed out of the locker room, clattering down the concrete runway and onto the field. Bobby Bell, Jack Rudnay, and I snapped to Jerrel Wilson for punts, and to Len Dawson holding for field goals, while the kick returners caught the balls and loped upfield several yards with them, loosening up. After twenty-five minutes the rest of our teammates joined us for calisthenics and drills—to pop our pads a few times before the real contact began—then we returned to the locker room for a brief ten minutes.

The atmosphere was altogether transformed now. Intensity and expectation hung heavily; players milled about adjusting straps, repairing tape jobs, making final stops at the urinals. Now, the adrenaline of some of the younger players began to spill out into words. Players grabbed each other's shoulder pads.

"You and me, baby."

"Have a good one."

Hank Stram entered from his own room. No inspirational anecdotes or impassioned rhetoric, but a few intense sentences reminding us what was at stake in the game.

"There's nothing more to say at this point, men. You all know what this game means and what it's going to take to win it. Let's go out there and get the job done."

A quick team prayer and we returned to the field for the main event.

We came out rolling. Jan Stenerud booted a 24-yard field goal the first time we got the ball, and later in the first period Len Dawson converted an interception by Willie Lanier into a seven-yard touchdown pass to halfback Ed Podolak. The quarter ended 10–0, but Miami won the second period. A one-yard plunge by Csonka and a 14-yard field goal by Garo Yepremian just before the gun made it 10–10 at half time, and the momentum continued on a pendulum until the end of the game. A nine-minute drive in the third period put us ahead 17–10, but Griese, Csonka, and Jim Kiick came back to tie it again with a minute left in the quarter. In the fourth, Elmo Wright gathered in a 63-yard Dawson pass to the three, from which point Podolak put us ahead once more, 24–17. But again Griese reciprocated. Hitting receivers twice on third-down plays, he moved the Dolphins to our five, then flipped the ball to Marv Fleming for yet a third tie, this one with a minute and a half to play.

As I lined up for the kickoff, I still felt confident. The Dolphins had played as well as they were capable, while we had missed opportunities. I was certain the game was still ours. Darkness had settled in, and the stadium lights had long been on. I was in a familiar world. I felt total absorption in what was happening on that acre of grass marked off by white chalk lines, but I felt no desperation, no painful anxiety that we might lose. When I had taken the field against Texas in similar circumstances in the Cotton Bowl, I had been *consumed* by my desire to win, and frustrated that I could not more single-handedly guarantee that we would. Now, as I awaited the kickoff with a minute and a half left in the game, my yearning for victory was calmer. To win would be wonderful, and would confirm my sense of what should be, but to lose would not be devastating. To be a professional meant to be less emotional, I had discovered. I could even be aware, somewhat objectively, of the drama of that roller-coaster game. Anyone who had abandoned the turkey and presents under the tree to watch this contest was seeing a good show.

As the ball sailed over my head, I dropped back to get into position for a good blocking angle on my man. We were returning the ball to the left, and I did not want to set my block too soon, allowing my man to recover and make the tackle. I saw that play unfold with extraordinary clarity. I saw Ed Podolak charging toward me with the ball, plenty of running room ahead of him, and my fellow blockers in perfect position to seal off this side. When Podolak was about fifteen yards away, I peeled back and drove my shoulder into my man's legs. As he toppled neatly over me, I looked up to Podolak streaming past, then cutting to the left sideline. I lost sight of him in the tangle of bodies around me, but the sustained roar of the crowd, building in intensity, told me that the return was a long one.

Podolak made it to the Miami 22 before being bumped out of bounds. When Stenerud trotted onto the field with thirty-five seconds to go, the victory seemed ours at last. But Jan, who had put us in the playoffs with his field goal against Oakland, and

whose toe had provided the margin of victory in four other
games, proved himself fallible this time. His miss from 32 yards
sent the game into sudden-death overtime. On the sidelines I felt
a quiet intensity that I shared with my teammates. The game
suddenly had assumed historical significance; my mind flashed
to the sudden-death championship game between Baltimore and
New York in 1958. It was exhilarating to be involved in a similar
one now. We received, and moved the ball to Miami's 35, when
Stenerud returned for a second try. This time Nick Buonaconti
blocked the attempt. Now I was worried. I began to sense that
whatever imps inhabited stadiums to play tricks with the ball
had determined that we would not win after all. We had already
missed more opportunities to win than a team was entitled to.
For the first time I seriously considered that we might lose. But
Yepremian failed, too, from 52 yards. As the overtime went on,
my sense of unreality increased. The lateness in the year and in
the day brought on unaccustomed darkness. The stadium lights
bathed everything in a soft glow; I was sleepwalking in the twi-
light zone. I trotted on and off the field with the kicking teams,
then watched some more of this strange game. I felt no tiredness
at all and lost all sense of time. When the fifth period ended, I
was surprised to discover there was still a clock. Would the
game continue forever?

It didn't. Halfway through the sixth quarter, Csonka sprang
free on a draw play 29 yards to our 36. The crisis of the moment
returned. Three plays and six yards later, Yepremian jogged onto
the field one more time, for the 44th play of overtime. Eighty-
two minutes and forty seconds after the opening whistle, Yepremian's ball exploded off the grass, soared upward into the glare
of the stadium lights, and slipped between the uprights to end
the longest game in NFL history.

I felt deflated but not crushed. There would be no Super Bowl
this year, but there were no tears in the locker room because of
that. The feeling had been very different at the Cotton Bowl two
years before. The end of a long season—twenty-one games from
preseason to playoff—brought relief. Julie and I would drive to
California to resume our off-season life a few weeks earlier than
we had anticipated. It hurt to lose. It hurt to miss out on the opportunity to be crowned the best football team in the world, and

on the $15,000 paycheck that went to the Super Bowl victors. But it did not hurt with the deep emotional pain of a Cotton Bowl defeat, when the stakes were entirely personal. We were professionals who had completed a season. More seasons would follow.

No more chances for the Super Bowl would follow, however. My high school team had won the state championship the year before I made the varsity; Notre Dame had won a national title when I was a freshman, Kansas City the Super Bowl the year before I was drafted. Throughout my football career, I always arrived just a little bit late. But failures in Kansas City were easier to take than they had been in high school or college. "Professional" implies many things: a professional is the best in his field, is one who gets paid for what he does, is engaged in a "profession," not just a hobby. My most difficult adjustment to professional football came from the recognition that the game was no longer a quest for self-discovery or an emotional crusade shared with a group of teammates. It was my employment. Wins and losses were beyond my control, and my primary concern had to be with what I could control: my own performance. Much in the game remained the same—physical challenges, team camaraderie, glamorous travel, painful training camps— but something crucial was different. I was paid for what I did, not what my teammates did. That basic fact created a very different game.

My contribution to the Chiefs over those four years came almost entirely on special teams. I started just one game during a regular season, and four in the preseason, but I covered kickoffs and punts, blocked on returns, and occasionally snapped the ball for punts, field goals, and extra points in over seventy games. Football fans have become aware of the "suicide squads" or "kamikaze teams" in recent years. Network telecasts focus an isolated camera occasionally on a particular special-teams player, following him down the field on a kickoff as he dodges blockers, busts up the wedge, and drags the ballcarrier to the ground. For a few seconds he is a star, but I doubt that many fans remember his name from one week to the next. He makes no pro-bowl

teams, holds out for no huge raises at contract time, and tends to
disappear altogether within a few years. Toughness is the name
of the game in special-teams play, but toughness is cheap in the
NFL.

The kicking game came to be recognized only in the late sixties as a major contributor to a team's success. The importing of
European soccer-style kickers such as the Gogolaks, Garo Yepremian, and Jan Stenerud made the field goal a much more potent
weapon than formerly, and specialization reached new levels.
Placekickers were no longer performers at other positions—as
Lou Groza, Lou Michaels, Paul Hornung, and others had been—
but were specialists who raised kicking to a major art (George
Blanda, continuing to kick for Oakland, was a notable exception). Coaches began to pay more attention to the entire kicking
game—signing not just punters and placekickers, but kick-return
specialists as well, and spending more and more practice time in
preparing the kicking teams. Coaches came to realize that the
special teams were in on 20 percent of the plays in a game. The
special teams not only could score many points but also determined the field position that produced or prevented other scores.
In Kansas City we were told that the special teams represented
a third of the game, and were as important as the offense and
defense. But we had difficulty believing that.

However important we knew the kicking game could be in deciding contests, we also knew that the reason we played on the
special teams was that we were not starting on offense or defense. The coaches were not going to risk a knee injury to Buck
Buchanan or Willie Lanier by putting them on the kickoff team.
Those of us who did sprint downfield covering kicks and dodg-
ing the bodies flying at our knees were Buck's and Willie's
backups—more expendable commodities. We knew that no one
besides a kicker or kick returner ever made the team solely for
his special-teams play, and that good performances on the kicking teams one year did not guarantee a spot on the roster the
next. When I joined the Chiefs in 1970, the best special-teams
player from the year before was a linebacker named Caesar
Belser. Caesar was cut during the training camp in 1970, but
wound up back on the team that season through fortunate cir-

cumstances. After the same thing happened in 1971, he was cut for good in 1972. All his recklessness and fine play mattered little when the time came to fix the forty-man roster; the special teams were created from those who made the team but were not starting.

We who played on the special teams were ambivalent about our roles. On the one hand, we felt like second-class citizens. We all felt we were good enough to be starting on offense or defense and were frustrated we had no opportunity to do so. We also understood that we could not create such opportunities for ourselves by spectacular play on the kicking teams. But on the other hand, the kicking teams gave us our only chance to play. We were proud athletes who had played football very well for many years, and who demanded excellence of ourselves. To demonstrate our abilities by blocking and tackling on punts and kickoffs—while the stars were resting on the sidelines—offered meager satisfaction. But it was all we had.

Certain code phrases summed up the coaches' expectations for special-teams players. "Reckless abandon" was the major one. An offensive performer had to play intelligently, a defensive player to react quickly to any surprise. But a special-team performer was expected to play with "reckless abandon"—to sprint downfield as fast as he could and hurtle his body against opposing players without regard for personal safety. This was the ideal. The best way to think of special-teams play is to picture two athletes, standing well over six feet tall and weighing 240 pounds and up, running 40 yards as fast as they can—right into each other. Such a collision—head on and at full speed—would have an impact of something like 14,000 foot-pounds per second, analogous to the 550-pound hammer of a pile driver dropped ten feet. Thought of objectively, reckless abandon makes about as much sense as challenging an oncoming train to a game of "chicken." The coaches like to yell, "Sacrifice your bodies," to special-teams players as they take the field. Notice it is *our* bodies they are talking about. The biggest hits in any game come on kicking plays. A crazy man who can bench-press four times his IQ lines up on the kickoff next to the kicker, collides headfirst 40 yards downfield at full speed with a two-hundred-pound run-

ning back, in an explosion of sound that brings spontaneous
"oohs" and "aahs" from 75,000 voices. That wasn't my normal
style, but I did it once—against Denver in 1973.

It was unintentional. As I lined up for the kickoff, it was just
another play. I was next to Jan Stenerud, facing George Daney,
a backup guard, on the other side of the ball. On either side of us
our teammates fanned out in an arc with Jan as the apex: Kerry
Reardon, a backup safety; Clyde Werner, my roommate and a
backup linebacker; Al Palewicz, another linebacker; and so on.
Opposite, the Broncos were deployed in the familiar alignment:
backup linemen, linebackers, and defensive backs like us. I
didn't even know most of their names. They were as anonymous
to me as we were to them, and as we all were to nearly everyone
watching the game on television. From previous kickoffs I expected the right guard to drop back ten yards, then try to cut
me, but I knew I also had to be wary of the center and of the
left guard crossing over. Seeing the blocker was the first step toward avoiding the block.

With the referee's whistle, we settled into our two-point
stances facing the middle of the field. As Jan crossed our vision
we turned and took off. Within five yards, I knew that the right
guard was my man. I sprinted downfield in my lane, watching
for the moment when he would set to throw. I ran right at him
until we were just a few yards apart, then veered sharply to my
right. He lunged and caught my left ankle, not upsetting me but
spinning me around. I regained my balance and continued down
the field. The contact had slowed me down, allowing some of
my teammates to reach the wedge first and occupy the blockers.
Just inside the thirty, the ballcarrier ten yards away and coming
straight at me, I started to gather myself, expecting him to cut to
one side or the other. But teammates on either side of me were
closing in; the back had no choice but to take me head on.

The collision was impressive. My forehead met his breastbone
in an explosion that boomed all over Arrowhead Stadium. I
dropped him instantly on his back, myself on top of him, but I
had no time to enjoy my mighty deed. Neither of us was injured,
but I was in agony. I got to my feet and could not even see
through my own pain if the runner was hurting. I stumbled toward our sideline, while my teammates pounded me on the back

and shook their fists in exultation, and the fans in Arrowhead gave me the biggest ovation of my career. But I could only feel the throbbing of my pinched nerve. I was sure that I had been compressed to about five ten. After the game, my aunt, uncle, and cousins visiting from Minneapolis were much impressed by their hard-nosed relative. But it had been an accident.

I had discovered long before the Denver game in 1973 that to be the toughest sonuvabitch in the NFL would not bring me any closer to starting at center. It might make it possible for me to go through life making spastic jerks with my head and shoulders, after an intense but futile two-year career. The crazy men who earn a season of notoriety by their "reckless abandon" on special teams tend to disappear after a year or two. Special-teams performers who play with their heads rather than simply using them to ram into odd-colored jerseys tend to last a little longer. They were the majority throughout the league. Coaches undoubtedly prefer the players with self-destructive tendencies, and teammates regard them with a certain awe—an admiration not coupled with any desire to emulate them. Special-teams maniacs elicit a sort of horrified fascination in others, for their willingness to do something so dangerous yet so stupid—and with apparent enjoyment. Gordon Liddy would have been a coaches' dream as a special-teams player.

There is another way to play on special teams, however—one that I and most of those I played with discovered. The maniac can act as an emotional catalyst to fans and teammates on occasion in a way the saner player cannot, but in every other way the sensible player can be just as effective. Kicking plays have specific aims. When we kicked off, we wanted to tackle the returner inside his own 20-yard line; when we received, our goal was to bring the ball out beyond our 30. On punts we hoped to hold the other team to no return and to spring our own at least ten yards. All of these goals could be achieved without risking spinal injuries.

The kickoff is the most dangerous play in football. The kicking team sends nine players sprinting downfield, the kicker and one other hanging back as safeties. The return team has five blockers up front, each assigned to a man, and four blockers in a "wedge" directly in front of the two kick returners. The attackers must avoid the blocks of the front line, then penetrate the wedge to make the tackle. The entire play takes just a few seconds, but in that short time high-speed collisions and bodies flying from the blind side create major risks of injury. Together with George Daney I was the wedge breaker on the kickoff team. We lined up on either side of the kicker and went directly to the ball, while those flanking us had to be more concerned with keeping in their lanes to prevent a long return through an uncovered opening. Many teams use their fastest or toughest or craziest athletes as wedge breakers. George and I were the fastest linemen available; Hank wanted the combination of size and speed. The coaches' dream of a wedge breaker is the guy who, after avoiding all the blockers up front, hurls his body broadside into the wedge, taking two or even three blockers down with him, leaving the ballcarrier unprotected as he meets the next wave of tacklers. As far as I was concerned, the coaches could keep dreaming. My body was not available for sacrifices. I planned on using it for several more years after football ended.

I did not cause many hearts to flutter with excitement or alarm, but I was an effective special-teams player. When I sprinted downfield under kickoffs, my priorities were two: protect myself and tackle the ballcarrier. Why should I risk hip pointers, twisted knees, and a jammed neck just so someone else could make the tackle? The pleasures of special-teams play were few, and making the tackle was the primary one. In the first 20 yards I had to spot the players who would be throwing at my legs. Having already had one knee surgery and several minor reinjuries, I felt my knees were more important than tackling the returner inside the 20. Once I successfully penetrated this front line, the wedge awaited me. Instead of a mangled knee, too much recklessness here could lead to a serious neck injury. Instead of simply diving into the wedge, I gathered myself under control, fended off the blockers, and went for the tackle. I sought that fine line between caution and recklessness. I was aggressive and intense without being careless. And I was successful. I never saw statistics, but I suspect I led the special teams in tackles at least two of the years I played, and I won three game balls for special-teams play. I tried to be hard-nosed but clear-headed; as a result I played well without sustaining a serious injury. Uncontrollable factors made injuries far too common. I felt no need to court additional opportunities to hurt myself.

Professional football taught me the limits of toughness. For thirteen years—through grade school, high school, and college—I had defined myself in relation to football largely by my toughness. I created a sense of my own powerfulness and of control over my own life in large part through knocking other people down, never allowing any physical fear to inhibit me, and being able to play with pain. By the time I was twenty-two and a Kansas City Chief, I no longer felt the same psychological need to dominate other players that had driven me for so long. Having proven myself to myself through earlier hard-earned successes, I still enjoyed knocking opposing players down, but those acts were no longer important in such essential ways to my psychological well-being. I could exult in the same old primitive pleasure to be had from overpowering another player, but I did not depend on those moments as I once did. I could also take pleasure in the perfect craftsmanship of a great block or tackle. I still played the game hard, but my motivation to do well was the same desire for excellence that I felt in other activities.

I also learned in my professional experience that toughness had a double edge—and one of the edges was potentially self-destructive. Pain is a major part of the professional football player's world. But much more than the amateur, the professional has to be able to determine when the necessary playing with pain has crossed over to "playing with" his physical well-being. Pain cannot be avoided. It is as much a part of the football player's everyday world as inky fingers are of the printer's. The human body was not designed for professional football. Joints in the neck, shoulders, elbows, wrists, lower back, knees, and ankles are not constructed to withstand the stress that professional football places on them every day. Players tape their ankles, but that can simply increase the stress on the next joint up: the knee. Players pad their legs and shoulders, their hands and forearms, but they cannot prevent all the bruises, muscle strains, slight twists and sprains that inevitably result when huge, fast men collide with each other and beat on each other

with their forearms and fists. The injury rate in the NFL each
year is about 90 percent. I suspect that 75 percent of all offensive linemen who have played in the NFL more than two years
have some kind of neck problem. The human neck is not a very
effective battering ram to withstand the collisions of two
260-pound linemen on every play. The player at any position
who comes to practice on any day without some injury—major
or minor—is the exception.

If players did not play with pain, no NFL club could field a
team on Sunday. But playing with pain can become a dangerous
trap. Players do not enjoy pain. Masochistic tendencies are not a
prerequisite for success in the NFL. But players who have made
it this far in their careers are liable to have developed a personal
code of toughness by which they find satisfaction in not allowing
pain to incapacitate them. To play hurt is to transcend the limitations of human frailty to some extent, to deny momentarily
your own mortality. Outrageously tough players acquire a special status among other players that is usually unknown to the
public. When I joined the Chiefs, the older players were still
telling stories of a former teammate, Sherrill Headrick, who had
retired in 1967. Headrick was the all-league middle linebacker in
the first three years of the old AFL's existence, and he played
like a crazy man. "I have to take a pee," Headrick once groaned
in the defensive huddle, then added, "I think I will," as the front
of his white football pants blossomed with a widening yellow
design. In another game Headrick suffered a compound fracture
of his thumb. He came to the sidelines, a jagged bone poking
through torn and bloody skin, and told the trainer to yank it
back into place, put some tape around it, and let him get back
into the game. This procedure was repeated several times
throughout the remainder of the game. How stupid, I thought as
I heard this story, to risk a truly serious injury in such a way.
But I was also deeply impressed by Headrick's ability to play
with what had to be extraordinary pain. I had valued toughness
far too long not to appreciate it in even so bizarre a case as this.

Playing with pain in the NFL is motivated by more than personal codes of courage. Professional football players are terrified
by their own mortality. To be incapacitated by an injury is to be
reminded of that mortality; it forebodes the end of a career. In-

jury—whether a major one or the cumulative effect of injurious wear and tear over a period of time—is undoubtedly the largest cause of careers ending. The football player who is "too old" at thirty-two would not be too old if he had not worn his body out over the previous ten years of playing football. Older players "lose a step" because of the wear and tear on knees, not simply because of age. The average career in the NFL is 4.2 years; for running backs it is much shorter because a single knee injury can make the crucial difference between getting around the corner on the sweep or being caught by the linebacker, between making that vital cut sharply and quickly or just slowly enough to be trapped. Professional football players play with pain because the pain of not playing would be even greater.

An incapacitating injury is frightening because someone always waits to take the injured athlete's position. The players not starting but playing on special teams and waiting for an opportunity to play regularly are usually talented and capable—and therefore threatening to the starters. I found myself in this position with Jack Rudnay, and during one summer our relationship produced a fairly typical drama. As I came to training camp in 1973, I had played three years with the Chiefs and was becoming more and more frustrated by my lack of a starting role. I had seen every other center around the league in game films and was convinced in my own mind, whether anyone else was or not, that I could play as well as or better than any of them. But I also knew that Jack Rudnay was a fine center—the best, I felt, in the NFL. I was not going to win his position away from him; the only chance I would have to start would come if he were hurt.

But Jack was also my friend. We shared the camaraderie of our offensive line group, but more besides. Jack had the kind of quick verbal wit that most appealed to me, and we enjoyed bantering back and forth in the locker room and during meetings, playing with words to alleviate the tedium. We also respected each other's abilities, and we shared feelings about upcoming games. We discussed strategy against different opponents, evaluated centers on opposing teams, worked together in numerous little ways. We evolved pregame rituals that were necessary to both of us: loosening each other up, going through a set routine

together the same way each week in the kind of ritual pattern
that is important to most players. Without saying so, we both
understood that I would like to be playing, but we also both
knew that Jack was playing very well and would continue to
play ahead of me as long as he was healthy.

In the third preseason game that summer, at home against
Minnesota, Jack twisted his knee badly. I finished the game at
center, unaware of the extent of the injury, but afterward I
learned that it appeared serious. Surgery seemed a possibility; if
not that, Jack could still miss a half dozen games. After three
years I finally had been given the opportunity to start. Yet, instead of joy, I felt ambivalence. I had yearned to start, but I
hated to be doing so now only by virtue of Jack's misfortune. I
felt guilty, as if I had subconsciously willed this awful injury to
my friend. In college I had felt no troubling complications like
this when I had been driven to succeed. Because starting was
less necessary to me now, I realized more fully the pain that another must experience for me to have the opportunity.

For his part, we never discussed this, but I am sure Jack felt
uneasy about my now starting in his place, even if only in
preseason games. If he should undergo an operation and miss
the entire season while I had a good year, what would be our
status when we came to camp the following summer? I do not
know what deliberations went into the decision, but Jack did not
have surgery.

I started the next preseason game against Green Bay and
played very well against a good middle linebacker, Jim Carter.
The following week I started again against Dallas on the road.
The Cowboys' stadium was a miserable place to play in the summer. The partial dome, covering the stands but not the playing
field, kept the air perfectly still, trapping the damp heat which
rose from the field. Suffocatingly hot, even in the evening, that
stadium drained me more than any other place I played in four
years. Besides starting at center, I kept my place on all the special teams—not just chasing Lee Roy Jordan and trying to handle Bob Lilly and Jethro Pugh on certain plays, but running
down under punts and kickoffs besides. Late in the fourth quarter, exhausted by nearly sixty minutes of two-way playing, I ran
downfield under one last punt. I arrived too late to make the

tackle, but in my wearied effort to leap over the tangle of bodies I came down wrong on my left leg. My knee gave out, and with it my stolen opportunity to be the starting center.

With two maimed centers, but my injury the worse, Jack was forced back into play sooner than was good for him. He started the last preseason game against St. Louis, while I dragged my leg along the sidelines. For the season opener against Los Angeles, I watched from the stands as Jack limped through a subpar game that he should not have been playing in, either. Now our roles were reversed. Jack may have returned to action sooner than he ought, out of anxiety over his job; I now found myself in the same position. The team could not risk continuing very long with one bad-legged center; a reinjury to Jack's knee would be disastrous. I feared that if I did not return quickly, Hank would shop around for another center. If the new one should prove to be good, where would I stand when I returned?

I suited up the following week against New England, dragging my swollen and heavily taped knee behind me in a reprise of my senior year in high school. I had thought that I would be activated but kept off the special teams for a couple more weeks —allowing my knee to heal, but making me available if Jack were hurt. But I was assigned immediately to all the kicking teams—and I dared not object, for fear of jeopardizing my position on the team. I was amazed that season to discover that although I could barely walk at times, I was able to play football. After a week of feeling crippled in practice, I could have my knee drained on Saturday—of as much as 125 cc's of fluid—then get through the game the next day on instinct and adrenaline. But I also came to realize that I was the only person in the organization whose primary concern was for myself. The trainer and the team doctor were paid by the club to keep the players on the field, not to guarantee our good health. I alone would have to determine if my injury was truly too serious to allow me to play. Toughness might help me through several seasons of professional football, but to guarantee healthy limbs for my life after football, common sense would be a better guide.

The experiences of two teammates helped me to understand this fact most clearly. John Lohmeyer was a rookie in 1973, a boyish, lanky defensive end from Emporia, Kansas, whose quickness and good attitude established him as a prospect for the future. In the twelfth game of the season, at home against Cleveland, John picked himself up from the turf after making the tackle on a kickoff, feeling an unusually sharp pain in his neck. On the sideline he informed the team orthopedist, who quickly diagnosed a pinched nerve. He twisted John's neck in several directions, then dismissed him with a snort.

"You young players don't know how to play with pain," he concluded.

John was skeptical—this was the same doctor who was said to have operated several years before on Fred Arbanas's wrong knee—but he stayed in the game, playing on all the special teams, risking all the full-speed collisions that were a part of the kicking game. When the pain did not let up as the game wore on, John became more convinced that it was caused by nothing so ordinary as a pinched nerve. Finally, at the beginning of the fourth quarter, he removed himself from the game.

The good doctor still doubted the seriousness of the injury, but told John to come to his office the next morning for X rays. John showered, dressed, went home, slept as usual, then appeared at the doctor's office Monday morning as directed. Sitting in the waiting room after the X rays had been taken, he was startled by the doctor busting through the door from his back office.

"Don't move! You've got a broken neck!"

The next time I saw John Lohmeyer, he was in a hospital bed, heavily sedated, with bolts in his skull to which weights were attached by wires, keeping his neck in traction. I could not decide if he looked more like Frankenstein's monster or a victim of the Inquisition, but he presented a frightening image of near-catastrophe. He had been very lucky. A local high school boy who had broken his neck playing football that same fall had been paralyzed from the neck down. John's break had been worse, but the more mature development of his neck muscles had prevented the spinal injury that could have left him a quadriplegic. His teammates were outraged by the incompetence of the doctor, and also by the manner in which the incident was hushed up. On Tuesday, the Kansas City *Times* devoted two uncritical paragraphs to the injury—in the *second* half of an article about the Chiefs' being unable to fly to Oakland early because of the fuel shortage. The *Star*, the afternoon paper, never described the injury at all—although it did include a story on Wednesday about the player activated to take John's place. "Holmes will replace John Lohmeyer, injured rookie defensive end," was all the article said of Lohmeyer.

Besides sharing the general outrage over such incompetence and callousness, I also saw most clearly that every player had to be his own physician. The Bill Walton case in professional basketball a few years ago brought before the public the important issue of the medical treatment of pro athletes. But the real issue became lost in the sideshow of mutual recriminations, Walton's negotiation of a free-agent contract with San Diego, and his claim to sole responsibility for Portland's NBA championship in 1977. The principle of medicine meant to keep athletes playing rather than to heal them fully was really at stake.

Injuries are a too common element in all professional sports, but particularly in football. Both of my best friends on the Chiefs—Sid Smith and Clyde Werner—missed an entire season after surgery for torn knee ligaments. Clyde missed another season after I left the team—this time with a torn Achilles tendon. Returning to play after suffering such injuries is simply part of the game, but the player alone must be able to decide when an injury is too serious, or one more injury is too many. Next to Sherrill Headrick, E. J. Holub had to be the toughest Chief of them all, but I felt that E.J. would have benefited from a little more caution. When I first saw them, E.J.'s knees looked like well-marbled meat at the butcher shop. Or, as a magazine article about the most operated-on knees in sport said a couple of years ago, as if he'd lost "a swordfight with a midget." Simply to count the elegant "S's" swirling around his kneecaps, and the more brutal slashes and short arcs of his various incisions, could not reveal the true number of E.J.'s operations. Some of those incisions had been reopened more than once. He had had his first knee operation in high school in 1956, and his ninth during the off season before I joined the team. He had two more before he retired in 1971, and was looking ahead to several more in the future, as doctors attempted to keep him from becoming totally crippled. With five other operations—on his hands, elbows, and a hamstring muscle—E.J. seemed to have donated his body to medical science *before* it could become a cadaver.

Through my rookie season and the following training camp, E. J. Holub was a remarkable figure to me. He routinely drained his own knees by slitting them open with a razor, wearing a feminine napkin over them to absorb the seepage. He never complained of pain, never made excuses for the obvious handicap to his playing, truly seemed to love playing the game as much after ten years in the NFL as he had after one. Clearly the sacrifice of his knees to so glorious an experience was worth it to him, and I suspected that he would never change his mind about that. But I wondered about his judgment. In a world gone soft by too much comfort, I could not help but admire this throwback to the hardier heroes of our past. A hundred and fifty years ago, E.J. probably would have rassled bears with no holds barred, and challenged Big Mike Fink to a duel with bare fists until only one man was left standing. But I knew also that E.J. would be crippled for the rest of his life: at this writing he is delaying an operation to give him an artificial left knee because he won't be able to ride a horse afterward. He also can't do a lot of the things the average accountant can do. Like walk without limping, run on the beach with his kids, sleep without pain at night. E.J. feels no regrets, but I decided while I was still playing that I could never risk my long-term health as he had done. I was not as tough as E. J. Holub—but I was grateful for my softness.

E.J. is an extreme case, but he simply has a monstrously large portion of the toughness that was part of nearly every professional football player's makeup. An ability to withstand the torturous demands of training camp and a long season, and to continue playing with minor and even major injuries was necessary for survival in the NFL. That shared toughness also was to some extent the basis for the masculine camaraderie that grew among us players over a period of time. As professional athletes we were very much aware of ourselves as an exclusive group. Insiders and outsiders were clearly defined: the insiders included us players and perhaps the coaches and a few proven others; the outsiders comprised the rest of mankind. Admission to the charmed circle of the elect could be gained only by sharing the physical risks that marked our football lives.

The center of our world, the locker room, was closed to most outsiders, although we indulged occasional intruders. When front-office personnel came down the elevator to the locker room, they trod on our turf, becoming the outsiders in our world. The organization's general manager and other executives did not come down very often. They undoubtedly felt their exclusion, their not belonging, and preferred to deal with us on their own ground, in their paneled offices upstairs where they ruled.

Reporters were also tolerated outsiders who invaded our domain. Because it was common knowledge that the reporters for the Kansas City *Star* and the *Times* could write only what Hank Stram wanted them to, we had little respect for the men who wandered about with pad and pencil asking questions. It was less what they wrote than what they didn't write. Not just the paltry coverage of John Lohmeyer's injury, but the absence of any sharp criticism of Stram's policies when the team began losing. I never knew how Stram managed to control the local press—whether by corporate decisions, refusal to talk to unfriendly reporters, or the writers' own timidity. Part of the control was of us players. Anyone who said anything detrimental to the team that showed up in print was fined a thousand dollars.

Sometimes we felt sorry for the reporters; one individual did write an article that was openly critical of the team—just before he left for a different job. But the general feeling among the players was more one of mild contempt for both the club executives and the reporters. We considered them parasites. These were men who made a living off *our* sweat, torn-up knees, and prematurely ended careers. They took no physical risks; their jobs were secure; they could not understand our world because they had never experienced it. They might pass judgment on us, but their judgments received no respect from us. They had to be tolerated, but not liked or admired.

Another kind of outsider was tolerated for brief periods. Two or three days a week a man known to me only as "the doughnut man" appeared with four dozen doughnuts that he left on a table for the players. He lingered about for ten or fifteen minutes, chatting with the players who came over to eat his maple bars and jelly rolls. Not a lover of sweets myself, I only watched when he came by. It struck me that this was an important fifteen minutes in his day. On returning to work, he undoubtedly enjoyed reporting to friends, "Bobby told me . . . ," or "Willie said this morning that . . ." He probably felt a sense of personal importance to be accepted on a first-name basis by some of the best football players in the NFL. But he was not the players' friend. They liked him for his doughnuts. Everyone benefited from the arrangement: the players ate the pastries and the doughnut man felt amply rewarded. I found these scenes strangely sad.

In peculiar ways, even wives were excluded from the players' world. In fact, football players' wives have a particularly tough lot in many ways. Whenever I met someone in Kansas City, I was aware that I was regarded as a Kansas City Chief first, and a person second. Living in Kansas City only during the season, in apartment complexes with transient populations, I simply did not get to *know*, in any genuine way, people who were not my teammates. The problem for the players' wives was much greater, however. Julie told me often that she always felt treated like a Kansas City Chief's wife while we were there—which was two times removed from being a real person. The novelty of that role was enjoyable for one season, while the superficial glamour of the professional football world remained intact. Julie went through her year as a rookie wife, awed by the veteran wives in the same way I was by their husbands, but gradually accepted. By her second year she had several good friends among the wives and felt very content. But in our third season together, one friend's husband had been traded and another cut, and Julie had a frustrating year. As an independent woman, prepared for a career of her own in teaching but unable to teach because we moved twice a year, Julie found it doubly frustrating to be regarded as a reflection of her husband's career. We were finally driven to decide that if she could find a teaching job that off season in California, she would accept it and we would suffer through the separation.

The difficulty for her and for the other wives was compounded by the fact that they were cut off in important ways from their husbands' occupation. Whether we willed it or not, wives were excluded from our world as clearly as other outsiders were. Their physical exclusion from the locker room only represented a larger, and more unfair, exclusion from the sacred mysteries of our football world. I was among the straightest of the straight on the team, one of the most committed husbands. Yet I found myself often drawing a line that kept Julie on one side and football on the other. Because much of her own identity was forcibly tied up in football during the six months each year we were in Kansas City, Julie wanted to share in my football life as much as possible. But there were certain things I felt could not be shared, because I was sure she could not understand. If I complained to Sid or Clyde about how much I ached or how much my knee hurt, they had had similar experiences and knew how to respond. We bitched or moaned together, or tacitly recognized that those aches were part of the game; the bitching was simply a form of therapy. If I complained to Julie about those same problems, she responded with pity and sympathy, or maybe with outrage against the coach or trainer for not caring better for me. However appropriate and loving these responses, they were the wrong ones. If I complained to Sid or Clyde about my lack of playing time, we bitched together about this frustration, but continued to understand the relative abilities of those who played ahead of us, the many factors that went into having the chance to start, the necessity of patience because the matter was beyond our control. If I complained to Julie about not playing, she became incensed at the injustice of Hank Stram's treatment of her husband, or insisted that I should go talk to the coach. Again, appropriate and loyal responses, but the wrong ones. Whenever I talked to Sid or Clyde about football, we drew on more than a dozen years of shared experiences. We shared the same code of stoical resignation and physical toughness, understood what were real injustices and what was bitching simply for its own sake, realized what was necessary for changes to be made. When I talked with Julie about football, I needed to explain too much. And I might have to reveal some of my most private, least easily expressed feelings, to make the explanation clear. The necessary stoicism and toughness ingrained in me for two thirds of my life had made me very protective of my vulnerability. I could not pour it out, even for the wife I loved, without great difficulty.

I always felt this exclusion of wives, even of my own wife, to be not just unfair to the women, but potentially dangerous for marriages. But I never saw a way around it. For Julie and me football was only a part of our life, not its entirety. For the long-serving veterans, particularly those who lived in Kansas City year round, I assumed the problem must have been greater. Football players and their wives can too easily develop nearly separate existences during the football season. Many individuals have transcended this obstacle, but it is fair to say that in general playing professional football is not good for personal relationships. What most helped Julie and me was recognizing the strangeness that football created, and being able to talk about it. Toughness was necessary in football, but not in marriage.

My private football world underwent some subtle transformations during my four years in Kansas City. Toughness continued a necessary quality for survival, but it lost its nearly religious importance. I learned to play football as a game on Sunday with its necessary preparation, not as an all-consuming crusade for self-discovery. I learned that toughness must have its limits—for the sake of both my physical health and my relationship with my wife. I learned to be satisfied with modest success—although I never rose above second-team center and special-teams player, I did not feel a failure. To be playing professional football at all was a fairly rare accomplishment, but also my sense of my own worth was not so dependent as it had been in high school and college on the level of my achievement in football. I was continually frustrated by my lack of a starting role, but I did not feel personally diminished. I even learned to find satisfaction in the small opportunities available to me— game balls, a blocked kick against Denver, numerous tackles on the kickoff team. Lilliputian accomplishments perhaps, but they had to be enough. I became more detached in my relationship to the game than I had been in high school and college, but that detachment was a necessary precondition to a peaceful departure from football after eighteen years' involvement.

I cried but once in all the time I played pro ball—and this was the only time I was ashamed and embarrassed by my crying. In 1973, as we were losing to Cincinnati 14–6, Jack Rudnay was briefly hurt as we moved in for a score. I raced onto the field, with the ball on the one-yard line and a chance to move within a point of Cincinnati. As we lined up for an off-tackle dive to the right, I hunched myself into a tight coil, conscious of Mike Reid, the Bengals' excellent, superquick tackle in my outside gap, whom I would have to cut off. On Dawson's signal, I snapped the ball, feeling a solid whack against my butt, as I lunged to drive into Reid's legs. As I extricated myself from the pile of bodies, I could not tell what had happened, but Cincinnati's players began trotting to one sideline and my teammates to another. I still did not know what had happened. Then Bob Johnson, the Bengals' veteran center, jogged by and said, "Tough luck. I know how it feels." With a sinking feeling I suddenly realized the exchange between Dawson and myself had been fumbled. We had given up the ball a yard short of a touchdown.

I was stunned. The snap had felt good, but Dawson claimed he did not get the ball. When a bad exchange occurs between a quarterback with seventeen years of experience and a backup center with four, it is the center who looks like a horse's ass. I felt miserable. My sister, Kathy, who lived in the area had come to the game, but I did not even want to talk to her afterward. On the plane back to Kansas City after the loss, Ed Budde sitting in front of me turned to look over the seat back.

"Nice snap."

He had meant it playfully, but for some reason that astonished me almost as much as it did Ed, I burst into tears. Perhaps it was simply a physiological release after brooding an hour over that horrendous play. Perhaps it had something to do with the fact I liked and admired El Budde a lot. But I was extraordinarily embarrassed. Ed, too, was obviously embarrassed, as Clyde, sitting next to me, probably was. The tears came and went quickly, and I leaned forward to apologize to Ed and tell him I did not know what had happened. I felt painfully sheepish. I had cried over other football games in college, when all my intense emotional involvement had been crushed by a defeat. But this was the only time I cried in Kansas City—and was the only time I was ashamed to have cried. If nothing else, I had learned in four years that pro football was not something to cry about.

EIGTH

The Owners and the Owned

I CAME into the NFL during a players' strike and left during the next one. Between those two events lay a series of experiences that taught me the differences between football played to fulfill childhood dreams and football played as a business. The first strike, during the summer of 1970, kept the veterans out of training camp until just before the beginning of preseason games. A settlement, for the most part favorable to the owners, ended the walkout and changed very little for the players. The second strike, during the summer of 1974, was not resolved that year at all. The strike collapsed due to insufficient support from the players, who worked the entire season without a contract with the owners, then resumed negotiations the following off season. Many ripples were felt from that second strike. Mine was not the only career that ended abruptly that summer; much better players than I suddenly found themselves released or traded under puzzling circumstances. Although I had come to realize it slowly, I understood by then that in the NFL the game was business; coaches were employers; athletic departments were replaced by millionaire owners; and playing for "God, country, and Notre Dame" became playing for pay.

I did not make this discovery all at once. In my naïve, emotional relationship to football I probably learned the truth more slowly than most performers in the NFL. I did not relinquish my emotional commitment to the game easily. It had to be yanked away from me by a series of events whose significance I could not misunderstand. The first was my original signing. A businessman in South Bend contacted me during my senior year and offered to negotiate my contract, without charge. He had performed this service for numerous other Notre Dame players in the past, and it was clear from his persistence that doing this was important to him. I accepted his offer. The first I heard from him was a call to meet him in his office. There, with autographed glossy photos of Notre Dame greats covering the wall behind his desk, he outlined the Chiefs' first contract offer.

"I talked to Hank Stram on the phone. Hank and I are old friends from the days when he was an assistant at Notre Dame under Terry Brennan. He offered a five-thousand-dollar signing bonus, and a three-year contract for fifteen thousand, sixteen five, and nineteen thousand.

"I talked to Ara about this, and he said it was not enough. So let's sit tight and I'll see what I can do."

I was not very familiar with the NFL pay structure, but I assumed Ara understood the going rate. I knew that since the NFL and AFL had merged a few years before, large rookie contracts had disappeared, but I hoped my agent would force a figure that Ara would consider appropriate. He called me a few weeks later, with great enthusiasm in his voice.

"I've gotten you a good contract, Mike," he opened. "You'll get five thousand for signing, and a three-year contract for fifteen thousand, sixteen five, and nineteen thousand."

My parents had taught me to be respectful to my elders. I was too embarrassed to mention that he was repeating Stram's original offer. Instead, I mumbled that those figures sounded fine, and signed the contracts. I was getting more money than I had ever had in my life, and a salary that would certainly support me in graduate school. I knew that Ara would be willing to help me negotiate a new contract if I said that I was not satisfied with this one. But I felt obligated to the man who had been representing me; we had a gentlemen's agreement.

Then came my being waived at the end of my first training camp. When I realized afterward that by agreeing to play on the taxi squad I had eliminated any possibility of being returned to the forty-man roster, I was furious with myself. I was beginning to acknowledge that I could no longer assume that what my coach wanted for the team was necessarily in my best interest. But I also glimpsed for the first time the fact that, as an employee of an organization that held me under contract, I would have to learn to fight against management when it became necessary. I realized that even had I understood what was at stake when Coach Stram asked me if I would accept placement on the taxi squad, I would not have been confident enough in my bargaining position to say no. I would have assumed that he would answer with a ticket home. I not only had to understand my new relationship to my coach as my employer, I had to learn how to operate within that new framework.

Even after this experience, I could not feel that Hank Stram had ever treated me unfairly. I knew I had been an easy employee to manage, and that Hank had taken no advantage in signing me to my original contract or in placing me on the taxi squad for three hundred a week that I had not placed in his hands. But when I was fined with the other special-teams players in 1971 after the Detroit game on Thanksgiving, my relationship with my coach was permanently altered.

The Chiefs gained $250 of my money, but Stram lost my loyalty; in the long run we both lost on the arrangement. I understood why he had done what he did—that he felt it would goad us to the divisional championship we all wanted. But this particular ploy was not necessary, and its cost was much too high. My relationship to my coaches had always been intensely personal, but now for the first time I felt merely *used* by one. Hank had treated me not as an individual person but as an object stamped "Property of the Kansas City Chiefs." From this point onward I felt that my own interests would have to come first in my consideration, the team's second. If my coach was not going to look out for me, I would have to look out for myself. This realization came as a much greater shock to me than it did to my less naïve teammates, who seemed to have understood the true relationship from the beginning.

But if I took longer to learn, I did not forget the lesson. My next major encounter with my coach as employer came during the summer of 1973, when I had to negotiate a new contract. This time I handled the discussions myself. I met with Hank periodically throughout the summer, coming to his office when he sent for me, patiently waiting between bargaining sessions. I was well prepared for the negotiations. Because I did not live in Kansas City year round, and because I was in graduate school in the off season—working toward a genuine career outside football—I was less vulnerable than the players who depended heavily on their continued playing for the Chiefs. I also had a firm figure in my mind, below which I had resolved not to go. The Players' Association had published data recently that reported the average salary for fourth-year players to be $27,000. I decided I was at least an average player, and would not settle for less than $27,000, $30,000, and $33,000 over three years. I knew that I would have to sign a three-year contract in order to get any significant raise at all.

In our early sessions, Hank offered me 10 percent raises each year over three years, claiming that any larger increases would be out of line with the other players' pay scale. We players did not discuss our salaries among ourselves, but I had heard enough unofficially to know that I would not in any way be jeopardizing the team's salary structure. Some of my teammates were woefully underpaid—all-league performers making less than $20,000—but the team's salaries ranged up to $65,000, $75,000, and $125,000 for the top-paid player. When Hank pointed out that raising my salary $8000 from my $19,000 base constituted an impossibly large jump, I argued that I should not be penalized for having signed a bad original contract. We talked around and around these issues, resolving nothing in several sessions, but maintaining a cordial relationship in our discussions. I knew that Hank basically liked me, but I also knew that he approached contract negotiations as an enjoyable challenge. I sensed that we were playing a game for control of me, and was determined to win this one.

The low point in our negotiations came the day of our second preseason game. After a stalemated afternoon session of contract talks, I did not play a single down—on special teams or as backup center—that evening against Detroit. Midway through the fourth quarter, Hank substituted freely on offense—except at center. He could have simply forgotten about me, but I did not think so. After the game, Clyde and I and our wives sat in the Arrowhead Stadium parking lot in Clyde's van, drinking beer from a cooler and bitching for three hours about Hank's little stratagem. I had been furious after the game, but this quiet session, lasting long past midnight, purged me of my anger and strengthened my resolve to remain firm in our talks. A couple of weeks later, Hank called me into his office once more, agreed to my terms, and signed the contract I wanted. I felt for the first time that I had finally learned how to play the professional game properly.

My relationship to Hank Stram was a complex one during my four years with the Chiefs. Although I learned that I had to regard him first of all as my employer, I knew, too, that he was more than that. Hank seemed to regard my striking in the summer of 1974 as a personal betrayal, but until then he had liked and respected me. For one thing, I had graduated from the one school for which Hank seemed to have a special respect. He had been an assistant coach at Notre Dame in 1957–58, and I sensed that he would have been tempted to trade his Chiefs' job for the head coaching position there, were it offered. Hank also liked me for my good attitude, my coachability, and my commitment to graduate school during the off season. Our relationship was always cordial and friendly.

But he was also my employer. On the professional level a coach cannot simply be a friend to his players. Nearly everyone on the team had some grievance against Hank, that grew perhaps inevitably out of the coach–player relationship. Many felt underpaid, others underplayed; most of us chafed under his system of fines. Two of the team's stars—one white, one black—had compared contract offers they had received after being drafted one year in the same round. The offer to the player from the small black school in the South had been considerably lower— not an act of conscious racism probably, but one based on the assumption that the black from that background would be more easily dazzled by dollar signs. No planned racism, but shortsighted economics. The result was the same, and meant the loss of a player's loyalty.

Like my coaches in high school and college, Hank Stram

talked about the Chiefs as a "family." But in the NFL, "families" are even more unstable than they are in the larger society. A player can be a member of the family only so long as he remains indispensable. My first painful recognition of this basic fact came in 1971 when a good friend, John Huarte, who had preceded me at Notre Dame by five years and was now my teammate, was suddenly traded in midseason to the Chicago Bears. I felt as if a relative had died. It was shocking to see a friend, with wife and four children, traded as easily as we had traded baseball cards when my brother and I were kids. I talked to John on the phone and discovered that he was less upset than I was; in fact, with the Bears he would have a better chance to play. But to have my life disrupted by a trade was a profoundly unsettling experience. In time I came to realize that the "family" of Kansas City Chiefs included few prodigal sons. In my first year with the team, Mike Garrett, the Chiefs' best running back the year before in the Super Bowl season, was traded to San Diego because of a personality conflict with Hank. There was nothing extraordinary about such an event, but it was startling to me, as I began to encounter the reality of professional football.

Hank Stram was actually more loyal to his players than most coaches. The most successful franchises in recent years—Oakland, Pittsburgh, Dallas—have continually produced winning teams because new, younger players are worked into the lineup every year, as older veterans, often with good years left in them, are dumped to make room. The entire team has never grown old together and lost its high quality. By the very nature of the game, heartlessness can be smart management in the NFL. Loyalty to the veterans who have served the "family" well over the years will only lead to losing seasons. Hank Stram was fired from the Chiefs after the 1974 season because he had made this mistake. The great Chiefs teams had been built in the early nineteen sixties—with Len Dawson, Jim Tyrer, Ed Budde, Dave Hill, E. J. Holub, Buck Buchanan, Jerry Mays, Bobby Bell, and so on. But in the early seventies, when most of these athletes were entering their last years, Hank remained loyal to the players who had brought him to the top. When they all grew old

together, the team began to lose, and wholesale replacements
could not save it.

Hank Stram was a complex man to play for. He could demonstrate this kind of loyalty, but simultaneously alienate players by
fining them, signing them to meager contracts, or otherwise ex-
ercising his control over them. I always felt that Hank loved his
players in a way. After the last game of the 1972 season in
Atlanta, I was moved to see him circulate among the players in
the locker room, bidding us goodbye and wishing us an enjoyable off season, with tears in the corners of his eyes that could
not be feigned. But Hank also needed to feel absolute *control* of
us, and of everything to do with running the football team.
Hank's assistant coaches were not allowed to speak to the press;
any official word had to come from the man himself. Hank was a
small man who lorded it over giants, and that sense of control
seemed necessary to his self-identity. Perhaps it was a misfortune that Stram came into pro coaching in the shadow of Vince
Lombardi's great Green Bay teams. Lombardi became a secular
saint among many football people, and I often conjectured that
Hank was denying his own personality to try to model himself
on the hard-nosed, all-powerful Packer coach. The Chiefs had
been thrashed by Lombardi's Green Bay team in the first Super
Bowl in 1967, when Hank was coaching in an upstart league trying to gain parity with the long-established NFL. Lombardi
could have been a potent figure for Stram to compare himself to.
Hank suppressed his strongest quality—his personal enthusiasm
and love for the game and for the players—under a persona he
created half out of the Lombardi mold and half for the media's
consumption. Hank Stram projected the image of an autocratic,
dapper, sophisticated "winner" strutting on the sidelines, while
deep inside those exquisitely tailored suits and that Napoleonic
manner was a kind and enthusiastic man trying to break out. He
gave us glimpses of the inner Hank, but more often kept him in
check.

He kept *us* in check, too—with an extraordinarily complete
and intimidating fine system. In training camp, what we did,
when we did it, how we looked, how much we ate, and most
other things besides were not just prescribed but reinforced by
huge fines. One player foolishly ignored the regulation against

having women in the dormitory—and more foolishly yet was
caught at bed check when we all knew the coaches would be
looking in on us. A twenty-five-hundred-dollar fine. Other players more innocently slept through a meal—a five-hundred-dollar
fine, and probably ten dollars for a new alarm clock. Sometimes
the threat of fines produced strange dramas. Jerry Mays was
late one night driving back from Kansas City with curfew loom-
ing. When his speeding car was pulled over by a policeman,
Jerry in panic leaped out of the car to run back and explain the
emergency. The policeman, seeing a six-foot-four, 260-pound
wild man running at him, felt a different kind of panic. He
jumped from his car, knelt behind the opened door, and leveled
his gun at the charging maniac. Jerry stopped abruptly, then
began shouting.

"No, no! I'm Jerry Mays—Kansas City Chiefs—late for curfew
in Liberty—I've got to make it!"

The understanding policeman let him go.

Sometimes avoiding fines became a game—but a rather desperate one, considering the stakes. The fine system continued
after the season started, most noticeably in the weekly weigh-ins
—with a fine of a hundred dollars for every pound a player was
overweight. Tuesday was the day. Linemen who played at 275
on Sunday but had to be 265 on Tuesday, came in early Tuesday
morning, wrapped themselves in rubber suits, sat in the sauna,
ran laps, and took diuretic pills in an effort to make weigh-in.
When all such measures were insufficient, trickery was resorted
to. A small wad of tape placed at a particular point under the
scale could change the reading by a number of pounds. Because
my problem was always to keep my weight *up*, I checked carefully to see who had weighed in before me. If I knew the fix was
on, I went first to the weight room to find a two-and-a-half-
pound weight or two to slip inside my jock. If I should step on
the scale and register 235, I was afraid the coaches would think
I was getting too light to play center.

The fine system was but one of the methods by which Hank
directed our lives. Others were more frivolous. No coach could
have been more conscious of the media than Hank Stram was
during the four years I played for him. His Super Bowl victory
had thrust him into the celebrity limelight and he enjoyed the

glow. He wanted to project not just a personal image but a team image as well, with results that sometimes seemed ludicrous to us players. When we traveled, Hank wanted us to appear as a well-groomed, conservative family. We wore team pants and blazers—black and white with a red arrowhead insignia over the breast pocket. In an age of Super Fly garb and other exotic fashions for men, flamboyant attire was not possible for the Kansas City Chiefs. We also had strict hair codes: no facial hair at all, sideburns no longer than the middle of the ear, hair that did not show under our helmets. The blacks' afros had to be conservative as well; the penalty for violations by anyone was a five-hundred-dollar fine. One of my black teammates, when newly traded to the team, was outraged. He had had a pencil-thin mustache since he was fourteen; it was part of both his personal identity and his black heritage. But in a time in which most coaches were being forced to surrender their desires for crew-cut cleanliness under the pressure of changing times, Hank still demanded that we look squeaky-clean. His own preferences were reinforced periodically by comments from fans—such as the letter from a woman that he posted prominently in the locker room my first year with the team. After commending us for our nice appearance in several paragraphs, she wrote a line that will linger in my memory always.

"It is obvious that your young men practice hygiene daily."

On the field our image was even more carefully created. Hank was intensely aware that professional football had entered the media age, in which *image* was all-important. Unlike other teams, we had our benches in Arrowhead Stadium on the sideline away from the locker room—because this was also the sideline opposite the TV cameras. He was to have maximum exposure. Our uniforms were carefully—obsessively—color-coordinated. At home, we wore red helmets, red jerseys with white and gold numerals, white pants with red and gold stripes, white socks with red and gold bands, and red shoes with white and gold bars. On the road, the color scheme was reversed: the same red helmets, but white jerseys, red pants, and white shoes. The red shoes were a particular embarrassment to me. I felt more like a clown sometimes than a football player. A team's temperament could be projected by its uniforms; I suspected that Oakland was so tough at home at least in part because the players *looked* so mean in their black jerseys. They probably felt mean in them as well. It was difficult to look or feel ferocious in red shoes. The first time we put the shoes on before a game, George Daney called over to me, "You go out there first and see if they laugh."

We were not just costumed for the TV cameras, we were choreographed as well. We may have been the only team in the NFL that *practiced* for the player introductions and the national anthem. On Saturdays before games, after running lightly through our two-minute offense, kicking game, and other specialty alignments, we practiced lining up in numerical order along the sideline marker, standing at attention for the anthem with helmet under left arm and right arm hanging free. We were spaced precisely one yard apart between the two 30-yard lines; Jim Lynch and I—numbers 51 and 50—usually straddling the midfield stripe. Perhaps we looked impressive, but I felt silly —and I felt even sillier one day in 1973 when Hank announced we would rehearse the player introductions. He had seen the University of Michigan on television recently, and was impressed by the Wolverines' massed huddle of frantically fired-up players, onto the top of which each of the starters would throw himself after being introduced, to be absorbed into the swarm of snarling enthusiasm. Hank described the setup, then said, "Let's try it." The starting defense was sent over to the tunnel entrance where the introductions would begin, while the rest of us were instructed to crowd into a tight huddle and chant with ferocious intensity. But in that huge empty stadium, before 78,000 unfilled seats and a few maintenance workers looking curiously on, with the game more than twenty-four hours away, we collectively felt silly. And began to act so. With George Daney and Jack Rudnay in our midst it was impossible to stay serious. George began screaming and howling as if it were the Super Bowl and he had just popped half the uppers in Kansas City. Jack joined in and then the rest of us; by the time Marvin Upshaw, the first player to be introduced, ran toward us, all he could do was break into a wide grin and join the silliness. But Hank was not amused. We tried a new system: dividing up into two sides with a corridor between, through which our teammates would run after being introduced, to be popped on the shoulder pads or slapped on the palms. That seemed easier to organize. We practiced it a few times, then went with it the next day.

Such attention to appearances was distracting, and seemed foolish to us, but it was an obsession with Hank, whether for personal reasons or because he understood more clearly than any of us the impact of the media on our sport. The actual playing of football games had not changed much in twenty-five years, nor could it change much, and we were football *players*. But the presentation of the game to the public had changed enormously, and Hank Stram may simply have been among the first to take this fact fully into account. His own image was very consciously created and maintained—from his dapper appearance, whether on the practice field or the sideline at game time, or at the banquet table, to his often repeated desire always to surround himself with "winners." Enamored of celebrities, he continually brought "stars" in other fields out to Liberty to meet the team. Tom Laughlin, the lead actor in the popular film *Billy Jack*, came one day; another time, Robert Goulet and Carol Lawrence, appearing at the Starlight Theater in Kansas City, came to visit. Hank introduced these celebrities to us, and invited them to say a few words. For us, the meeting created an opportunity to take a break from a grueling practice. For the celebrity visitors, it must have been intimidating sometimes to confront sixty dirty, sweating, enormous football players under those circumstances. Robert Goulet—flawlessly coiffed, attired, and manicured—seemed particularly uneasy, and made a clumsy effort to demonstrate that he was just one of the boys. "Go out there tomorrow night," he told us, "and knock the"—here he slipped into an urgent, conspiratorial whisper, looking right and left to make sure anyone who heard the next word would not be offended—"shit" —he slipped it out softly as if his mother might be lurking along the sideline and would leap forward with a gasp, to wash his mouth out with soap—"out of them." Gosh, we sometimes even used worse words than that!

Hank wanted us to think of ourselves as winners, who associated with other winners, and he also wanted to create his own image as a celebrity and winner. One of his finest moments in training camp came one afternoon while we stood around waiting for him to appear. Someone spotted a helicopter in the distance. As it drew nearer and nearer, we all began to recognize what was happening. In minutes, the copter was hovering overhead, then settling down onto the practice field, to emit the little man himself, obviously pleased with the drama he had created.

"I insist that you be on time for practice," he announced to us, "and I have the same obligation myself. Even if it means renting a helicopter."

How long ago had he planned this charade, I wondered? and would the wire services pick up the story?

Having created an image for himself, Hank worked too hard sometimes at maintaining it. We would have preferred the real Hank Stram to the quasi-Lombardi or the media celebrity. Occasionally his efforts completely misfired. The week after John Lohmeyer's neck injury in 1973, we played Oakland on the coast to decide the divisional championship. Perhaps Hank had seen *Knute Rockne, All-American* too many times and decided to do the Gipper one better. He tape-recorded a message from a groggy, heavily drugged John in his hospital bed that not only did not fire us up, but appalled us by its miscalculated manipulation of a nearly tragic event. As I trotted onto the field after listening to the message in the locker room, Jack Rudnay said to me with disgust, "That's about as low as anyone can go." Also that year, Hank hired a nephew fresh out of college as his administrative assistant—read gofer. Among Dougie's duties was to tape-record all of Hank's inspirational talks to the team—which we heard via rumor were played back for his family's comments at the dinner table. After a speech, Dougie casually circulated among the players, subtly asking, "Well, what did you think of Hank's talk?" before slipping back to his boss's office to report. Dougie also passed on to Hank the players' feelings about other matters that he overheard. We were not overly fond of Dougie.

Hank Stram became a victim of his own need to embody his image of a great coach. His strengths as a coach, and the qualities that made him highly successful in his first ten years with the Chiefs—in which he was the winningest coach in pro football—were his organizational abilities and his genuine love for his players and the game. Players traded to Kansas City from other teams constantly remarked on the Chiefs' first-class organization. Hank had created a stable, well-run system, surrounded himself with competent assistants and great players in the early years, and achieved well-earned success. His players were loyal to him and liked him, and he liked them in return. But he became too caught up in his own success and in the pressures to sustain it. And he was betrayed by the conflict between coaches and players that was inevitable on the professional level. The coach's interest and the players' interests were bound to conflict at times. The players who made the Chiefs great in the sixties grew old, but Hank could not bear to replace them. The younger players became frustrated by not playing; and, caught up in image making, Hank had failed to gain our loyalty as he had from our older teammates. He tried to control us in ways we felt were unnecessary; his absolute control over our salaries, our playing time, even many of our personal habits troubled us at times. Eventually Hank's policies backfired. In 1974, for the first time since 1963, losses outnumbered wins.

This is a player's perspective on what happened to the Chiefs in the seventies. From *his* perspective, Hank was caught in an awkward position between the players and the owner. In an interview in 1981, Hank observed that the coach is often compromised by a general manager who has closer contact with the team owner. He complained that before his firing by the Chiefs in 1975, the bureaucratic interference with his running of the club had been a continual frustration. To the players, Lamar Hunt was an unobtrusive owner, a quiet man, not much older than some of the players, an owner who occasionally accompanied the team on game trips or visited the locker room, but who seemed to leave the decisions to Hank. But we were not present at Hank's private meetings with Lamar, where his ownership may have more fully exerted itself.

Lamar Hunt is one of the major sports entrepreneurs of our time. NFL owners tend to keep much lower profiles than their baseball or basketball counterparts—probably because they do not wish to draw too much attention to themselves and to the incredible profits they are making from their franchises. Lamar Hunt is one of the least obtrusive of them all, but he has had a greater impact on the recent history of American sport than perhaps any other owner. At twenty-six, armed with the millions he inherited from his self-made oil-billionaire father, H. L. Hunt, but unable to purchase an NFL franchise, Lamar decided to create his own rival league. He is generally credited for not just founding the AFL, but sustaining it with his bankroll through the lean early years, until merger with the established league gave it permanent stability. AFL franchises that were founded on a few thousand dollars came to be worth $30 to $40 million. Lamar Hunt made fortunes not just for himself but for many of his fellow owners with his entrepreneurial spirit.

The players' relationship to Lamar was an easy one. The first time I met him, he approached me on the field as we warmed up before my initial preseason game, and introduced himself—as if it were natural that he should know who I was, but I might not know him. The extent of our relationship for four years consisted of cordial "Hi, Mikes" and "How are yous"—a very superficial sort of friendliness, perhaps, but friendliness nonetheless that always made me feel he was a decent man as well as a wise owner for his noninterference in the team's operation. He rarely intruded on my consciousness during the entire time I played for his team. I was very aware of being owned, but little aware of him as owner; my contact was almost entirely with the subordinates through whom he manipulated the team. On only one occasion did I directly encounter the wealth and power he represented. In the summer of 1973, Lamar had the entire team to his Dallas home for a barbecue the night before a preseason game against the Cowboys. His kindly intention was a mistake. As we rode the team bus up the long drive to his mansion, past fountains as ornate as any in the Countryclub Plaza back in Kansas City, past a carriage house that looked more elegant than the homes most of us lived in, I felt rather strange—a bit like a field hand come up from the bottom lands because ole massa was rewarding us with a holiday celebration. We were invited to wander through the house—a $2-million palace that we heard Lamar had picked up for $1 million because the seller needed instant cash. One room in particular epitomized the house for me: a bathroom done in ornate gilt, white marble, and mirrors, at the end of a long corridor with gilt-framed mirrors on either side: a mini-Versailles that was appalling in its aggressive extravagance. As we strolled through such conspicuous opulence in room after room, I overheard one of my teammates mumbling half to himself, half to whomever might be listening.

"The next time I talk contract, they're not gonna tell me they got no money."

He summed up our feelings for many of us. The invitation from Lamar was generous and unnecessary, but more than anything else it pointed out with unmistakable clarity the financial gulf between the owner and the players he owned. We were indeed "owned" in some peculiar ways. Each of us was bound by the standard player contract, which tied us unilaterally to the club for the duration of the contract plus an option year, but in effect limited our mobility permanently. We were not just restricted to playing for the Kansas City Chiefs as long as the organization should desire our services, but were also bound by the club's and the league's rules and regulations, subject to stiff fines or even suspension without recourse. The court of last resort in any dispute was the commissioner's office, but the commissioner was hired and salaried by the owners. We all understood where his interests lay. Beyond all this, seeing the tangible evidence of Lamar Hunt's wealth reminded us of the fortunes that Lamar and other owners were making off *us*. Lamar Hunt was rich long before he founded the Dallas Texans and the American Football League; he was rich long before he was born. He had risked a tiny fraction of his inherited wealth to sustain the shaky league through hard times. In one sense he was an extraordinary benefactor to the players, in providing nearly twice as many jobs in professional football than existed before he formed the AFL. But we players risked much more than Lamar ever had, every time we walked onto the field. We risked our livelihood. Despite this simple truth, we understood that Lamar Hunt's annual profits—from attendance, television, parking and concessions, and other miscellaneous sources of football income —surpassed the combined salaries of all the players on the team. When Lamar Hunt filed his income taxes, he was allowed by the IRS to depreciate us players as equipment that wears out over time. We players were entitled to no comparable tax break, even though our owner could endlessly replace us, while we had only our own bodies until they wore out. Lamar had taken minor financial risks in the early sixties, but his profits had been risk-free for some time, and would continue to grow. No matter how good or bad the team might be, the television contract alone would guarantee significant profits. We players, on the other hand, risked our entire careers in every game and even every practice we participated in. Twenty-four hours after eating barbecued ribs at Lamar Hunt's home, I injured my knee in a preseason game against Dallas. As a three-year veteran I earned slightly more than two hundred dollars for the game. I wonder how much Lamar Hunt made.

Being owned was a palpable feeling at certain times during my four years with Kansas City. When I had my hair cut shorter than I liked it, got up at 6:30 A.M. for a training-camp breakfast I did not want to eat, or drove to the Glenwood Manor on Christmas Eve in 1971, I felt slightly owned. When I was told by my coach in effect that I could pay a $250 fine for what he had determined was incompetent special-teams play, or not play football in the NFL at all, I felt as oppressively owned as a feudal lord's serf. But even in more calmly rational moments, when I negotiated my contract or dwelt on my frustrations over not playing more but having no power to play elsewhere, I felt my ownership by the Kansas City Chiefs as a constant fact of my life—the condition of being a player in the NFL. What made the situation bearable was my separate existence apart from football—my graduate studies and eventual career in teaching. My teammates with no such alternative were less fortunate. To be partly owned was frustrating enough; to be wholly owned would have been frightening.

In the same interview in which he complained of front-office bureaucrats, Hank Stram also made clear his feelings about what has happened to pro football more generally in recent years:

> The life is draining out of the game. Some superrich guy buys the team and meddles in it. Some jock-sniffer, who's not even a football guy, runs the front office. The assistant coaches are technicians who divide the team up into offense, defense, special teams and kicking game. They're the theorists. And the players are big,

strong, weight-trained mechanics who do exactly what they're told. The coach is just the guy standing in the middle holding a clip-board, with nothing to do.

Where the hell is the humanity in the game? I remember when guys got into the game so they could express themselves. It was heroic.

Hank used similar words to us on occasion, particularly in my last year when we began losing key games that were costing us a playoff spot.

"Some of you have too many distractions," he'd tell us in the locker room after a loss. "You're worrying more about your businesses off the field than about football. You're professional athletes, and you should be committed a hundred percent to your profession. But you're not. Some of you also are more con-cerned about how much money you're making and how much the other guy gets. There used to be players who played for the love of the games—who couldn't wait to get out on the field and hit somebody, and didn't give a damn about agents and con-tracts. You had better start making that kind of commitment right here, right now, or you won't be around long."

Ah, for the good old days when men played for the love of the game! E. J. Holub was retired now; so was Sherrill Headrick, the man unfazed by compound fractures. One of my older team-mates told me that Sherrill had played each year for minimum raises. Each spring he walked into the general manager's office to ask, "Well, what do I make this year?" then signed a contract. Those were heroic times, ah yes—and not so long ago—before players' unions and no-cut contracts and other such perversions of the grand old game began to interfere. If only we could turn back the clock!

But I had seen E. J. Holub unable to walk normally a year after he retired. And I had seen Sherrill Headrick, too. A team-mate had pointed him out to me at training camp—on one of his periodic visits to borrow money from his still-solvent former teammates. Sherrill had been broke virtually since he left foot-ball. And I had read in the paper that Hank Stram had negoti-ated a new contract for himself (with the help of an agent), for $1 million over ten years. Anyone for the good old days?

Professional football underwent many significant changes in

the seventies. But, Hank's comments to the contrary, during my years in Kansas City the humanity of the game remained where it had always been—among the players. Pro football was a business, but the players made it something more. Long seasons of pleasure and pain, jubilation and frustration, wins and losses created a world of shared experiences that we players alone fully participated in. From July to December we spent more time with each other than we did with our families, doing something that was alternately painful, challenging, and immensely rewarding. The players who shared these feelings and experiences were not "mechanics," as Hank had claimed, but individuals with hopes, fears, and aspirations never far beneath the surface. We were stamped out of no mold. Like any other group of individuals we had unique personalities and temperaments, but the nature of our profession also made us very much aware of ourselves as a special group with much in common that we shared with no others. We *were* a sort of "family" after all.

The bond among teammates is perhaps unique in its intensity and simultaneous fragility. The year after I graduated from Notre Dame, I returned to the campus on a free weekend, to see old friends and watch a football game. After the contest, a routine 51–10 thrashing of Army, I walked into the locker room to greet my former teammates. The year before I had been offensive captain, a leader particularly to the underclassmen who now comprised most of the team. But as I walked into the locker room, I instantly felt an outsider. Joe Theismann, Tom Gatewood, Denny Allen, and others said, hi, and shook my hand on their way to the showers. Dan Novakov, my backup at center the previous year and the starter now, stopped briefly to ask how I was doing. But there was no spark. These athletes who had shared a long season of successes and failures with me, that had ended less than twelve months before, were merely acquaintances now. Not quite strangers, but not quite friends either.

I saw the same thing happen several times in Kansas City. Players cut or traded became instant outsiders—no longer part of the team but also reminders to their former teammates of their own career insecurity. Players who returned to see old teammates did not find teammates at all. Jerry Mays, after playing ten years in the defensive line, six of them as all-league and all of them as an inspirational team leader, walked into the locker room just before game time one Sunday in 1972, two years after he had retired. His old friends welcomed him, but with a near-formality that signaled a changed relationship. He walked about the locker room, exchanging greetings with players not as if they were friends too long separated, but more as if Jerry were a politician drumming up votes. Hank Stram had asked him to say a few words to the team—at a pivotal point in the season we needed a victory, and perhaps the old captain could touch some dormant emotions.

"You know," Jerry began, "I've been out of football less than two years, and you wouldn't believe how much I miss it. You men are the luckiest people in the world; I'd give anything to be back here with you."

Amazing! I was not surprised to hear that Jerry Mays had loved playing football. Although I did not know him well—I had played with him only one year—I remembered clearly the kind of football player he had been. He had played every down at full speed, had given 100 percent on every play for ten years. But I also knew that Jerry had gone straight from the Chiefs to his father's construction company in Dallas, where he held down a high-management-level position. He had traded football for a high-paying, challenging career, yet he now claimed to be missing football terribly.

No one could miss two-a-day practices in Liberty, Missouri, or the dregs of a long, unsuccessful season. Jerry might have longed for the euphoria of a Super Bowl championship or the glory of being a football star, but probably what he missed most of all was the fellowship of his teammates. For ten years he shared many of the most intense experiences of his life with a group of other men who became close to him in ways perhaps no one else did. But that bond, for all its intensity, could not survive the end of football. Only teammates shared it. All others were outsiders.

That bond was one of the major pleasures of my professional career. I did not feel a closeness to all my teammates, certainly. As in any group of forty, personalities and temperaments invariably clashed. Some of my teammates seemed aloof, a few were obnoxious, many I simply did not know well. But most were agreeable, intelligent, interesting men. Our backgrounds, values, and interests off the field varied greatly; in many cases we shared only the common bond of our football experiences. But that bond could be a potent one while we continued to play together.

I shared this bond even with players I did not particularly like. But other, more personal, bonds as well reinforced this all-encompassing one. By the inevitable affinities of our racially conscious society, the black players associated more with other blacks, and whites with whites. The team had its rednecks and more militant blacks, but for the most part they submerged their feelings. Within the democracy of the locker room and the playing field—not a perfect democracy but a better one than could be found in the larger society—interracial friendships were possible. Middle-class whites from the North and poor Southern blacks could meet on common ground in the locker room. Most blacks, I discovered for the first time, were bilingual; they spoke a language among themselves that tended to be private and exclusive, but could revert to standard English to include others. I felt cut off from the experiences of many of my black teammates, but others gave me a sense of who they were. Willie Lanier was a proud, intelligent, impressively articulate man who helped teach me the importance of self-protection in the NFL; Emmitt Thomas was quiet, dignified, and gently easygoing—until he stepped onto the football field, where he was the best cornerback in football. James Marsalis was self-demanding and serious, Curley Culp brooding, Buck Buchanan almost magisterial. Out of my racially narrow background I discovered in Kansas City some of the diversity of black life in this country, and felt at least a small connection to it.

Shared experiences on the football field created particular bonds. Special-teams players felt certain connections to one another; offensive and defensive units did as well; kickers could feel excluded from such bonds by virtue of their specialized role. The team was further broken down into smaller units by position. The offensive linemen comprised the group to which I felt the closest connection. We were the "Blutoes," as George Daney named us. Ed Budde bore the nickname Bluto, but we collectively adopted the name as well. We thought of ourselves as a distinct group within the team. We were well aware of our low pay relative to most other positions on the team—particularly to the running backs for whom we blocked—and of our relative obscurity in the public's eye. But we also maintained a great pride in what we did, and an appreciation of the difficulties of each of our positions. We shared pinched nerves, battered hands and forearms, a fear of quick defensive linemen and a respect for strong, hardworking ones, a disgust with self-inflated running backs, and an understanding that collectively we were the slowest, bulkiest, but hardest-working and most important group on the team (we never argued our relative importance with other teammates, but only assumed it). We even had a coach, Bill Walsh, who was one of us and who shared our view.

In one sense we all had the same temperament. In order to be offensive linemen we all had to be hardworking, persistent, and tolerant of pain. But my fellow linemen were distinct individuals as well. At right tackle Dave Hill—or Butter Bean—was a huge man who played with finesse. He was the same off the field as on—an easygoing Alabaman, slow-talking and slow to anger, but quick to laugh. His bookend at left tackle was Jim Tyrer, at six six and 280 even bigger than Hill by an inch and fifteen pounds. Tyrer was known as "Pinky," a strikingly incongruous name for a man so large; he had obviously been named for the thick red hair that topped his huge frame. Jim had enormously broad shoulders and back, tapering to narrow hips, thin legs, and positively skinny ankles that looked altogether too delicate to support so massive a structure. Jim's head was also unusually large —a full size bigger than anyone else's on the team. With his red helmet on, he looked, according to one opponent, like a huge red garbage can being thrown at him on every play. Jim did not like to be kidded about his head; dignity was the quality he emanated, but he tolerated the characteristic buffoonery of the other linemen with good grace. Jim projected responsibility, stability, self-control, and farsightedness. He came to work every day in a suit, the uniform from his off-the-field job as president of his own company. He was the class of the offensive line. No one could have anticipated how his life would change after football.

The starting guards were Mo Moorman and Ed Budde, a pair of six five, 265-pounders. Mo was the youngest of the guards and

tackles, twenty-eight in my last year, 1973, while Hill and Budde
were thirty-three, and Tyrer thirty-five. Mo was hard-nosed and
surly when he played; if I should ever have seen Mo Moorman
butting his head against the side of a brick building, I would
have sent for gauze and iodine, but also would have evacuated
the place. In the locker room he was often surly as well, or at
least morose, and harder to reach than his fellow linemen, but
he could be won over by the others' humor.

Ed Budde, on the other hand, exuded an engaging geniality
that covered his underlying toughness. He had been *the* bad-ass
guard in the AFL as a young man, and still was as tough and
strong as any guard in the league, but off the field he was now
almost teddy-bearish in his gentleness and easy humor. His
greatest anxiety was not over losing games but over losing his
hair. Ed had done enough research on weaves, transplants, and
methods of preserving what hair he still had to write a book on
the subject. I could infuriate him with playful maliciousness by
complaining about always having to shampoo my hair twice to
get it clean—because it was so thick. "You'll get old, too," he'd
remind me with mock anger.

Players like Hill, Budde, and Tyrer were only seven and nine
years older than I, but measured by football time they were old
graybeards who were nearing the end of long careers and had
storehouses of anecdotes and experiences to pass on to youngsters like myself. The locker room was the center of our world—
the site of our meetings, our pregame rituals and postgame cele-
brations or despairs, and of several hours each week of just
lounging around. In college, I did not spend much time in the
locker room. Its rows of lockers, using up most of the floor
space, were very different from the lockers along the walls in
Kansas City, leaving the large communal space in the middle. In
college, the locker room was the place to change clothes before
and after practice. The center of my world—where I came to
know the people around me—was the floor of my dormitory
where I lived. But in Kansas City, we spent hours together in
the locker room. At Arrowhead Stadium it was a spacious, red-
carpeted rectangle, lined on all four walls with walnut-grained
stalls in which each player had a stool, a locked cabinet for his
valuables, and several hooks and shelves for his clothes. Off one

end was the training room with its whirlpool tubs, taping tables, and therapy machines. Off another end were the showers, a sauna, a row of sinks and mirrors, and gigantic whirlpool. On the walls throughout the complex hung numerous plaques, with inspirational and cautionary sayings. One announced, "Fatigue makes cowards of us all," another warned about how fat can sap a player's ability. The misquoted Gospel According to St. Lombardi—"Winning isn't everything, it's the only thing"—was proclaimed. There were also more elaborate contributions to the team philosophy. The most memorable was a quotation from Teddy Roosevelt that hung over the whirlpool tub in the training room:

> Far better is it to dare mighty things, to win glorious triumphs, even though checkered by failure, than to take rank with those poor spirits who neither enjoy much nor suffer much, because they live in the gray twilight that knows not victory nor defeat.

Reading these lines, I always felt ambivalent. On the one hand, they spoke to some of my own feelings that drove me through many years of playing football. But to see them etched on a plaque and hung on the locker-room wall made them seem slightly silly, certainly pretentious. In Roosevelt's time they summed up a prevailing attitude; in our time they seemed better reserved for the private hearts of individuals than to be broadcast as if they were the guiding principle of the Kansas City Chiefs' organization.

One other plaque hung in a particularly prominent place:

> What you see here
> What you hear here
> What you say here
> Let it stay here
> When you leave here.

The locker room was the inner sanctum, with access denied to all but the elect. It was the center of the Kansas City Chiefs' "family," and family secrets were to remain in the family.

There were secrets that had nothing to do with policy or team philosophy. The Chiefs, like any team, had their folklore, which was passed on by the elders to the younger players. Sometimes

the locker room became our old-time, small-town general store
where we sat around on our stools like old men and wide-eyed
kids, hunkered down just out of the hot sun, scratching in the
dirt with sticks and telling stories. It was in sitting around on my
stool waiting for meetings, that I heard tales of Sherrill Headrick
and E. J. Holub. I heard, too, about Willie Lanier as a rookie,
when he picked out Ed Budde as the man he had to prove his
toughness against. He and Ed went after each other on play
after play, stunning their teammates at Liberty with their feroc-
ity, neither conceding any edge. It was Bluto vs. the Bear in the
main event day after day. Willie kept up his fearsome head-
knocking into the season. One of his main antagonists was
Hewritt Dixon, the powerful, 230-pound running back from
Oakland. Willie tackled him so viciously in their first encounter
that Dixon became ever after a Bear hunter. Whenever Dixon
ran a sweep, the older Chiefs told me, he began hunting for the
Bear as soon as he touched the ball—to find Willie before Willie
nailed him. Hewritt Dixon was a lion to the rest of the league,
but Willie Lanier had tamed him to a pussy cat against the
Chiefs.

Willie paid the price for his early recklessness. He began having severe headaches, and after one memorable hit knocked himself unconscious. Finally, he told himself, no more. He had
proven whatever he had to prove, and decided he would never
risk permanent injury for the sake of a mere football game. He
began wearing a helmet with thick padding on the outside, and
he modified the violence of his hitting. He settled down—to play
simply as the best middle linebacker in football, not as a human
destroyer.

I heard, too, the story about a game the Chiefs had played
against Denver a few years back. The man across the line from
Ed Budde was Dave Costa, an excellent defensive tackle, but
also a notorious "white knuckler." As Ed came to the line for the
Chiefs' first offensive play, he confronted Costa shaking in his
stance, snorting and grunting through clenched teeth as he impatiently held himself in check until the ball snapped. As Ed settled into his stance, he looked across the line at Costa, a man
he'd known off the field as well as on for several years, and
greeted him in his friendliest, most casual voice.

"Hi, Dave, how're the wife and kids?"

As Costa went limp, trying to register this startling, inappropriate remark, the ball snapped and Ed exploded into him, dumping him squarely on his back.

Another story, told with great relish by Dave Hill to the young offensive linemen, concerned George Daney, Mo Moorman's backup at right guard. George and Mo had been first-round draft choices in the same year, 1968, but only one could become the starter. George, who had been six four, 230 pounds, and able to run 4.6 in the forty, became ground down over the years by the frustration of not playing regularly. He bulked up to 260, told himself that the only way he was going to survive emotionally was not to give a damn—and became the team clown.

In one game, when Mo was hurt, George had to replace him briefly. After Len Dawson called a pass play, George broke the huddle with the rest of his teammates and trotted up to the line. The defense was in an "odd" alignment—placing a man over the center and leaving George uncovered. The guard's responsibilities were clear: check the middle linebacker for a blitz, then help the center block his man if no one was coming. But George was not always a serious student of the game. As the ball was snapped, he turned inside to help E. J. Holub, then saw too late the linebacker blow past him. George turned just in time to see Dawson, arm raised and ball cocked, obliterated by the untouched linebacker.

One of the other linemen helped Dawson to his feet. The quarterback, having already played a dozen years, was not as sprightly as he once had been. And he did not like to be hit. He had been known to chew out even Jim Tyrer and Ed Budde when his pass protection had broken down. The blow that Dawson had just received had been so violent that his helmet had been twisted around on his face until he could spit through the earhole. He was furious. He readjusted his helmet, boiling to a rage and preparing to let loose a few well-chosen curses, when George cut in.

"Way to pick up the blitz, Lenny."

This was George Daney, the clear choice as my most unforgettable teammate. When I first met him, he told me he had gone to the University of Texas at El Paso where he had a double major—brain surgery and welding. To most of the team, George was a screw-off who didn't give a damn, but those who knew him better saw a more complicated person. In his earliest years, as a first-round draft choice and a fine athlete, George had had high expectations for himself, great enthusiasm for and commitment to the game. But year after year of not playing regularly, of being thrown onto the special teams and told in unspoken ways that he was not good enough to start, wore him down psychologically even more than physically. It wore me down, too, but George had greater imagination than I in his ways of compensating. In playing the clown, he made the hard times more bearable for the rest of us. In the middle of a brutal practice, mired in the endlessness of two-a-days in Liberty, George lined up once in the end zone for offensive-line drills. We were to begin with a few easy wind sprints, then move on to passblocking. On Coach Walsh's signal, all of us sprinted out of our stances for twenty yards. Except George. He ran directly into the goalpost, knocking himself flat on his back, as the rest of us howled. In another practice, in a different year but under the same conditions, we assembled for drills only to discover George was missing. A familiar voice directed us to a deep pit that had been dug for a new goalpost. At the bottom sat George, grinning like a happy child, completely delighted with himself.

George's occasional partner in insanity was Jack Rudnay; together they were known as Heckle and Jeckle. A favorite trick of theirs during the season enlivened some of the tedium of team meetings. After we had broken up into groups and dispersed to separate rooms for game films and chalk-board discussions, Heckle and Jeckle loved to remove a few acoustical tiles in the ceiling of our meeting room, then crawl through the rafters with a fire extinguisher to a spot over the meeting room of the defensive line or running backs—for a surprise attack. As George gently lifted a ceiling tile, Jack aimed the extinguisher for a quick blast at a chosen player, then George slipped the tile quickly back into place.

But George was more truly a solo artist. His life seemed a constant anticipation of some new prank or joke to break up his teammates. There was nothing malicious in him; he was like an enormous elf with a genius for both verbal and physical wit. In

1973, the routine of daily meetings, which involved more waiting around for meetings to begin than actual meeting time, was broken for several weeks by the construction off our shower room of a giant whirlpool—six feet deep, twelve feet across, fed by eighteen jets powerful enough to propel someone across the pool who did not hang on to the edge. George appointed himself unofficial foreman of the job, overseeing the digging, pipe-laying, and tiling, and providing running commentary as long as the project lasted. One of the final stages was the tiling of three steps down to the pool's bottom—particularly steep ones to drop six feet in only three steps. When the construction was completed, George called for a christening ceremony. While several of us stood around, and one walked slowly down the steps into the pool, George intoned the benediction.

"One small step for man—one giant step for Hank."

Our five-foot-eight mentor was not present, of course, but Bill Walsh, our line coach, was. I watched him try to fight back a grin, out of loyalty to his boss, then give up and burst into laughter with the rest of us.

To most of his teammates George seemed a happy idiot—uncaring about anything serious, immune to both the pain of training camp and any commitment to his career. But George's antic behavior was a mask that hid the hurt of his disappointment. No one hated training camp more than George. No one suffered more in the obstacle course, the wind sprints, the drills and weights and mile run. No one desired any more deeply than George to be playing regularly—to be respected as a first-rate football player and a valued member of the team—or realized more fully the frustrations of being owned. No one understood more clearly than George the brevity of football careers and their inconsequence in establishing lifelong security. All the time he was playing the clown for the entertainment of his teammates, George was also establishing himself in business away from football, preparing for the future. George Daney was a fool like Shakespeare's fools—one of the wisest of us all.

George Daney, Jack Rudnay, Ed Budde, Mo Moorman, Jim Tyrer, Dave Hill—these were anonymous linemen to much of the public, to nearly all of the public outside Kansas City, but they were the human center of the Kansas City Chiefs for me.

Also Sid Smith, Larry Gagner, Francis Peay, Wayne Walton—others like myself and George who did not start but were part of the family.

Professional football was much more businesslike and less emotional than football at any other level at which I competed. But ironically, professional football was more genuinely personal, too. For one thing, I lived with these men more fully than with any other group of teammates. For four years we lived together nearly twenty-four hours a day for six weeks in training camp, then spent six hours a day together during the week and longer on weekends for three and a half months during the regular season. I was not a student during these many weeks; even if I read during my off hours with an eye to my return to graduate school once the season ended, I was first and foremost a football player for these months, sharing with my teammates the hopes and frustrations of a long season.

But I did not just spend more time with my teammates in Kansas City than I had at Notre Dame or in high school. My relationship to them had fundamentally changed. As a professional I was much less self-absorbed than at any time previously. Football had become much more a game I played with others. The implications of my being paid for playing made the game itself not mean as much, but those "others" meant comparably more. Playing football in high school and college, I was caught up in *abstractions:* toughness, courage, self-worth, personal identity. Playing football in Kansas City I was much more consumed by the physical actuality of the game. Aches and pains were not tokens of anything; they were aches and pains. Victories were not symbolic triumphs, but events that moved us closer to the playoffs. Playing or not playing, winning or losing, signified much less to me than they ever had before. They were simply the facts of my existence. In this new football world, I was less obsessively aware of myself, and more aware of my teammates as people. They were not obstacles to my desires, heroes to be emulated, competitors to be beaten out or humiliated if I could. They were human beings, with personalities and temperaments, vices and virtues, hopes and fears of their own. I knew something of their lives off the field. They had wives and children perhaps; some were deeply committed to their families, others chased women and stayed away from home as much as they could. Some I did not like, most I did, but all shared something in common. They were human. And I was more fully aware of their humanity than I had been with any of my groups of teammates in the past. I was less successful as a player in Kansas City than I had been in high school or college, but I gained something important in exchange for personal success—a fuller appreciation of the men I played with.

My exit from the Chiefs was not a pleasant one, coming as it did during the players' strike. My last training camp—in the summer of 1974—was the strangest one of all. The players' contract with the owners had expired at the end of the 1973 season, but virtually no progress had been made in negotiating a new one before the opening of training camp. The Players' Association had presented a list of sixty-three demands to the owners in March, and the owners had responded very cleverly. They released it to the press. What had been intended as an extreme bargaining position to be compromised in the course of negotiations appeared to the public as a series of outrageous demands by greedy prima donnas. We were demanding $25,000 per man for the Super Bowl winners, up to $3000 a game for preseason pay, a $20,000 minimum salary. We wanted something called "adjustment pay": on retirement a player would receive up to $5000 for each season he had played, to help him adjust to the outside world through education or investment in a business. We demanded the elimination of the option clause, the waiver system, the compensation clause, the standard player contract, all fines, and the commissioner's authority over the players—the entire system built up over fifty years. We were trying to destroy the league, it appeared.

We never had a chance with most of the press. The owners had bought much goodwill over the years, through cooperating with reporters covering the teams, and by lavishly entertaining them during Super Bowl week. The relationship between players and reporters, on the other hand, was an uneasy one under the best of circumstances. The players resented the newspapermen's ivory-tower judgments. The reporters responded with their own

contempt for overpaid, overpraised, and undereducated boors.
Without the support of the press, we could expect little from the
public. The owners scored early and big by publishing our
demands—in violation of proper bargaining protocol, of course
—and then sat back to try to break the union.

When training camp opened in July in Liberty, the Kansas
City Chiefs stayed home. For me, the decision to strike had not
been a pleasant one, but it had been easy. Throughout the
spring I had thought about the implications. Hank Stram had
even called me one day, to remind me that Mo Moorman had retired at the end of the previous season.

"You'll have a great opportunity to win that right guard spot,"
Hank told me. "You've been telling me for years that you
wanted a chance to play. Now you have it, if you come to
camp."

However much my selfish interest lay in reporting to camp, I
could not betray the union that was fighting for me, and the
players who were risking their own careers for the sake of our
collective welfare. Several of the sixty-three demands indeed
looked preposterous, but what was truly at stake in the strike
was not. Football players in the NFL had the lowest salaries and
benefits and the least power among athletes in any of the major
spectator team sports. We were demanding monetary increases
—in minimum salary (from the current $12,000 for rookies,
$13,000 for veterans), preseason pay, per diem, and playoff pay;
and in contributions to our pension and insurance funds—starting our demands high, to have something to give away at the
bargaining table. Any labor union negotiated such matters as
these. But our more serious demands were for *freedoms*. We
wanted our contracts to be binding on the clubs as well as on us
—particularly in the case of injured players, who currently were
paid their salaries only for the year in which they were injured,
not for the duration of the contract. We wanted veterans after a
certain number of years in the league to have the right to veto
trades. We wanted more rights for waived players—for example,
a guaranteed salary if they made the team but were cut in midseason, and the right to negotiate a new contract with another
club after being cut. We wanted to abolish above all else the
"Rozelle rule," which gave the commissioner the absolute right

to compensate a team for losing a free agent to another club— the policy that had made free agency in professional football a virtual impossibility. And we wanted impartial arbitration in resolving disputes between players and management. Pete Rozelle was the sole arbitrator in such cases—a man hired and paid by the owners, whom the owners in fact had just rewarded with a ten-year contract for a reported two hundred thousand a year. Could this man be fair to the players?

The players were willing to negotiate even these "freedom" issues. I became unbearably frustrated at times when I saw how the press and the public perceived the striking players. I wanted to ask every workingman, "Do you think it fair that the salary of the man who decides on any grievance you have with your employer is paid by your employer? Do you feel that football players should have *no* control at all over where they work, and that injured players should not be somehow protected? You have workman's compensation and unemployment benefits; aren't we entitled to anything at all?"

But as striking football players we found ourselves in an anomalous position. We were middle-class individuals using working-class tactics to increase privileges it was generally perceived we already had in excess. We were not striking for a living wage, but for greater luxury. The fact that the owners were making exorbitant profits was immaterial; in fact, through clever bookkeeping they could claim their real profits were much lower than in fact they were. We players were the spoiled ones. How could someone making fifty thousand dollars a year expect any sympathy from the teamster making eighteen, who already had to dish out ten dollars to watch us play? The only salaries the public knew about were the well-publicized ones made by Joe Namath, O. J. Simpson, and other superstars. But if Joe Namath was making four hundred thousand a year, forty-one players had to make the teamster's eighteen thousand to produce a league average of twenty-seven thousand.

When training camp opened, I flew back to Kansas City to take part in the strike. Clyde Werner and I slept on the living-room floor of my grandfather's one-bedroom apartment, eating as cheaply as possible at local cafeterias. We practiced with the other striking vets at a local public park, running through plays,

doing drills and wind sprints and distance running to stay in
shape, but certainly not driving ourselves as we would have
been driven had we been in Liberty. When Ed Podolak, our
player representative, returned periodically from Washington to
report on the negotiations and the state of the strike, we met to
discuss the issues. We did not select our meeting places wisely,
however. One session was held at a nightclub owned by Dave
Hill. We chose a quiet corner in the early evening before the
place became busy, but still our discussions were much more
public than they should have been.

What Ed reported and what we read in the papers did not en-
courage us. The owners, in refusing to negotiate on any of the
freedom issues, seemed determined to break the union, and the
players were making it easier for them. All of Kansas City's veterans but two had honored the strike. Wilbur Young had just negotiated a lucrative contract for himself, in which he agreed not
to strike. And Jim Kearney apparently was unwilling to risk the
livelihood of his large family. But around the league, support for
the strike was not everywhere so strong. In Cincinnati, Paul
Brown, the Bengals' owner, had renegotiated most of his key
players' contracts. As a result, twenty-five of the forty-two veterans went to camp. In Miami, a similar situation prevailed; we
read in the paper the comments of one Dolphin player attacking
the union as he returned to camp—the same player who we
knew from other sources had just signed a contract for a hundred thousand a year. "I got mine, so screw you," was his basic
sentiment. An all-pro offensive tackle in Dallas announced in the
press that he had prayed for several days, and the Lord had told
him that his duty was to go to camp. Did the Lord have anything to do with the contract which we knew he had just negoti-
ated for a huge raise? As the strike continued, more and more
players around the league caved in. Had we supported the walkout 100 percent, the owners would have been forced to settle,
and would probably have done so after a few weeks at most. Instead, it dragged on into the preseason, the players' position
becoming increasingly weakened as more and more defected.

The Chiefs' preseason opened on August 5 at Arrowhead with
a team of rookies. The striking veterans set up picket lines just
outside the stadium gates, and passed out pamphlets to the fans

who drove up. We had hoped the fans would stay away altogether in support of our cause; we wanted those who came to at least see our side of the dispute. We had read in the paper that a poll by the Milwaukee *Journal* revealed that 88.7 percent of its readers sided with the owners, and that another poll by a radio station in Worcester, Massachusetts, reported 83 percent on the owners' side. The media exert a great deal of influence in such ways. It was not until after the strike had collapsed that a Harris poll—much more reliable—revealed that over 50 percent supported the players. It is difficult to know how much the earlier misrepresentation eroded player strength and reinforced owner rigidity in the strike.

Most of the drivers accepted our offered pamphlets in silence and drove on. Some mumbled words of support, but many kept their windows tightly rolled up, and a few more aggressively and angrily refused our handout.

"What the hell do you guys have to complain about? How much do you make anyway?"

"Why don't you quit your crying and go back to work?"

"You guys give me a pain. Hell, if I made what you do, I'd take it and be damn grateful."

It was difficult to remain silent. To become angry would defeat our purpose in being there, but attempts at calm explanation were rebuffed. One driver rolled his window up with angry jerks as I tried to talk to him; another hit his accelerator to spurt ahead out of earshot. The real issues in the strike were clear to me and reasonable: some basic protections and freedoms that every worker in the country was entitled to. But much of the public saw only greed.

After forty-five days and two preseason games, the players' executive council announced a "cooling-off period." The veterans would report to camp for two weeks, during which time greater effort would be made to reach a settlement without the hostility of picket lines at games. In fact, the association was beaten. Anxiety about careers had undermined the players' resolve. As the ultimate team game, football is less dependent on individual players than basketball or baseball, and the basic insecurity that is part of the players' lives drove many back to camp. Each year 23 percent of the veterans fail to make the team, and in 1974 many players feared they would be included in that number. The owners had been hurt by a loss of 50 percent in attendance in the first two games, but the players stood to lose much more. The erosion of support within its own membership had made the positions of still striking players increasingly precarious. Several name players had been conspicuous strikebreakers. Mike Curtis, the Colts' all-pro middle linebacker, had announced back in June that he would not strike. Quarterbacks Bob Griese, Terry Bradshaw, and John Hadl had given up on August 5. In all, 427 of the 1300 players in the league had defied the strike, whether out of fear, greed, or principle. Rather than see the strike force dwindle away to an embarrassing remnant, Ed Garvey and the players' own elected officials decided on the "cooling off." With my fellow Chiefs, I reported to William Jewell College on August 14, nearly four weeks into training camp.

Hank Stram greeted us positively. He was subdued, but seemed determined to be upbeat. He had taken the strike as a personal betrayal: by not reporting to camp we had been disloyal to him. But he had to salvage the season now, and he would make the best of it.

"I'm glad you're back," he told us at our first team meeting. "What's past is done and it's time now to play football. There's one thing the strike has proved. The Kansas City Chiefs are a team; we play as a team and we strike as a team. But we're here to play football now, and we have a lot of catching up to do. Let's forget the past few weeks and go to work."

This was Wednesday. We had a game with the Rams in L.A. on Saturday, three days away. Hank left a couple of assistants in Liberty with us to run practices, and took the rookies to Los Angeles. On Saturday night I watched the game on television at the corner bar in Liberty with a group of my fellow veterans. It felt odd to watch strangers in *our* uniforms on the screen, while we drank beer and played shuffleboard at half time. But it was also satisfying to see the rookies drubbed by the Rams' veterans by a 58–16 score. We were not disloyal. These were not our teammates, but rookies trying to take our jobs—who had been given a great advantage in being allowed to play all of three games without the veterans present. Now that we were back in camp, we were fighting for our careers.

The rest of training camp felt slightly unreal—like a dream that seemed very true to life but was just a little bit strange in ways I could not put my finger on. Here was a training camp without the exhaustion and the endlessness. Here was a training camp in which I hung out with the older veterans in the evening at the corner bar, not with the younger players at the pizza place. Tension hovered in the air. I felt a closeness to players I had had little to do with before, but virtually no connection to the rookies and something strained in my relationship to the entire coaching staff. Here was a training camp in which there was a starting position open in the offensive line. But here was also a training camp in which everything seemed up for grabs—including my place on the roster.

I had come to camp the previous summer feeling *too* secure. I wanted a chance to play, knew there could be no opportunity for me in Kansas City, but realized I was not liable to be traded. As a backup center I was only a marginal player, but I was necessary insurance in case Jack Rudnay was hurt, and I was also the only offensive lineman who could play all five positions in an emergency. With only three backup linemen, such versatility was valuable to the team. But this year I knew my position was not secure. A rookie free-agent center in camp was not very good, but anything seemed possible in this turbulent summer. Around the league, a number of shocking cuts and trades had already taken place. Bill Curry, the Players' Association president, had been cut by the Houston Oilers after supposedly flunking his physical exam. He was later signed by the Rams after passing an identical test. Kermit Alexander, an association vice-president, had been cut by the Philadelphia Eagles. Ken Reaves, Atlanta's player representative, was traded to New Orleans. In all, five union officials were waived, and two were never signed by other clubs. Coaches and owners around the league were sending signals to the players.

I did not start our first preseason game at right guard after returning to camp. I had expected to, because George Daney had been slightly hurt during the week, but just before game time Hank announced George would start. I played most of the game, however, when George reinjured himself. My opposition across the line was Charlie Krueger, a fifteen-year veteran at de-

fensive tackle I had watched play on television as a kid. Charlie
was at the end of his career, not nearly the defensive tackle he
had once been, but playing well against him encouraged me
anyway. Nothing much was said to me by any of the coaches
during the following week, as George continued to run with the
first team. Our next game was against the Cowboys in Dallas—
in that unnaturally still sauna of a stadium where I had hurt my
knee the year before and where I always felt snakebit. George
and I both assumed that he was to start, but just moments before we were to take the field, Hank approached me.

"You start at guard tonight, Mike. You played well last week
and you earned it."

I was not ready for this. I needed a few days of knowing I
was to start, to prepare myself mentally. I felt disoriented as we
took the field, and I played like it for the rest of the game.
Jethro Pugh gave me trouble all evening. Like Krueger, he was
near the end of a long career, but I made him look like the all-
pro he once had been. My chance to play had been dropped in
my lap and I fumbled it. I tried to tell myself that it was only
one game, but I knew that with a single game left in our abbreviated preseason the coaches would not be in a position to ex-
periment much longer.

My major concern had been over the right guard position,
where George and I, and a rookie, Tom Condon, were the candidates. But I was also more generally anxious about my survival
on the team. I had forfeited whatever personal loyalty Hank
Stram had felt toward me, there was another center in camp,
and I had failed to make myself indispensable at right guard.
On Monday after the Dallas game, a big cut was announced. I
listened anxiously to the list of names read off by the reporter on
television. Mike McDaniel, the rookie center, was among them. I
had been in McDaniel's position four years before, but I felt no
compassion for him now. For the first time that summer, I felt
secure again. Whatever should happen at right guard, I was still
necessary to the team as backup center. My ability to play all
the line positions and perhaps to start at guard increased my
value.

I reported to practice on Tuesday the most relaxed I had been
in weeks. I joked with Bill Walsh, who checked our weigh-ins,

dressed for practice, and chatted with teammates as we waited
for the meeting. At the proper hour, I filed with my fellow offensive linemen into our meeting room to look at films of St. Louis,
the week's opponent. I laughed with Jack Rudnay and George
Daney about something while we waited for Bill Walsh to appear, enjoying the fact that life had at last returned to normal.
Bill came in a few minutes late, and his first words were unexpected.

"Mike, Hank wants to see you."

Silence struck the room. There was no mistaking the import of
those words. Even if we had never heard them before, we knew
them well. They were the call of the Turk. Sitting near the front
of the room, I had to work my way around an obstacle course of
chairs to the door in the back. No words were said or looks
exchanged—just awkward silence until I was out of the room. In
Hank's office, our talk was brief, and one-sided.

"I've placed you on waivers, Mike. I've been trying to arrange
a trade for you but have not been able to work anything out. I'm
giving you your chance to play somewhere else now, like you've
wanted. You've made a fine contribution to the Kansas City
Chiefs. Good luck."

That was it. I mumbled a goodbye and walked out, still too
stunned to react. As I undressed at my locker, to put my civilian
clothes back on, my mind was suddenly flooded by things I
wished I had said.

"Why didn't you have the decency to call me into your office
before I got dressed for practice, weighed in, went to the meeting? Were you trying to make an example of me before the
others on the team? What do you mean you're giving me a
chance? You know as well as I that every roster in the league is
swollen after weeks without cuts. My chances of being picked
up anywhere are almost nil. Don't pretend you're doing me a
favor."

I was furious. I was bitter. I was hurt. I was dumbfounded.
The act made no sense to me. To leave the team with only one
center? How could he do that? I considered the possibility that
maybe I was just not good enough anymore—that after four
years having not made myself a starter, maybe I ought to be cut.
But I did not want to think about that. I was in my eighteenth

year of playing football and now my last memory was to be of bitterness and hurt. Of being cut. Of being told I was no longer wanted on the team. That my eighteen years had added up to zero. I called Julie and listened to her cry, then vilify Hank Stram. I told my grandfather, and called my parents and Julie's parents. They all said the same thing.

"It's not the end of the world."

However true, I did not want to hear a cliché. I did not want eighteen years of my life to end with a platitude. I flew home to Palo Alto, knowing that I had three weeks to decide what to do. Classes at Stanford would start then; I had one last class to take, Old English, before my coursework was done and I could concentrate on my dissertation. But something in my life was left unfinished. Eighteen years was a long time to do anything, but my football career had been lopped off short.

When the Hamilton Tiger-Cats called to offer a contract, I discussed with Julie the financial advantages of signing, and the problems of separation. She left the decision finally to me, and even if I thought I was torn, I knew what I had to do. After eighteen years of playing football, I needed to end my career by quitting when *I* was ready, not when someone who owned me said I was finished. I called Hamilton and said I'd play. There was something I still had to do before I could say goodbye to football.

PART FOUR

The End of Autumn

NINE

A Tragedy for Heroes

I LEFT THE CHIEFS on September 3, 1974, and retired after finishing out that season in the Canadian Football League. One of my teammates with the Chiefs left Kansas City the same time I did. But Jim Tyrer departed under very different circumstances. The Chiefs' Media Guide for the 1974 season summed up pretty clearly the differences between our two careers. In a brief biographical sketch, the team's director of public relations tried to encapsulate what was most notable in each player's background. About me, the guide said:

> Versatile performer, backup center and filled in at offensive guard several games last two seasons . . . Good specialty team player . . . Was on taxi squad in '70 but was activated the last game of the season . . . Has played regularly in every game behind veteran Jack Rudnay since '71 season . . . Outstanding blocker who can play center or guard . . . Was walk-on player (non-scholarship) first year at Notre Dame . . . Became starter mid-way of junior year . . . Taught English at Stanford the past two summers while working on his Ph.D. . . . Married and plans to teach after receiving doctors [sic] degree.

Little to report here, but Jim Tyrer's case was very different:

> Has been a Chiefs starter ever since his rookie year, 14 seasons ago . . . Named to two straight AFC-NFC Pro Bowls, '70 and '71 . . . Regarded as one of the finest offensive tackles in the game . . .

Named Consensus All-Pro in 1970 . . . Selected as AFL's Offensive Lineman of the Year by National Football League Players Association in '69 . . . Has been selected to All-AFL team and has
participated in Pro Bowl nine times . . . One of the most consistent
performers on the Chiefs squad . . . Was co-captain of team in '70,
'71 and '72 . . . College All-American at Ohio State . . . President
of his own company, Pro Forma, a merchandising firm and representative for various professional athletes in commercial ventures
. . . Married, four children.

No faint praise here. Jim Tyrer had truly been a great player—
one of the finest offensive tackles to have played the game. For
thirteen seasons—only one less than the team had existed—Jim
Tyrer had been at the heart of the Kansas City Chiefs. But he
had been slipping for the past couple of years, and at the beginning of his fourteenth, at the age of thirty-five, Jim had been
called into Hank Stram's office and given a choice: retire, or accept a trade to the Washington Redskins. Jim chose the trade.

The last time I saw Jim Tyrer face to face came moments
after his conversation with Hank. When he returned to his
locker, to clean it out as if he were just another rookie who had
failed to make the team, he betrayed no emotion. He said little
—muttered a few words to Dave Hill, accepted the farewells of
a handful of teammates, and left quietly. There was no slouch-
ing in his massive frame, no head hanging or nervous agitation.
In his eyes I had seen no shrinking of his giant stature, but just
faintly, more behind the eyes than in them, I had seen his hurt.
Or thought I did; perhaps I only imagined I saw what I knew
had to be there. Jim Tyrer had been a proud man, and he was a
proud man still. Whatever he felt deepest in his soul where only
he could see—and not avoid seeing—was closed off to the rest of
us.

The next time I saw Jim Tyrer was on telelvision. In Hamilton
we caught Buffalo TV stations, and one Monday night I
watched part of a Redskins game. The figure I saw on the screen
was the same Jim Tyrer I had known—and it wasn't. This one
wore a strange uniform—jersey and helmet a different shade of
red than the Chiefs wore, gold pants instead of white, strange
insignia on the side of the helmet. He stood along the sidelines,
noticeably gigantic even among his giant teammates as he had

been among us. But he was on the sidelines, not in the game.
After thirteen seasons as a starter, an all-pro, and a team captain, he was standing on the sidelines, waiting for fourth down
when he would trot onto the field with the punting team. The
television cameras never showed his face, but to me his back
spoke eloquently. It looked rigid, as if his skeleton were holding
in some desperate emotion by sheer force. It looked so lonely,
turning neither to the right nor the left, acknowledging no one
around him, standing like a lone sentinel. Protecting what?

The next I learned of Jim Tyrer was six years later. I had
heard a few rumors in the interim, mainly from Clyde Werner,
my old roommate and friend who continued to play with the
Chiefs for three years after I left. The rumors said that Jim was
having financial problems. One business had bankrupted, and no
other had fully redeemed it. Someone told Clyde that Jim had
had to sell his lavish home for a more modest one. Someone else
supposedly saw Jim in downtown Kansas City, attempting to
peddle Martha's—his wife's—furs to a dealer. Just rumors perhaps, nothing more. But when I picked up the newspaper on
September 16, 1980—six years and two weeks after Jim Tyrer
and I left the Chiefs under such different circumstances—what I
read could not be dismissed as rumor. What caught my eye first
was a familiar face—a photograph of a head I remembered well.
It was, after all, the biggest head on the team. The tight-lipped
smile and bushy hair were familiar, too. But the headline that
accompanied the photo could not have been any less appropriate,
matched with that particular photo. The line was cryptic, but
said it all: "Ex-Chief tackle Tyrer kills wife, self."

What makes a man kill his wife and himself? What *drives* a
man who had always seemed to place his four children first in
his life, who kept them in expensive private schools in bad times
as well as good, because he felt the public schools inadequate
for them—to leave these children orphans? Several possible explanations come easily to mind, too easily perhaps. His businesses had failed. First one company then another had collapsed, using up everything he had managed to save from
fourteen seasons of professional football. At forty-one years old

he was out of work, broke, heavily in debt, and unable to meet his financial obligations. Everything he had struggled for over twenty years—his home, his children's education, his own livelihood—was in jeopardy. There seemed no way out. Why not end all the misery with a gun to the head? It would be so easy. . . .

But why kill Martha, too? Depression over financial setbacks cannot account for the murder as well as the suicide. Perhaps Jim was jealous. Could Martha have been having an affair, and Jim discovered the truth and shot her? He was no longer a football star; perhaps he no longer held her interest in quite the way he once had. Had he vented his frustrations on her? Or had he been preoccupied with his financial troubles, neglected her, driven her to seek companionship elsewhere? Did friendship lead to more? Had Jim found out? Did the collapse of his marriage in addition to his business seem too much? Had the only solution seemed to be to kill both of them? Vengeance and despair?

But what about the children? How could Jim have left four orphans, one of them still in high school and two others not even that old. Seventeen years old, and eleven and thirteen. And the fourth, a sophomore in college, only nineteen. Jim's behavior was clearly irrational. Also violent. He had played a violent sport for more than half his lifetime. He had been a huge man who used his enormous body as a weapon against other people. He had hurt people with that massive helmeted head, had undoubtedly caved in a few knees, broken a couple of bones perhaps. He had become accustomed to violence, inured to violence. Violence had become simply a part of his life, but for the past six years his outlet for violent aggressions had been taken away from him. The violent tendencies he had nurtured for more than twenty years had not suddenly dissipated when he quit football. The violence was always there, just beneath the surface, waiting to be rekindled by the proper provocation. Killing his wife and himself had been irrational—call it "temporary insanity," caused perhaps by a fight with Martha. Just a routine marital argument, but Jim was under a lot of stress, was depressed by his financial difficulties. In a weak moment, his rage conjured up the violence lurking within him. It exploded in a murder and suicide.

But that explanation does not satisfy either—in fact it is perhaps the worst of them all. Jim Tyrer was not a violent man. And football violence is very different from murder and suicide. All three of the "explanations" are scenarios that come readily to the mind of anyone who has read potboiler novels or watched television. Simple melodramas of uncontrolled passion and its tragic consequences. Is the truth about Jim Tyrer present anywhere in any of them? Probably not. If Jim Tyrer had been simply depressed or jealous or irrational, his actions and feelings would not have followed patterns so neat as these. The depressed businessman, the jealous husband, and the irrational man of violence are not persons but figments of television melodrama. The truth of a human life is always more complex. Perhaps Jim was indeed depressed; many friends and acquaintances reported that this was so; maybe he was even jealous or "temporarily insane." But none of those descriptions can fully account for the violent end to two lives. Jim Tyrer was human, not a character in a soap opera. How can we understand what drove him to do what he did?

Anyone's life is a mystery to others, in many ways even to himself. Who can see himself so clearly, so objectively, so wisely, that he knows exactly who he is? And if knowing one's own self is difficult, how much more difficult is it to understand another's life? So we pretend. Armed with psychoanalytical and sociological knowledge, we explain more than we know. Out of the extraordinary complexity that is a human life, we isolate a few causes for certain behavior, classify them by familiar names, and claim to have explained why that individual acted the way he did. How should we classify Jim Tyrer? I guess we should put him in the category of men who were great football stars—who were all-state in high school, all-American in college, all-pro afterward—but who then killed their wives and took their own lives a few years after retirement. A rather small group that would be.

Jim Tyrer was the unlikeliest suicide-murderer to those who knew him. Among all the Chiefs I played with, he seemed the most responsible, the most controlled, the most conscientious and stable. He struck his other associates in football the same way. Len Dawson was astonished by what happened. "He was such a strong, stable guy," Dawson told a reporter. "He was a great family man. Doing something like this is completely contrary to his character." Hank Stram was equally stunned. "It's so amazing," Hank declared. "Jim was such a solid guy. He had his feet on the ground. He knew what he wanted and how to do it." Hometown friends and acquaintances shared the shock. The athletic director at his old high school called him a "great individual," and mourned, "It's hard to understand why this would happen." Dave Hill summed up everyone's feelings when asked why he thought Tyrer did it. "I have no idea. I have no earthly idea."

The external circumstances of Jim Tyrer's life offer little help. They read like a Frank Merriwell story. Jim was born in 1939 in Newark, Ohio, a town of 30,000 in the rolling hills of the Licking River valley, thirty-four miles east of Columbus. Newark in the forties and fifties when Jim was growing up was among the stablest and most conservative of communities. Having been founded in 1802, it was one of Ohio's oldest settlements, the destination of pioneers crossing the Alleghany Mountains to the promised opportunities of the West. First as the hub of the canal system between Lake Erie and the Ohio River beginning around 1825, then later as an industrial center after the first railroad connected the town with other commercial centers in the eighteen fifties, Newark had thrived for a century and a half, without boom or bust but steady growth. During Jim's childhood, the populace engaged in manufacturing, agriculture, and trade in balanced proportions that guaranteed economic stability. Two thirds owned their own homes; 40 percent had finished high school or gone to college; 98.7 percent were white. What the town's Chamber of Commerce says today was felt forty years ago as well: "This is a community for good living."

Jim grew up with his mother and father and a sister in this settled world. And he played football—as any big athletic kid in such Ohio towns inevitably would. First at Roosevelt Junior High then at Newark High School, Jim Tyrer established himself as a great athlete and citizen. He starred not just in football, but in basketball and track as well, and was a good student besides. When he expressed his interest in being a dentist, his friends teased him that his hands were too large. But large hands—and a comparably large body—made him a great athlete. He grew to six four, 240 pounds by his senior year, and was an outstanding two-way tackle on the football team. He was named All-Central

Ohio in 1955 and 1956, and All-Ohio in '56. In addition, he was second-team All-Central Ohio in basketball his senior year. He impressed his coaches and teammates with his attitude as much as his ability. When he was honored in 1970 as the first member of Newark High School's Hall of Fame, he was remembered as a "quality boy" and a "coach's dream" by his old mentors. A former teammate described him as a "terror on the gridiron, but meek as a kitten off the field." The sports editor of Newark's daily newspaper remembered him this way: "He was always friendly, and never too busy to shake hands and to wish everyone well. He was a gentleman always. And he played his games fair and square."

The drama of Jim's high school career did not take place entirely on the field or in the gymnasium. After one football game against nearby Marietta High School, a drunk driver hit Newark's team bus on its way home, pushing it over an embankment. The driver of the car was killed, and several of the coaches and players on the bus shaken up. But big Jim played the hero's role, if only in a small way. He managed to open the emergency door of the bus, and assisted his teammates and coaches out of the wreckage to safety. Right out of Frank Merriwell's playbook.

Tragedy struck closer to home during Jim's junior basketball season. While Jim was shooting a free throw in Newark's 58–54 victory over Lancaster to grab the Central Ohio League championship, his father was stricken by a heart attack in the stands, and died shortly afterward at a friend's house. The seventeen-year-old son was devastated, but he decided late the next day to play in that night's game against Mount Vernon, saying it would have been his dad's wish that he do so. Jim must have read the official Schoolboy Athlete Hero's Cliché Manual. His Wildcats won 68–62, as Jim scored 24 points and played outstanding defense in one of the best games of his career, before exhaustion forced him out of the game.

Jim's vices seem to have been minor, barely able to expose his feet as mere clay. He did get sick on the bus coming home from one football game—but after drinking six pints of chocolate milk, not a six-pack. He was an admirable sportsman, until his very last high school football game, from which he was ejected for fighting with another All-Ohio player from Marietta. This seems to have been virtually the only blemish on his career.

Pride, excellence, and dignity marked Jim Tyrer's life from his childhood on. At Ohio State, this pattern continued, as Jim became one in a long line of OSU all-American offensive tackles in 1960, his senior year. And the pattern continued on the Dallas Texans, and then the Kansas City Chiefs when the team moved there in 1963. Jim was drafted by the Texans just behind E. J. Holub and Bob Lilly (who signed with the Cowboys instead), and ahead of teammates Jerry Mays and Fred Arbanas in the first of the young team's big drafts that guaranteed its future. Tyrer was a franchise builder. His first year as an all-AFL performer was his second in the league, and he earned that honor for nine more consecutive seasons, and was eventually named to the league's all-time team. He played in the Texans' 20–17 AFL Championship victory over the Houston Oilers in 1962, professional football's second longest game. He played in the first Super Bowl ever, a 31–7 loss to the Green Bay Packers in 1967. He played in the Chiefs' rebound victory in Super Bowl IV, 23–7 over Minnesota. He cocaptained the team during my first three years as his teammate. He played in the first two AFC–NFC Pro Bowls ever held. He earned, in short, nearly every honor possible for an offensive lineman, gained the highest personal rewards, and shared in the loftiest team honors available. He rose as high as one can go in professional football.

Jim Tyrer's story has a familiar ring to it. Both in fiction and in fact, the same or a very similar story has been played out so many times that it has become as recognizable as the plot for a new crime drama on TV. Jim Tyrer was an All-American Boy, then a Big Man on Campus, then a Professional Football Star. But his six years after retirement do not go together with that image. His life became less public then; our information is more sketchy. Jim did not keep in touch with very many of his former teammates, or very often with those he did see. That special bond was broken; new ties would have to replace it. Jim involved himself with his family as he had done throughout his career. His four children—Tina, Bradley, Stephanie, and Jason—were the center of his home life. Their education was extremely important to him, worth the sacrifices for expensive private schools. Jim was a good football father to his older son, Brad, proud and supportive but never pushy. Brad in 1980 was a starting tight end as a junior at Rockhurst High School, following in his father's footsteps, but not dragged through them. Jim was active as a fund raiser for the Rockhurst Fathers' Club, and was a first-rate football coach for a local YMCA team—not an easy achievement for one who had become accustomed to excellence in his own long career. The Tyrers were churchgoers, and Jim even spoke at conferences of the Fellowship of Christian Athletes, urging high school athletes to thank God for their talent.

Martha was the perfect partner for Jim—as able, intelligent, and energetic as he was. She and Jim had been high school and college sweethearts, lovers in a classic wholesome romance. They began dating at Newark High School, then married in 1960, between Jim's junior and senior years at Ohio State. During the following school year, Martha was Sweetheart of the Year for Jim's fraternity. She graduated from Ohio State in dental hygiene, but gave up her own career for her husband and then for her children. She was an avid and knowledgeable football fan, a friend and counselor to other football families in Kansas City. She took active part in her sorority's alumni affairs in Kansas City and in Jim's fraternity activities. Her major interest outside the home was a group called Young Matrons for which she served as president in 1980. But her home was the center of her life. She devoted herself to supporting Jim in his career and to guiding her children through their school and athletic activities. "Mom always put all of us first," Brad said. She and Jim had outwardly lived a Barbie-and-Ken storybook romance and married life.

Martha paid the ultimate price as an athlete's wife. Football wives are too easily forced by the public's perception of them to become merely extensions of their spouses' careers. Martha Tyrer was a model wife to her husband, but in the end she became just an extension of his depression and despair. Martha Tyrer was the ultimate victim, as Jim was not. She was killed without an opportunity to prevent it. Her husband was the one who acted to the last, she the acted-upon. In a sense, Jim Tyrer is a symbol of all athletes who fail to adjust to their retirement. Martha Tyrer is a symbol, too—of the athlete's wife consumed by her husband's career.

Jim prepared for retirement. He tried to be a full-time businessman, starting his own company, Pro Forma, while he was still with the Chiefs. Maybe this was not a good idea for a business. Pro Forma was to represent athletes in landing endorsements and handling commercial activities. But how successful could such a business be in Kansas City, when the advertising center of the country was in New York and the television center in New York and Hollywood? Perhaps the company was doomed to failure. Next, Jim became a manufacturer's representative, but became quickly dissatisfied. He opened a tire business, but was little more successful. A mild winter killed the market for snow tires. He sold out. Three careers, three busts, leaving only debts, depression, and self-doubts. With Martha, he tried selling Amway household products. He told George Daney that he never gave his businesses a fair chance, pulling out too soon, before they had a reasonable opportunity to develop into something. Just days before the tragedy, he was asking old friends such as George and Dave Hill if they knew anyone looking for a "good man." How ironic. Jim had been the best there was as a professional football player for ten of the fourteen years he played. Now he was trying to convince some prospective employer that he was merely a "good man," as any out-of-work and minimally talented person would do. But he also wanted a starting salary of forty thousand. A scouting position had opened up with the Chiefs, but the twenty-five-thousand-dollar salary did not even tempt Jim. His standard of living had become fixed at the all-pro tackle's level. "I can't start there," was Jim's only comment about the scouting job.

In the days before the murder-suicide, Tyrer clearly seemed depressed to those who saw him. Fred Arbanas had lined up an opportunity to sell national accounts for the Yellow Pages, but Tyrer never showed up to take the test. He was a college graduate, but had been out of school for twenty years. He told Arbanas that he always did poorly on those tests; he was competing with kids right out of school, barely older than his daughter. His minister and friend at the Presbyterian church he attended detected paranoia and arranged psychiatric counseling. George Daney saw him on the Wednesday before the fateful Sunday. Jim was obviously down. He kept asking George how he looked; he was concerned about the forty pounds he had lost. They talked about football. Jim had continued his contact with the Chiefs' organization, buying season tickets, attending Chiefs' functions. That Sunday he took his eleven-year-old son, Jason, to the game in Arrowhead Stadium, won 17–16 by the Seattle Seahawks. Someone reported that Jim stayed afterward, wandering around the empty stadium before he went home. For the last time.

No one knows what passed through Jim Tyrer's mind between the end of the Chiefs' game and five the next morning. Son Bradley was awakened by a gunshot and by his mother's scream. Two more shots rang out as he hid under the bed for nearly an hour, thinking burglars were in the house. At five-fifty he ventured to his parents' room. There he found his mother and father both dead. Both shot. Bradley was seventeen years old—the same age Jim had been when his own father died of a heart attack suffered during a high school basketball game.

The police reconstructed easily what Jim Tyrer did the morning of September 15, 1980. The weapon was a .38-caliber revolver. He fired a first shot that missed Martha while she slept, then when she awoke and started to get up from the bed, Tyrer shot her in the head. He then placed the gun in his own mouth and fired a third time.

The police deduced *what* Jim Tyrer did, but are we any closer to knowing *why* he did it? His retirement from football cannot explain everything, but it offers at least a partial understanding. The image of Jim's last day that most haunts me is that lone figure wandering through that empty stadium after watching the Chiefs' game with Seattle. Arrowhead Stadium is an enormous place. On Mondays during the season, we ran around the ballpark on one of the upper concourses—two laps to a mile. The structure is a half-mile in circumference on the inside. Empty or nearly so, the stadium is particularly cavernous and lifeless—row after row of empty seats ascending away from a vast expanse of green carpet broken only by a white line every five yards. An empty stadium can be so utterly silent; the voices of the few maintenance workers and concessionaries that lingered on while Jim wandered through Arrowhead would have only accentuated the silence, the vast emptiness.

It is hard to imagine a place where one would feel more alone. On the desert perhaps, or stranded at sea. But within the bounds of civilization few places could be so lonely. I can imagine few places also, where one could feel smaller than in an empty stadium. To be almost the only person in an arena that seats 78,000—that contained nearly that many people just a short time before—must have made Jim Tyrer, all six and a half feet and an eighth of a ton of him, feel that he was one of the tiniest of creatures. Jim left no record of his thoughts as he wandered through the empty stadium in the coming dusk of a Kansas City autumn. Yet, could he have looked down on the field without remembering his own career lived out upon it only six years before? He had been one of the cocaptains on the team that played the first game ever held on that field. He had helped make the building of that stadium possible by being one of the best offensive linemen in football for eleven years before that first game in Arrowhead. On that field and others like it, he had spent much of fourteen years of his life—between the ages of twenty-two and thirty-five, when he was in his prime, when he was the fastest, the strongest, the most physically capable he would ever be.

He had played football on that field while 78,000 cheered him from the stands. He had been a giant then—made a giant not so much by his physical height and weight as by the adulation of those 78,000 fans who focused their attention on him. A little bit of every one of those 78,000 individuals was in him, swelling him so large that he and a handful of teammates filled that immense stadium with their presence. His name during introductions had brought loud cheers from the stands; his ability on the field had brought great respect from his opponents; his presence in the locker room had brought warm friendship from his teammates.

As Jim Tyrer looked down on that vacant field, could he have avoided comparing that time with his present life? It is impossible to know just how Jim Tyrer saw himself, but whatever he saw must have seemed a pale reflection of the man he had been when his life had centered on that strip of green carpet he looked down upon. His impatience with his businesses after football could have been caused by the vision of excellence he retained in his mind from his years of playing, and which he still demanded of himself. Friends he had visited recently had discovered Jim was still upset about his dismissal from the Chiefs in 1974. After having given thirteen years to the organization, Jim had seen his left tackle position handed over to a rookie, while he was given the choice of retirement or trade. Six years later that ingratitude still gnawed at him. As he looked down on the field where he had been a star such a short time before, from a vantage point at which he felt himself a diminished person, a failure, wouldn't Jim Tyrer have been painfully struck by the change in his life? Whatever specific problems were causing his depression—business failures, debts, unemployment, personal problems—could only seem greater when compared to the life he had lived just a few years before. That powerful awareness of his diminished life could well have driven his troubled mind to welcome self-destruction.

Jim Tyrer's was by no means the first sports tragedy in this country. Though not exactly part of an epidemic, his startling death was not unique. Whenever we read of the untimely death of a great athlete, we are more moved than by the same fate befalling an ordinary citizen. What a loss, we think; how appalling for one who had risen so high to fall so low. The early death of a sports hero is not just a death, but a "tragedy."

Professional football has seen eight players die on the field or from game-related injuries—all since 1948. Heart attacks dropped Stan Mauldin, Dave Sparks, and Chuck Hughes during games, and J. V. Cain in the middle of a preseason practice. The oldest was twenty-eight, the youngest twenty-six. Hughes died on national television in a game between Chicago and Detroit in 1971, while I was with the Chiefs. It seemed extraordinary to me that an athlete just a few years older than I, playing the same game in the same league—for a team, in fact, that we would be playing in a few weeks—could suddenly drop dead. Heart attacks were for burnt-out corporate executives, not young football players.

Two other NFL players, Mack Lee Hill and Melvin Johnson, died following surgery for minor game injuries. And two more, Howard Glenn and Stone Johnson, suffered broken necks on the field, dying within days. Mack Lee Hill, Melvin Johnson, and Stone Johnson all played for Kansas City—the Chiefs have been particularly prone to tragedy. All of the stricken men were in their mid-twenties.

Because none of these players was a star, their deaths were not mourned as intensely as they would have been had the athletes been greater players. Ernie Davis, on the other hand, the brilliant running back from Syracuse who won the Heisman Trophy in 1961 and died of leukemia in 1962 before playing a down in the NFL, was given a full-scale hero's funeral. Sports fans nationwide mourned Davis. *The New York Times* eulogized him as a "legend," *Sports Illustrated* saluted his courage, President Kennedy sent a message to be read at his funeral; the entire nation expressed shock and sadness and great respect for the dead football star.

More recently, the death of Brian Piccolo from cancer led to a book and a movie, *Brian's Song*, that moved readers and viewers all over the country to tears. And the death of California's all-American quarterback, Joe Roth, in 1977 after a three-year battle with malignant melanoma left West Coast football fans mourning the tragic loss of a fine young man and talented football player.

The deaths of great athletes such as Ernie Davis and Joe Roth are widely regarded as poignant tragedies. Young men stricken in their prime—deprived of years of glory and well-deserved rewards. Brian Piccolo and the eight who died on the field or from injuries incurred there seem tragic, too, but Davis and Roth simply more so because of their greatness. What a tragedy that such goodness and talent should be snuffed out so young, the public collectively mourns. Think what they could have accomplished had they only been given the normal human life span. Why is it that only the good die young?

I do not see Ernie Davis and Joe Roth as tragic figures, however. Nor Brian Piccolo, Chuck Hughes, Mack Lee Hill, Stone Johnson, or any of the others. But Jim Tyrer was. Davis and Roth died at the peak of their fame. Davis in particular was acknowledged the best college football player in the land, the star of the future in the NFL. His fame could rise no higher; if he had achieved everything expected of him with the Cleveland Browns, he would merely have sustained the plateau he had already achieved. Ernie Davis died without disappointing anyone, without fumbling in a big game or failing to rank among the top rushers in the league. Even more important, he died without growing old, without losing a step to his pursing tacklers, without suffering a crippling knee injury—without having to adjust to no longer being Ernie Davis, star running back. In a peculiar way, Ernie Davis' death was not tragic at all.

The British poet A. E. Housman wrote a poem a half-century ago called "To an Athlete Dying Young," that sums up the good fortune of men such as Ernie Davis and Joe Roth, who died at the peak of their athletic powers. "Smart lad," the poet calls the athlete who dies young, who does not merely become part of "the rout / Of lads that wore their honour out." Davis and Roth can never be numbered among the "Runners whom renown outran / And the name died before the man." Many ancient peoples routinely and ritualistically killed their kings in the prime of their life—because they believed that their own prosperity was tied to the vital health of their leader, but also because they wanted their kings to pass into the afterlife as still-vigorous heroes, not as dried-up old men. The king slayings were a religious ritual that recognized the advantage of an "athlete dying young." The ancient Greeks made this same recognition in a peculiarly open way. When a great hero was crowned with the laurels of his success and cheered by the appreciative populace, the people in the crowd would break into a chant: "Die now, die now, die now!" Everyone knew well the disillusionment that could so easily follow great achievement.

Athletes like Ernie Davis and Joe Roth are strangely fortunate in one sense. Ironically, by dying young they are spared awareness of their athletic mortality. What is *tragic* is Jim Tyrer deciding just six years after a glorious football career has ended, that life is no longer worth living. To have been all-pro one year, then less than a decade later to have been so depressed that suicide seemed the only option, is the essence of tragedy. Tragedy moves us because we see the mighty fallen low, because we recognize that success greater than we can ever hope to achieve for ourselves has not brought happiness to one who had it. To think of Jim Tyrer not at the moment when he pulled the trigger three times, nor at the moments of his glory with the Kansas City Chiefs, but in the years between those moments when he struggled with the loss of his greatness and could not accept himself as a lesser man—that is what is so haunting about Jim Tyrer's death.

The tragedy of Jim Tyrer is not unique. There was a disturbingly parallel case in another sport not quite ten years before Tyrer's murder-suicide. Bruce Gardner was a great pitcher at the University of Southern California. In a three-year career, between 1958 and 1960, he compiled a 40–5 won-lost record. In league games he was 18–1, with a 2.49 ERA—the best record of any West Coast pitcher since the nineteen thirties. In his senior year, the NCAA named him the best collegiate pitcher in the entire country. If that were not enough, Bruce Gardner was handsome, articulate, an outstanding student, and an excellent musician. He even played the lead in a USC dramatic production—the role of Joe Hardy in the play *Damn Yankees*, who sold his soul to the devil to become a major-league baseball star.

After graduation in 1960, Gardner signed a contract with the Los Angeles Dodgers. He could have signed out of high school with the White Sox for a fifty-thousand-dollar bonus but had been persuaded to go to college. At twenty-one, because he now had fewer years to give the Dodgers, he was less valuable, but he still signed for twenty thousand. In 1960 he pitched briefly with Montreal in the Dodger farm system before being drafted into the Army. The following year he was 20–4 at Reno in class C, but he injured his pitching arm in the service and aggravated the problem on his return to baseball. In the next two years he was 1–5 in Spokane; 10–4 in Great Falls, Montana; 1–2 in Salem, Oregon. I was an avid fan of the Spokane Indians, a Dodger triple-A farm team in those days, but I have no recollection of Gardner at all. Finally he was released by the Dodgers in 1964.

The greatest college pitcher in the country at twenty-one was washed up at twenty-five.

Bruce Gardner became successful at other careers outside baseball. He worked as a singer and pianist at night, performing some of his own compositions. He did well selling stocks and bonds until he grew disillusioned, then went into teaching. But he always talked about how much he wanted to play major-league baseball. He was still resentful of those who convinced him to pass up the White Sox' offer and go on to college. He talked continually to friends about baseball, baseball, baseball—about the major-league career he never had. The last job he held was as a physical education instructor and coach at Dorsey High School in the Los Angeles area. Even here he was successful. As coach of the junior varsity baseball team he won the league championship in his first season, and was liked and admired by his players. But on Monday, June 7, 1971, Bruce Gardner's body was found by a caretaker, sprawled between the pitcher's mound and second base on USC's Bovard Field, the baseball diamond where he had achieved his greatest glory eleven years before. He had a bullet hole in his left temple. In his left hand—his pitching hand—was a .38-caliber revolver, the same model Tyrer used. In his right hand was clutched his USC diploma mounted on a plaque. A few feet away lay another plaque—his award from the NCAA for being the best collegiate pitcher of 1960. His colleagues at Dorsey High School had had no warning that the always-smiling thirty-two-year-old teacher was planning anything desperate when he left school the previous Friday. They also discovered that he had filed his final grades before leaving, although school did not close until June 18. To the last, Bruce Gardner was conscientious and thorough.

A few of the particulars in Jim Tyrer's and Bruce Gardner's stories differ. Although they were born the same year and achieved all-American recognition in the same year, Tyrer was nine years older when he killed himself, Gardner was more successful in his careers away from sports, and Tyrer achieved stardom at the professional level, not just in college. But otherwise their tragedies are identical. And although I can recall no other athletes who committed suicide shortly after their careers ended, their tragedies should not be thought of as isolated instances of deviant behavior. Theirs are only extreme cases of a problem that faces all great athletes. Mickey Mantle, who has never been known as one of the more reflective, philosophical sports stars of our time, made some extraordinary revelations to two newspaper reporters a few years ago. Mantle had retired in 1968, after eighteen years as a Yankee, with a .298 lifetime batting average, 536 home runs, and automatic entry into the Hall of Fame five years later when he first became eligible. Yet, ten years after he left baseball, he was wondering aloud if he should have retired in 1964. For all that he had accomplished, he regretted not having a batting average over .300. And despite his continuing demand for public appearances and his financial success in a variety of enterprises, he still wanted to play baseball. "I just wish I could turn back the clock and be eighteen again," Mantle told one reporter. "I would even settle for twenty-seven." A few months later, he talked again about being out of baseball.

"I don't think I'll ever get over it. You get so used to being pampered and applauded all your life, and all of a sudden you're in your own living room watching somebody else get all that.

"Once you've had it, it's hard to forget. It's tough to realize you're through. I don't think anybody ever gets over it, and I can see how it can kill somebody."

What a chilling comment when we realize that less than a year and a half later it helped do just that to Jim Tyrer.

Mantle described a recurring dream that is so telling in its simplicity: "I still dream almost every night that I'm trying to make a comeback. . . . If I get a hit, I can't run to first base. They always just nick me."

Mantle's predecessor in center field, Joe DiMaggio, expressed a similar sense of loss. Marilyn Monroe, back from entertaining the troops in Korea, gushed to her husband, "Joe, you've never heard cheering like that."

"Yes," he replied, "I have."

Stardom was fatal for Jim Tyrer after a long professional career. It was fatal for Bruce Gardner after a spectacular college career. Such tragedies are particularly shocking and receive a great deal of public attention, yet every great athlete—and many not so great—faces the same problems to a lesser degree.

Athletics are a unique activity in our culture. In no other field
that engages large numbers of people must the participants give
up their involvement so young. No other activity creates such intense gratification and head-turning adulation so easily for so
many people. Yet no other activity takes away that gratification
and adulation so early, completely—and painfully. F. Scott Fitz-
gerald once said, "There are no second acts in American lives."
How true that is for athletes.

In sports the ordinary human problem of aging is intensified.
The George Blandas and Jim Marshalls, the Hoyt Wilhelms,
Gaylord Perrys, and Phil Niekros, seem to play forever. But the
fact is that the average career in the NFL is 4.2 years, and few
athletes in any professional sport play beyond thirty-five. In
1981, much was made of Craig Morton, the oldest player in the
NFC—at thirty-eight. Even Blanda, the oldest man ever to play
professional football, was only forty-eight when he retired—or
rather when he was forced to retire. At forty-eight, a businessman might be well established, looking forward to fifteen or
twenty more years before pensions and social security.

The athlete does not necessarily cease to be a productive citizen when he retires from his sport. He can go into any number
of alternative careers. But the major occupation and preoccu-
pation of his life, for which he has prepared himself through a
childhood and adolescence of developing his skills, and for
which he has committed himself intensely and risked serious injury over and over again—is suddenly taken from him. It is as if
an actor, after studying his craft for years and finally gaining his
opportunity on Broadway, were allowed a few years of acting
before he is forced to retire. But with age Olivier and Gielgud
continue on. They pass from leading men to the leading men's
fathers, but they continue to practice their art. They are not
forced to give it up—to find something else to do for which they
have considerably less talent and inclination.

The athlete's case is even less like that of other professionals.
The businessman does not make his decisions before 75,000
cheering or booing fans. When the lawyer blows a case, he does
not have 75,000 pairs of critical eyes, and millions more watching on television, judging his failure. When the doctor performs
a successful appendectomy, he does not have those seventy-five

thousands and those millions cheering wildly, and he reads no adulatory reviews of his surgical skill in the newspapers the next day. The professional athlete lives an intense existence, doing something difficult that few can do but many admire, feeling himself a special person—a hero. Then it is all taken away. Just like that.

After it was taken away from Jim Tyrer, he apparently never did find anything to replace it.

Retirement for many people in this country is a little death, a sort of prelude to the big death. For an athlete, that little death comes very early. The businessman who quits working at sixty-five has a life expectancy of seventy-two—seven years of retirement. Bruce Gardner had seven years of retirement, too. Jim Tyrer six.

If we think of a hero as an individual who embodies to a high degree the virtues and qualities most valued by his culture, and who serves as an ideal or model to ordinary citizens, it is clear that we live in unheroic times. Soldiers, politicians, millionaire capitalists—all have been perceived in former times as heroic individuals. But not today. When we look around for heroes today, we find mostly athletes. Big money is altering the public perception of sports, but for at least a little while longer, when we look for heroes, we will find Dr. J., George Brett, and Earl Campbell.

To the athlete playing football, the heroic stature of the game is one of its greatest appeals. I could not have invested football with such importance in my youth had I not been aware of the heroic qualities of the sport. Football heroes were a large part of my earliest awareness of football. Hoppy Sebesta, Billy Cannon, and Jon Arnett embodied the finest qualities I could imagine attaining. They were capable, courageous, tough, and talented—everything I wanted to be. The sport they played seemed a heroic activity—in which anyone who played shared in the greatness. In high school I heard my name yelled by cheerleaders; I stood on the field before my parents, friends, and classmates, proving myself worthy to represent them. In college, I read letters from grade-schoolers in Van Nuys, California, who followed everything I and my teammates did from two thousand miles away. I played on the same football field where Johnny Lujack, Leon Hart, and John Lattner had achieved a sort of immortality through their athletic excellence. In Kansas City, I started only one game in four years, but fathers and mothers approached me in restaurants to ask for my autograph for their sons, and 78,000 fans cheered in Arrowhead Stadium when I made a tackle on the kickoff team.

In the last ten years, many reporters who follow the game have reminded us that professional football is really just entertainment. That we should not take it seriously. Football players, they imply, are like movie actors. They put on a show that entertains huge numbers of people. They are vaudevilleans in shoulder pads, not heroes to be admired and emulated.

I think those reporters are wrong. I agree that more and more owners are coming to believe that professional football is simply entertainment, and I understand why the reporters who see the players' sometimes unpleasant human side are not inclined to think of them as heroes. But to much of the public that follows pro football, the players still have heroic dimensions. And the players are affected by the way the public perceives them. Professional football is a cutthroat business and a form of popular entertainment, but it is also a heroic activity. That basic contradiction is what complicates players' lives.

Football players entertain, but to much of society they are not mere entertainers. An entertainer is a celebrity; a football player can be a hero. A celebrity is famous for who he is, a football player for what he does. It's the difference between pretending and doing. John Wayne never fought in a war or cleared the bad guys out of a Western town. But football players have no stand-ins on the field. The bullets John Wayne dodged were fake; the tacklers O. J. Simpson dodged were real. And fans know the difference.

If athletes truly can serve as heroes in our culture, then two conclusions are inescapable. One, sports such as football can have a vital function that should be tampered with only with great care. And two, the football player himself is an extraordinarily privileged individual, but he also bears a potentially crushing burden. As to the first point, the more the owners and television networks package professional football as entertaining spectacle, the less it retains its connection to heroic sport. The essence of football's heroic element does not lie in elegant domed stadiums, flashing electronic scoreboards, and Las Vegas-type chorus-line cheerleaders. It lies in what the players do on the field—the runs and passes and blocks and tackles that demonstrate those qualities of dedication, courage, and almost superhuman physical ability that thrill the fans. As the games themselves become less the focus of the fans' attention than does the surrounding hoopla, professional football will indeed become more like mere entertainment. Super Bowl Sunday 1981 began with an hour-long review of the season and a two-hour pregame show, and concluded with an hour wrap-up. Nongame hours outscored the game, four to three.

In numerous little ways, the impact of the media on football in recent years has become increasingly obvious. Hank Stram's attention to how he looked along the sidelines and how we looked for the player introductions and national anthem are part of this. (Hank's transition to broadcasting seems particularly appropriate.) End zone dances after touchdowns are another case. The first of the dancers was a teammate of mine in Kansas City, Elmo Wright, a first-round draft choice in 1971 from the University of Houston, where he had earned the nickname "the Dancer" for his end zone antics after catching a touchdown pass. His technique was simple, more like running in place than dancing, but he infuriated opponents when he continued this as a rookie pro. An Oakland Raider defensive back broke Elmo's nose on one play, in what was obviously a deliberate response to one of his dances. Elmo had been dancing on the defender's grave after a touchdown; the defender was telling Elmo he was still alive.

Within a half dozen years Elmo Wright's simple dance had been adapted by half the running backs and receivers in the NFL into often elaborately choreographed routines. It was no longer dancing on the grave of the man you beat for a touchdown, but dancing before the television camera—to gain attention and perhaps some of the benefits that attention could bring. The television camera has become an incredibly obtrusive part of any football game. When I played, the standard response to seeing a television camera was to ignore it, not to indicate in any way that we were distracted from our serious purpose. Now the standard reaction is some kind of simple to elaborate performance. Thomas Henderson of the Dallas Cowboys was the most outrageous of the camera-conscious players in recent years. A camera pointed in his direction signaled it was time for *The Thomas Henderson Show*. During the 1979 Pro Bowl, when "Hollywood" Henderson was asked on the sideline why he carried on the way he did, he looked into the camera and said, "So that you'll want to talk to me."

Playing to the camera is not just egocentric behavior, but a conscious recognition that the camera creates stars—and stars get endorsements, acting jobs, and large salaries. Stars are celebrities, not heroes, but celebrities are paid better than heroes. This trend began while I was playing. Monday Night Football's rookie year was also my own, and it was striking to notice how much more intensely some people played before the prime-time TV cameras than on normal Sundays. Ed Podolak, my running-back teammate, announced in the locker room on one occasion that it was Monday Night, time for a big game. Stars were born on Monday Nights.

Professional football is moving in the direction of entertainment, but the transition is not yet complete, and football players who are aware of themselves as heroes face a peculiar dilemma. In four years in Kansas City, I felt heroic very rarely, but often enough to understand how it feels—and to suspect how it must have felt to the great players on the team. I shared with all my teammates the feeling of being conspicuously isolated on the playing field of Arrowhead Stadium, ringed by 78,000 fans who invested all their hopes and fears for the week's game in us forty Chiefs. I was only one of forty, but with 78,000 watching, and millions more at home, my share of the attention seemed large enough. I was also one of the forty who flew on chartered airplanes to distant cities, trooped conspicuously into first-class hotels while heads turned and jaws dropped just a little. We entered local restaurants in smaller groups, recognizable by our size as football players, by the insignias on our jackets as Kansas City Chiefs. Again heads turned to follow us; throughout dinner we were aware of a current of interest focusing on our table. We talked and laughed, ate and drank, self-consciously oblivious to our surroundings but aware all the time that we had become the center of much attention. At six five, 240, I was bigger than normal people anyway, but as a Kansas City Chief sometimes I felt gargantuan. At the rival stadium the next day, we walked from our team bus to the visitors' entrance through cordons of Charger or Raider or Bronco fans, looking us over with fear and admiration. In the stadium, they booed and jeered us, and widely cheered the home team—showing their respect for us by their hostility. Playing before a rabidly antagonistic crowd on the road could be as exhilarating as playing before supportive fans at home.

Simply by being a member of the team I shared in the acclaim, but the forty players were individual heroes to widely differing degrees. My own great moments on the field were infrequent and sometimes private. Even then, an outstanding play on one of the special teams that earned the fans' appreciation gave me a hint of what the great players on the team must have felt continually. To have been Otis Taylor leaping high over the outstretched finger tips of the cornerback to snag a long pass for a touchdown; to have been Willie Lanier flowing down the line of scrimmage stalking the ballcarrier, then meeting him squarely in the hole and driving him emphatically to the ground; or to have been Jim Tyrer blocking on play after play conscious of himself as the best in the game—to have been any of these men would have meant living an intensely exhilarating existence. To have heard boisterous cheering directed toward yourself time after time for ten, twelve, fourteen years would make it difficult not to believe you were truly a hero.

I glimpsed, too, the superficial reminders of heroic stature that great football players continually receive. Whenever a young boy asked me for my autograph, I signed reluctantly, knowing that he would most likely look at the name and be disappointed —reminding me of my marginal status on the team. Not so with the stars.

"Hey, there's Lenny Dawson!" one boy would call out to his buddies. "C'mon, let's get his autograph!"

Or, getting the signature of someone they did not recognize at first, they would suddenly light up when they read the name.

"Wow, Jim Tyrer! Hey, Jim, you guys were great against Oakland last Sunday!"

Such moments were insignificant in isolation. And signing autographs could become a nuisance. But no matter how much anyone claimed to be bothered by ten-year-olds with autograph books, the knowledge that all those kids out there *wanted* your autograph created an intoxicating feeling.

And not just kids. When you're a star, businessmen want to buy you drinks, the parents of your children's friends want to meet you and talk about football, men and women of all ages find you fascinating. Although it was difficult to *know* people in Kansas City, it was easy to meet them. Everyone, it seemed, wanted to meet a Kansas City Chief. If that Chief happened to be Len Dawson, Otis Taylor, or Jim Tyrer, all the better.

Professional football players—particularly great ones—can be rewarded and honored far beyond what their usefulness to society seems to warrant. People who object to the glorification of athletes in our culture are appalled by the salaries they earn, the recognition they receive, the privileged position they hold. But there is a catch. It's all taken away. One day you're a hero, the next you're merely human again. The retired football star does not become instantly anonymous. People still want to meet him, buy him a drink, talk about football. But he ceases to be a hero. He remains a celebrity for a few years perhaps, many if he is a Joe Namath or an O. J. Simpson. But he is no longer a hero—no longer doing what gained him his fame. He is the man approached by the kid, "Didn't you used to be . . . ?" He is famous for what he once did, not for what he is doing now, and that kind of fame becomes very hollow—ultimately meaningless.

As professional football becomes increasingly a business and a form of entertainment, the players may bear a reduced burden. The less they feel themselves to be heroes, the easier it will be to give up that feeling on retirement. But the players' gain will be the culture's loss: in a country with few heroes now, we may soon have fewer yet. And in another way, it will be the players' loss, too. As the game comes to mean less to them, the experiences of playing will be less rewarding. The pleasures and burdens of playing professional football walk hand in hand. It is ironic that one of football's greatest satisfactions can become its deadliest danger.

Jim Tyrer did not adjust. Why he committed murder and suicide while other retired athletes have not, we can never know for certain. But we can easily understand that Jim's heroic past had become a burden in his present, accentuating whatever problems troubled him. His great pride must have been wounded by his comparative failure; his privacy—fed by the code of individual toughness—gave his frustration no outlet.

Jim Tyrer never told me he felt like a hero while he was playing. Football players do not talk about such emotions, or most likely even think such thoughts while they are playing. To feel a hero is a *feeling*, not a consciously articulated response. But to have been as great a football player as Jim Tyrer was for so many years, and not to have felt an extraordinary specialness seems unlikely. Take that specialness away and substitute only setbacks, and self-destruction can follow.

Who's to blame? Not Hank Stram. His ultimatum—trade or retirement—made sense from management's perspective. Jim was not the tackle he had once been; the Chiefs desperately needed new blood in the lineup. The end of his career had to come some time; other coaches might have ended it sooner. Who's to blame, then? Himself? For not being strong enough after all to cope with his greatest challenge? Somehow weakness does not seem the proper explanation. Rather, Jim Tyrer was betrayed by his own strength and pride. When his pride had nothing to nourish it, it fed on himself. It devoured him from the inside out.

If Jim Tyrer was a victim, he was the victim of an entire culture. He was driven to suicide by all his coaches and teammates and athletic directors and school principals; by the millions of fans who watched him play, the little kids who begged for his autograph, the reporters who interviewed him, and the friends who praised him. The entire society that idolizes football players and takes them for its heroes helped kill Jim Tyrer.

Yet to leave it at that reduces Tyrer to a helpless victim, and his murder-suicide to a simple matter of villainy triumphant. This does not explain the event. Jim Tyrer's death was *tragic*. He was not a passive victim of a cruel societal force, but a great man betrayed by pride in his own greatness. His death moved the public in ways that the deaths of other individuals would not have. Had a shoe salesman or an accountant or a university professor killed himself and his wife under similar circumstances, we would not have reacted with such shock, such pity. But Jim Tyrer was a great man brought low. He gave pleasure to millions of football fans for many years—the pleasure of seeing excellence achieved in an extraordinarily difficult art. He gave football much, and football gave him much in return. Then it was all taken away when he was thirty-five years old. Jim Tyrer died of a rare ailment to which shoe salesmen, accountants, and university professors are immune. Jim Tyrer's violent death was a tragedy reserved only for heroes.

TEN

Adjusting

THE DEATH of Jim Tyrer shocked a lot of people into recognizing the problems of ex-athletes. The general public had seemingly assumed that all former players went on to coaching, telecasting, selling insurance, or making Lite Beer commercials —living the good life off their football earnings. But sports reporters began uncovering a number of startling stories. It turned out that Carl Eller, less than a year after completing a glorious sixteen-season career, was bankrupt. Jim Otto, the Oakland Raiders' center and Chiefs' old nemesis, was now a cripple incapable of working. After playing in 210 consecutive games (a league record), despite seven knee operations, Otto had been forced to retire in 1975. Only six years later he had one artificial knee, was awaiting another, and was unable to dance, jog, play tennis—or even walk without pain. He sold his ranch because riding a tractor hurt too much. But he regretted nothing, he claimed. He had loved the game and still did. He spent his time now watching his son, Jimmy, play high school football. "He plays reckless, just like me," Otto said proudly. Poor Jimmy. Poor Jim.

Ray Didinger of the Philadelphia *Daily News* took a long searching look at ex-athletes in America in 1981 and found some unnerving cases. The problem, he pointed out, was not a new one. Jim Thorpe, the greatest athlete of his era—some claim of all time—went from Olympic gold-medal winner and pro baseball and football star to alcoholic, barker in sideshows and dance halls, and dollar-a-day laborer, before dying penniless in 1953. Babe Ruth, the Sultan of Swat himself, became an embarrassment hanging on the fringes of baseball, playing sandlot exhibitions and batting phosphorescent baseballs into the audience at Coney Island. Sideshows, dance halls, and Coney Island have captured some nostalgic interest in recent years, but there was nothing charming or quaint about them for the great athletes who had to peddle their dying names in order to survive.

The settings and names have changed, but the problems of many ex-athletes today remain the same. Don Newcombe, the great Dodger pitcher of the fifties, had to fight through alcoholism and business failure before he regained an even keel after several years out of baseball. Denny McLain was the best pitcher in the game in 1968 and 1969. Arm troubles forced an early retirement and brought on several years of drifting and unsuccessful attempts at selling real estate and playing the organ in cocktail lounges, before he reestablished himself.

Professional football has left a striking number of similar cases:

Lenny Moore, the great Baltimore Colt runner and receiver of the fifties and sixties—a Hall of Fame inductee who scored more touchdowns than any player in history except Jim Brown—was forced to retire in 1967. In the following eight years he worked one season as a color commentator for CBS but was not retained, picked up a few dollars making personal appearances, borrowed money to open a cocktail lounge which quickly folded, and did a series of TV spots for army recruiting—before he was finally hired by his old team as director of promotions.

Duane Thomas, my former teammate on the College All-Star team, had a couple of great years with the Dallas Cowboys in the early seventies before his problems with management cut short his career. Now, he borrows money to pay his bills and dreams of striking it big in business or the movies—of being a "star" as he had been earlier. But he is unable to hold more routine jobs with more modest salaries.

Ernie Holmes was a key member of Pittsburgh's "Steel Curtain" defensive line during the Super Bowl years. Problems with alcohol and guns cropped up even while he was playing. He was traded to Tampa Bay in 1978, claimed on waivers by New England, then cut by the Patriots in 1979. After that, nothing but hard times: a series of short-term jobs, an unsuccessful café in his hometown, an attempt to take up professional boxing at age 32. He sits by the phone, waiting for a call from the NFL that will save him at least for a short time—but which never comes.

For John Reaves the phone did ring. The former all-American quarterback for the University of Florida found little success in the NFL with Philadelphia, Cincinnati, or Minnesota. He became despondent and irrational, took to mixing drugs and liquor, and ended up in a drug rehabilitation center after threatening three persons' lives. Following his release by the Vikings, he failed to catch on with any other NFL club, but could not accept life as a real-estate salesman. "He saw himself as a football player," his wife explained. "That's why now he must think of himself as a failure." When Ken Stabler temporarily retired in the summer of 1981, the Houston Oilers invited Reaves to camp. He went thinking he'd been reborn. In truth, his "death" had only been delayed a little longer.

Finally, Jack Concannon. All-American quarterback at Boston College—four years as backup with the Philadelphia Eagles— five pretty good years in Chicago—brief stints with Dallas and Green Bay before retirement in 1974. Then a failed bar business, foreclosure on his house, repossession of his car, and arrest for allegedly selling cocaine to an undercover narcotics agent. The ultimate irony: while Concannon awaited trial in prison, the guards would shove slips of paper through the bars, asking for his autograph.

These are just five cases, none as tragic as Jim Tyrer's but all indicative of athletes who failed to adjust to the end of their careers. These five represent many others. A counseling psychologist who works with the NFL Players' Association reports that there are "literally hundreds of these ex-players wandering around, helpless, bewildered, with no real prospects for the future." Unfortunately, a few of my former teammates with the Chiefs must be counted in that number. A former first-round draft choice, whose career was abbreviated by knee injuries, years later is still hanging out in gyms back in his hometown, playing basketball, vainly hoping for a comeback so that he can do the only thing he knows and that means anything to him.

A former starter who played nine years in Kansas City and elsewhere is now refereeing recreation-league basketball games, and trying to hold on until he qualifies for his NFL pension.

A former all-pro, wanting to stay on as a coach, was not even interviewed by the Chiefs when a position opened up. No other team would talk to him either. He did take that scouting job that Jim Tyrer wouldn't consider, but he will pay for it with endless travel and with feeling himself on the outermost fringe of the football world—the world in which he was not so long ago the greatest at his position.

That's the bad news. The good news is that the Kansas City Chiefs of the early seventies were an exceptional group of athletes. Many of my former teammates have been remarkably successful in developing their lives after football. Among the offensive linemen, Dave Hill is currently in the wholesale car-auction business, Ed Budde is a sales manager for a beer company, Mo Moorman has a beer distributorship in Louisville, George Daney sells specialty advertising and promotional items, and E. J. Holub is foreman of a ranch in Oklahoma (only Jack Rudnay is still playing). Obviously a wide variety of careers have taken the place of football in their lives, and in the lives of other ex-Chiefs. Len Dawson continues in the public spotlight as a color commentator on network football telecasts; Mike Adamle, a Chief in 1971 and 1972, has also found a career in television. Willie Lanier works for a stock firm in Richmond, Virginia; Jim Lynch is a partner in a food brokerage; Buck Buchanan and Bobby Bell own and manage restaurants; Emmitt Thomas is in coaching; George Seals, a defensive tackle with the Bears who finished out his career in Kansas City in 1972 and 1973, holds a seat on the Board of Trade in Chicago. And so on. Linebacker Bob Stein is an attorney in Minneapolis, defensive end Marvin Upshaw sells real estate, cornerback Kerry Reardon is a partner in a construction company, linebacker Caesar Belser is an executive for Southwestern Bell, kick returner Larry Marshall is in the retail liquor and grocery business, my old roommates Sid Smith and Clyde Werner are in housing construction in Houston and wholesale paper sales in Oregon respectively. It is ironic that the same team that has seen four of its players die unnaturally should be so successful in making the transition from football to the outside world.

To find new employment is not the sum of adjustment to retirement from the NFL. Jim Tyrer tried a variety of jobs in the six years after he left football, but when they did not measure up to his expectations, he abandoned them. Financial security is certainly the major immediate concern of any retiring football player. Some move into other careers in which the financial return is greater than their football salaries, but these cases are exceptions. For most, leaving football means at least a temporary cut in pay, perhaps a permanent one, and consequently an adjustment to a lower standard of living. Football players tend to be conspicuous consumers. Elegant cars, lavish homes, expensive clothes, and entertainment create an image that many athletes like to project. A certain casualness or carelessness with money —a willingness to spend freely in bars and to lose cavalierly at poker—is also cultivated by many professional athletes. Players can become competitive with each other in their buying. Salaries are indications of players' value; cars and clothes are indications of the size of salaries; buying extravagantly becomes a way of proving your value as a football player. Wives can be infected with such ideas also. At home games in Kansas City, the wives sat in a single section, where their husbands had their complimentary seats and where the wives could check each other out from week to week. Julie used to report to me after games on the mink-and-diamond derby that took place in the stands. Unable to compete, Julie assumed the opposite role, wearing Big Mac overalls instead of designer originals. But no matter how much we told each other the money was not important to us, we could not remain completely immune to the attractions of luxury. When I signed my contract in 1973 for $27,000, $30,000, and $33,000, we began to realize that we, too, might begin to have money crying to be spent. Being cut after the first year of the contract spared us (?) that particular burden.

An extravagant lifestyle may be affordable on a player's salary, but not on his nonfootball pay. Unfortunately, expensive tastes and habits do not immediately disappear with the exit from football. The ex-football player might feel poverty-stricken on a twenty-thousand-a-year income. Worse, he also might feel personally diminished by his lower salary. If he has developed a scale of professional importance based on the NFL's salary structure, a drastic reduction in pay on retirement can seem like a reduction in his human worth.

The quality of the job the retired football player finds is dependent on many elements. Lack of a college degree—the case for 70 percent of NFL players—obviously is a handicap. Employers may welcome the opportunity to buy the athlete a drink and talk football to him, but they will hire him only if he is qualified for the job. Whether the player works to establish himself in the off seasons while he is still playing can be another critical factor. To wait until retirement at age thirty or thirty-five, then to have to compete with twenty-two-year-olds fresh out of school for entry-level positions, can be a disheartening experience for the athlete who has become accustomed to thinking of himself as a talented and highly qualified professional. The football player's public image can actually work against him. The image of the wonderfully talented athlete attracts many people—including prospective employers—while he is playing, but the football player is also stereotyped as a not-very-bright fellow who can do one thing supremely well, but nothing else. If he does nothing to counter this image while he is playing, he may have few opportunities to prove it wrong when he retires.

Although employment with financial security is the most obvious concern of the retiring athlete, in many ways it is not the most important part of his transition from football. Psychological adjustment can be extremely difficult. The ex-athlete who finds himself in a career that is less challenging, less rewarding, less satisfying than football will find the loss of his athletic career painfully difficult. As my own experiences attest, playing professional football is by no means a uniformly pleasant experience, but it is an exceptionally intense one—much more intense, most likely, than anything a player will do afterward. The football player has higher highs and lower lows than individuals in more ordinary jobs. No employee feels so owned as the football player does, no physical labor is so brutal as training camp, no job is so insecure as a professional football player's. But on the other hand, in what other fields are workers so honored, rewards so immediate, or successes so clear-cut and intense? Within the corporate structure of NFL clubs there is the game itself, offering a unique and rewarding experience.

Most careers involve doing the same thing day after day. In the football player's life there is variety within sameness. The rhythm of the football season is as predictable as the cycle of the seasons in nature. Football begins in summer, with six to eight weeks of training camp in which a mass of hopeful players are tested and sifted and molded into a team of forty (or forty-five) men. With the approach of autumn comes the season itself—fourteen games when I played, sixteen now, in which twenty-eight teams in six divisions jockey for position to be eligible for the playoffs at the season's close. With the end of fall, eighteen teams go home for the winter, while the surviving ten work through three rounds of eliminations, culminating in the Super Bowl in mid-winter. Then comes a period of rest, followed by rejuvenation in the spring preparatory to a new beginning of the cycle the following summer.

Within this overall cycle, the three main phases—preseason, season, and postseason—have their own rhythms. Preseason begins in agony and ends in unity—through the weeks of double workouts, practice games, and the sequence of cuts that take place on a regular basis. The beginning of league games brings a new rhythm. In the course of fourteen or sixteen games any number of patterns can emerge. Sustained excellence by a perennial winner or futility by a consistent loser or ups and downs of all varieties are conceivable. The possibilities are countless, but the patterns are recognizable to the players involved. Few surprises can be totally unexpected—they occur within a range of foreseeable possibilities. Whatever happens has happened many times before. Similarly, for the postseason, in which the weaker teams, or the unluckier or less hungry ones, fall away one at a time until only two, then one emerges as the best of the twenty-eight. Each year the outcome is different, but the pattern is always the same.

While I played, these patterns broke down further into the rhythms of the week: rest on Monday; last Sunday's game film and light workout on Tuesday; films of the opponent and heavier workouts on Wednesday and Thursday, tapering off on Friday; light workout, test on the game plan, and travel or retreat to the Glenwood Manor on Saturday. Then Sunday the culmination: pregame meal, taping and dressing, warmups, taking the field, coin toss, player introductions, final huddle on the sideline, lineup for the kickoff, referee's whistle, ball sailing high and deep to start the game—everything in its proper order, its familiar pattern.

The season had its distinctive rhythm; the weeks did too. So also did the individual days. Game days always followed one pattern, midweek days another: dressing, taping, waiting around, meeting, waiting some more, meeting again and more waiting, practicing, showering, dressing, driving home. Each of these patterns, both large and small, occurred over and over again, creating a familiar, comfortable world. Sometimes the routine became tedious. In late November, there was little pleasure in taking the field for yet another Wednesday practice—to run the same warmup lap, do the same calisthenics and drills, run through the same plays we had run through five thousand times before. But there was also variety in the sameness. A Monday was different from a Thursday, a September game from a December one, a preseason workout from an end-of-the-year practice. The days when I felt strong, healthy, and satisfied could be wonderful; when I was hurt, weary, or oppressed by my nonplaying the routine was deadening.

But above all, playing football was an intense existence. It seemed impossible that a season could last even one game longer than it did. There were times to collapse with exhaustion, then times to soar with elation. Sometimes the emotional roller coaster grew uncomfortable, and I longed for the lower highs and higher lows of a more normal life. But to trade this intense existence for that more normal life requires an adjustment. Careers outside football can be both more routine and more chaotic. They most likely lack that seasonal rhythm, those comfortably recurring and predictable patterns. On the other hand, so many of the jobs football players find themselves in after retirement can be rooted in a tedious day-to-day sameness. While playing football, one is aware of the insistence of time. Not just the brevity of careers, but the concentrated focus on the *now* heightens the intensity of the football player's existence. During the season his life is measured out in fourteen or sixteen week-long episodes, each with a clear buildup, climax, and aftermath. The football player can easily become accustomed to an in-grained shortsightedness, in which the past is meaningless and the future irrelevant except for the game just ahead. In careers outside football, on the other hand, past mistakes can haunt the present, and the future is a seemingly endless string of days on the job. Retirement from football requires a reorientation, a fun-damentally different attitude toward work and time. It means a surrender of intensity.

A second fundamental adjustment stems from the intensely physical nature of professional football. Playing football in the NFL makes emotional and psychological and even intellectual demands, but compared to virtually any career outside the game it is most of all an intensely physical existence. As such, there is a simplicity, a clarity, and an immediacy in playing football that the athlete must give up on retirement. For most people, the body is a necessary burden most of the time. Men and women tend to be most aware of their bodies when they malfunction—when the sinuses act up or the lower back aches. Physical plea-sures are a part of life, but are peripheral to other things.

For the football player, day-to-day existence is above all phys-ical. His primary sensitivity to the world around him is not through sight or sound, but through the more intense sensations of touch. He knows intimately the hardness or softness of the ground he walks on, the strength and direction of the wind, the heat of the sun and the chill of its absence. I played football games in 90-degree heat and minus-13-degree chill factor, in blizzards that obscured everything more than fifty feet away, in rain that turned grass fields to mud and synthetic turf to treach-erous slickness, and on crisp, clear autumn days bright with sun but invigorated by a cool briskness in the air. Each experience was real, each different from every other.

To feel strong, fast, quick, or graceful was immensely satisfy-ing, but I also found intense pleasures in the little details of my physical universe. In a drink of cold water when I felt myself at the point of dehydration. In a sudden breeze, slapping refresh-

ingly against the sweat on my face, neck, and arms. In a plunge
into the swimming pool after a grueling practice at William Jewell College. In food and drink consumed in colossal amounts,
to satisfy a gargantuan appetite or replenish a large weight loss.
I never had to count my calories or nibble on lettuce leaves
when I craved meat and potatoes and cherry pie. Training-camp
meals were like Viking feasts, with mounds of food heaped on
platters, utensils optional.

Pain was a large part of my physical world, but ironically it
served its own positive functions. In its perverse way it made me
more aware of my body than pleasure did. Dull aches in over-
worked muscles could actually be satisfying. They told me that
the muscles were being developed, were getting stronger; when
the pain disappeared they would have reached a new plateau of
strength and endurance. Greater pains and near-total exhaustion
were terrible, but they could gratify in a different way. It was
profoundly satisfying—perhaps more in retrospect than at the
time—to have pushed myself beyond what I had believed were
my physical limits. To have endured a brutal practice in the humidity of Liberty, having drilled, hit, lifted, and run for two
hours until I felt there was nothing left, then to have walked off
that field still alive, still functioning, aware that had we been
required to run one more wind sprint, I could have done it; this
was an immensely satisfying experience that I will never have
again. Truly severe pains and injuries made me more acutely
conscious of my body than ever, though they brought no satisfactions. But they did accentuate the physical pleasures by contrast. They made the pleasures more intense, balanced the highs
with the lows, created a world of intense variety.

Mondays—when we had no game, no practice—offered some
of the most enjoyable moments of my professional career. Monday was a day of sensuous luxuriance, of physical pampering
that seemed almost decadent. I would come into the locker room
in the late morning, after sleeping in as long as I wanted. After
undressing, I put on only a pair of shorts, feeling totally free. On
bare feet I padded across the carpeted floor to the training room
where I leisurely treated any minor aches in the ice bath or
whirlpool tub. The trainer, Wayne Rudy, was there, and usually
a few teammates; talk was low-keyed and unhurried. Next I

walked outside the locker room to the weights in the outer tunnel, not to work hard but to loosen up, flex a few muscles, maintain their tone. The one exercise at which I might exert myself a little was the bench press. With a heavy weight on the bar, it was exhilarating to feel my entire body focusing its power to lift the bar off the rack, drop it to my chest, and thrust it upward with an explosion of effort. Legs, buttocks, back, shoulders, neck, arms, and lungs worked smoothly together, making me feel power running through the length of my body.

Mostly I lifted lighter weights through quick repetitions, then padded back through the locker room to the giant whirlpool off the shower area. Immersed up to my neck in the steaming-hot water, with one of the powerful jets directed at my lower back, I felt my entire body sag in relaxation. I moved around a bit, directing the jets at my neck, my shoulders, my upper back, and my legs, but then always coming back to my lower back, where most of my day-to-day stiffness and soreness centered. From the whirlpool to the showers was just a few steps. I turned the water on strong and left it on long—no anxiety about using up the hot water as at home, no feeling cramped in a tiny shower stall or bathtub. I cooled off from the heat of the whirlpool, luxuriating in the gentler warmth; I washed my hair and soaped all over, feeling clean, refreshed, relaxed. Around the corner from the showers were the sinks and mirrors, where I shaved for a more complete feeling of cleanness. My last act before dressing was to shake bath powder over my shoulders and feet, not worrying about messing up a bathroom floor as at home, but shaking and shaking, then rubbing it in. Finally, I dressed slowly and went home.

Such pleasures are the simplest, most elemental ones imaginable, and they were distinctly a part of my physical existence as a football player. Since retirement, I never have the time, the facilities, the lack of concern about waste and mess—the conscious indolence of those Mondays in Kansas City. Whether or not my teammates relished the identical physical pleasures that I most enjoyed, they and all football players shared in the intensely physical world of their profession. But this must be given up, too, for something less simple, less direct, less immediately satisfying. Ex-football players, in fact, fare worse physically in the outside world than ordinary citizens do. Their life expectancy is fifty-four, almost two decades less than the normal life span. Large appetites continue, but the exercise that burned the calories off does not. With less exercise, muscles turn to fat, hard flesh to mere bulk. Heart attacks come easily. Even if the danger of excessive weight can be avoided, damaged joints deteriorate. Gnarled fingers, surgically scarred knees, lingering pinched nerves prolong aches that are no longer countered by greater physical pleasures. From being a physical ideal, the football player if he is not careful can become a physical wreck. But even if he avoids that extreme, his life can never be as intensely physical as it once was. He must adjust to a world in which his body and his senses, which were the center of his existence while he played, are simply no longer as important.

A third major source of adjustment is the relative simplicity of the football world. Football players must deal continually with an undercurrent of anxiety about their job insecurity and lack of control over their own careers, but countering that complication is the basic simplicity of the demands placed upon them. What is necessary for success is clearly understood, what is expected from them is clearly laid out. The football player's world is like the field he plays on. A football field is precisely 100 yards long and 53⅓ yards wide. Everything the players can do on the field is governed by a set of rules that all understand and agree to. Violators are punished by any of six officials constantly watching for infractions. The object of the game is clear: to score more points than the opponent. The way to score points is equally clear: by touchdowns, field goals, extra points, and safeties. The manner of scoring touchdowns, the movement of the ball up and down the field—everything that can happen is clearly prescribed and understood by all who participate.

The football player's life is in certain ways much like the game he plays in its unambiguous simplicity. He understands fully the skills demanded for his job: blocking, tackling, running, passing, or kicking. He knows what he must do to maintain his ability to perform, that he must be strong, fast, quick. He has coaches who tell him what to do and when to do it, and who monitor his actions to see that he does. He has rules that govern his behavior not just while in uniform but away from the field as well. He knows exactly what is expected of him in all phases of his life, and he knows the penalties for failure in any of them. How different such a life is from most other careers! What are the rules in the business world? Not the federal and state and local laws, but the unofficial rules by which businessmen act? What personal qualities are necessary for success in business? and how are they developed? How is success measured in business? How much success is necessary for survival? On what basis are employees rewarded, promoted, given salary increases? There are possible answers to all these questions, but those answers would be uncertain, imprecise. Different businessmen would propose different answers; one businessman's answers might change over time.

The football player lives in a world of much greater certainties than he will find after he retires. Having become accustomed to simple rules, simple measurements of success, a relatively simple life stripped down to essentials, he must adjust to a professional world of greater ambiguity and complexity. He will likely find himself in positions at times where he does not know what he should do, where he does not feel that he has control over the outcome. Such situations would rarely have arisen while he was playing. He may well have discovered things he could not do as a player—not be able to handle a particular opponent, perhaps—but he would have understood that inability. And he would have known about ways to compensate for his disadvantage.

There is a potential danger in the simplicity of the football player's world. If he has done for many years just what his coaches have told him, and become comfortable in doing only what he was told to do, being cut loose to make his own decisions can be a shock. Through high school and college, a player's coaches can have virtually a father's influence over him. But as a professional, if he has not done so earlier, he must more fully take control over his own life. He must begin to think and act independently, to see football as merely a part, not the sum of his life. If he does not do this, to be suddenly thrust out from his authoritarian football world can be intimidating.

The football player lives in a world of "us" and "them." The obstacles to his success are clearly recognizable individuals,

whether rivals in training camp or opponents across the line of
scrimmage. As long as he continues to defeat these specific individuals, he will thrive in his career. In college particularly,
where I felt an overwhelming need to prove myself, I was able
to satisfy that most perplexing need simply by knocking down
other football players. Nothing could have been simpler. Every
pro football player enjoys the same kind of clarity and simplicity
in his professional life. Unjust fines create only an occasional
confusion. In a larger world grown increasingly impersonal and
morally ambiguous, his private universe demands straightforward personal conflict, in which his strength, speed, agility,
and cleverness are pitted against those qualities in another, with
superior ability prevailing. Where else is such comforting cer-
tainty possible? Where else is success determined in one-on-one
physical confrontations governed by rules, in which the "best
man" will usually win? Not in most careers outside football. On
retirement, the ex-athlete must adjust to much greater uncertainties in his new life.

At the end of a game a football player can total up his
successes and failures and determine his overall accomplishment.
If any doubts remain in his own mind, the game films will settle
them. I used to hate watching myself on film. Every mistake was
so glaringly obvious, so real, so right there in plain sight to be
examined over and over again as the coach ran the play back
and forth, back and forth, before moving on to the next. The
plays I executed well never looked as good to me on film. In
some ways the camera lied. It could not record the force of impact or the effort that went into a block. Plays on which in my
mind's eye I had been awesome often looked much more ordinary on film. One play in particular stands out in my mind.
Against Cleveland in 1972 I entered the game in the fourth
quarter when we had a comfortable lead. Jerry Sherk, the
Browns' fine defensive tackle, lined up on my nose, right on top
of the ball, so close that I felt smothered. I had little room to operate in, but on snapping the ball I exploded into Sherk, raised
him up, and dumped him on his back. My feet had not even
moved; they had had no chance to move with Sherk right on top
of me. But I had hit him harder than I had ever hit anyone on
the line of scrimmage in my life. When I came off the field at

the end of that series of downs, I felt terrific, my pinched nerve notwithstanding, and Jack Rudnay almost leaped on me in his excitement over the hit. But on Tuesday when we watched the game film, I nearly missed the great moment. After Bill Walsh had run one play back a couple of times, I finally realized I was watching my Big Play. I could barely see anything. I saw myself and Sherk obscured in the middle of the line; on the snap of the ball he simply disappeared. There had been Sherk, lined up on my nose, then all of a sudden in the next frame he wasn't there. He was buried under me, but the film did not reveal how he got there. I was hidden in a pile of bodies, my legs and lower trunk sticking out, not having moved from the spot where I had snapped the ball.

"Nice block, Mike," Jack called out in the darkened room, probably more from memory of the play than from what he saw on the screen.

"Yeah, good block," Bill Walsh added as what seemed an afterthought.

That was all. I had been looking forward to that moment when all my fellow linemen would marvel over my great play. But the camera robbed me of my pleasure.

But if the camera failed to capture the full reality of everything that happened on the field, it rarely lied about the end result. In fact, maybe it did not lie at all; it simply deflated my heroic illusions by revealing their merely human reality. The camera told each of us just how well we had done on every play. We could measure ourselves against the opponents we played and decide who had won the individual battles. We each had our own unambiguous challenge. We could determine our own success on an individual basis and within the context of the team's fortunes. We knew quite clearly how good we were, and each of us could feel self-sufficient—responsible for our own successes and failures—but also part of the team effort.

While I was playing football, we either won or we lost on Sunday, and I played well or badly. Whichever the case, next Sunday was a new game, with another clear-cut resolution. The life of a professional football player is intense, is simplified, is life on a large scale. In my childhood I discovered that football was unlike the other games I played. As an adult, I learned it differed from other kinds of work as well. When football is exchanged for a new career, the athlete must adjust.

All football players must make these adjustments. All must give up the familiar rhythms, the physical intensity, and the basic simplicity of their football world. The better players can find adjusting more difficult because their careers have been longer and more intense. They have had more opportunities to feel heroic, have had many more highs than lows and more pleasures than pains, have experienced success much more often than failure. They are the geniuses of their profession—the very best at a very difficult craft. Theirs is a physical rather than an intellectual genius, but genius nonetheless, and to have to give it up so early can be difficult. It is surely ironic that greater excellence can mean greater difficulty in adjusting to retirement. There seems to be a perverse law of compensation at work which punishes the talented.

But every football player shares this problem to some degree. Even those who never make all-pro, who never even start, have succeeded at a level that only a privileged few achieve. Of the millions who play football in high school each year, and the thousands in college, only a few hundred will go on to make it in the pros. When they retire, less honored players may not be giving up as much as the all-pros, but they too must trade the intensity, the simplicity, and the prestige of their football careers for something else. No matter how well prepared they are for life after football, they must make a psychological, emotional, and financial adjustment. If they are not prepared for the outside world at all, they may find adjustment impossible.

Most players make the adjustment somehow; the majority of my teammates in Kansas City have done it very well. However much they might miss football—miss the camaraderie, the special privileges, the intensity and simplicity—most of them have successfully made the transition to other careers. In discussing that change, they consistently cite the same keys to adjusting. Begin preparing for retirement long before it comes, they all say. Invest in your future while you are still playing. A few of my teammates in Kansas City did nothing but play basketball and golf during their off seasons. There is little future in that. Others were caught in a more insidious trap. A name athlete can capitalize on his fame while he is playing, but he discovers on retirement that he has become a depressed commodity. A few of my fellow Chiefs were vice-presidents in banks and other institutions, which sounded impressive to me during my first year, until I discovered that their titles should have read "Vice-President in Charge of Taking Clients to Lunch." Or "Vice-President of Nothing"—which is exactly what they were when they left football. One teammate, a perennial all-pro, held such a position with General Motors in Kansas City, and was fired within months after retirement. As George Daney says, "It seems like there are lots of opportunities when you're playing, but after you're done, the door slams in your face."

But there are opportunities, and those who seize them are the wise and fortunate ones. "Most athletes are a knee injury away from oblivion," according to George Seals, and George is but one of many who saw that a knee injury would not find them unprepared. They worked hard in their off seasons, establishing themselves in outside careers. When football ended, productive life did not. Detachment is a key—being able to see your own football career from outside, rather than being totally caught up in it. Football can be a seductive siren, whispering in players' ears the words that will drag them to their doom. "You're special," it breathes. "You're a hero; the world admires you and wants to take care of you. Don't worry about anything; sign autographs and let people buy you drinks. You can play forever." The athlete cannot afford to believe such lies for very long.

Willie Lanier was more detached than anyone I knew while he was playing with the Chiefs. He became one of my own mentors, telling me one summer that he was going to play at 225 pounds, even though the coaches wanted him at his customary 245. It was *his* body, not theirs. He was going to have to live with it for many years after football ended, and he would not let anyone tell him how to care for it. For eight or nine years Willie played with this sort of detachment—which in no way interfered with his being the best middle linebacker in football. But somehow—he does not know how he could have let it happen—in his last year and a half he began to care too much; he lost himself in the game. The change almost proved disastrous, for leaving football became a painful rupture rather than a transition to another career. After retirement in 1977, Willie floated for a couple of years, doing nothing, not taking care of himself, finding nothing to fill the void in his life. Willie had never seemed to me capable of having such a void. I knew no one in better control of his own destiny, who used his off seasons more productively. But in his last years in Kansas City, perhaps as he saw his effectiveness on the field slip a little, his great pride made him begin to care too much about football. And when he quit, he discovered that he expected himself to do things at such a high level of excellence that he could not adjust to taking his place as an average citizen. He struggled through this period, and eventually established himself with a stock firm in his hometown, Richmond, Virginia. But it was not easy; others might have given up. How strange it is that *caring* too much can become dangerous.

The final key to relatively painless adjustment is easily summed up: don't leave the game unfulfilled. How much did Jim Tyrer's bitterness over the end of his career affect his attitude toward life during those six years of his retirement? After being all-pro for ten seasons, his last memory of the Chiefs was of being forced to accept an unwanted trade. Ed Budde, his partner at left guard, retired voluntarily when he felt he was losing a step—so that he would not have to face such a no-win decision as the one given Tyrer. Ed has no regrets, and his story is repeated by others. George Seals woke up one morning after having just signed the most lucrative three-year contract of his career, and said, "That's enough." When he retired, he felt he was at the top of his game, and he never regretted the decision to quit. He feels very different from his old Chicago Bear teammates, whom he sees occasionally, who after having been cut are still bitter, and still living in their pasts. When they get together, all they can talk about are the touchdowns they scored or the blocks they made in big games years ago. Being cut makes the player feel he still has something to prove. But outside football, where can he prove it? Unfulfillment can be a deadly poison.

Football players have to fight what Jim Lynch calls the "one-more-year syndrome." They have to avoid being like gamblers who cannot quit when they are ahead, who always think that just one more hand will make their fortunes. For too many players that "one more year" leads to the kind of frustration that capped Jim Tyrer's otherwise outstanding career. Few in any sport walk away on top. The great baseball players of my childhood—Stan Musial, Mickey Mantle, Warren Spahn, Willie Mays—all played too long. Batting .270 at the end instead of .330, or being hit by players who couldn't even see the fastball three years before. Professional boxers are notorious for prolonging their careers—trying for one more comeback until they have been punched silly. Football players, too. Jim Otto, George Blanda, Jim Tyrer, countless others—all forced to leave the game because they didn't retire voluntarily when they should have.

As might be expected, George Daney's career ended in a manner appropriate to what preceded it. His retirement could have been staged by Mel Brooks or Woody Allen. Like George Seals, Daney woke up one morning in June 1975, told his wife Linda for the thousandth time, "That's it," but meant it for a change. His retirement called for no press conference, but he drove to Arrowhead Stadium to inform the Chiefs of his decision. The general manager was out, as were his assistant and the director of public relations. Downstairs George could find no one except Wayne Rudy, the trainer. George announced his retirement to Wayne.

"Why me?" Rudy asked.

"Wayne, you're the next in command," George told him, and left.

George went home, gathered up his wife and kids, and drove to the Lake of the Ozarks to celebrate. When he returned several days later, he learned that he had not officially retired because he had failed to fill out the proper forms. And he had been traded to Houston.

Several calls from Houston finally persuaded him to report, but George demanded one condition. He would not step onto the practice field without a contract. After seven years in the NFL, George was not going to be treated like a rookie or free agent desperate for a job. He flew to Houston, was given a thorough physical exam, then was told to dress for practice.

"I go nowhere without a contract," George told them.

The Oilers' trainer and doctor, not knowing what to do, finally sent a ball boy out to explain the problem to Bum Phillips. In ten minutes the boy returned with Bum's solution.

"You're fired."

George Daney went out the way he had played, with his own distinctive flair. But like Lynch, Seals, Budde, and his other fortunate teammates, he did not look back. He had done long before what every football player has to do if he is to make the adjustment to the outside world. He took control of his own life. The player who uses football rather than the reverse makes the successful adjustment. Every one of my teammates who talked to me about making the transition from football views his athletic career as a positive experience—but because he made it that way. There has been too much argument over whether football retards psychological and emotional maturity, or fosters values and qualities that aid the athlete outside the game. What it does is provide opportunities for character to be developed in either positive or negative ways, but it creates by itself neither bums nor saints. Individuals who take control of their lives, who use football rather than letting it use them, can benefit a great deal. If they can see beyond the intense *now* of their football world to the future that must follow it, they can prepare themselves.

It would be a mistake to minimize the difficulties. Bob Stein, a large part of whose law practice involves representing professional athletes, points out a problem that faces many players. "It is so difficult to achieve the level of success required to even make it to a professional football team, that it seems unrealistic in most cases to expect either a comparable success in another field within one lifetime, or developing one's sense of priorities to the extent that the 'second career' does not become anticlimactic and empty." My teammates who have successfully established themselves outside football are particularly sensible, intelligent men. And perhaps they have not told the whole truth. Perhaps deep down inside the corners of their hearts they still have longings for some of those pleasures and satisfactions that football gave them. But they have demonstrated that football players can move beyond the game without looking back too insistently. If the player recognizes that those distinctive and unique pleasures given him by professional football are only temporary, and that he is a different, more ordinary person than the public image he projects to sports fans, he can find that life after football need not be a painfully drawn-out anticlimax.

In my own case, football served me well for eighteen years. Outside the daily round of my existence—my family, friends, and schooling—football was the single most powerful influence in my life. Whether it created or merely reinforced certain personal characteristics, it played a large role in teaching me who I was. It gave me physical, emotional, and psychological pleasures; made pain and frustration and disappointment seem like manageable barriers; and gave me potent experiences of success and even of dreams fulfilled. Football was vitally important to me for over half my lifetime, yet it is in no way a burden I now bear. It is not an ideal past against which my present and future can never measure up. It is not the sole source of meaningful existence which I was forced to give up prematurely. It does not haunt my dreams and waking memories with either lost glory or expectations unfulfilled.

My football career rests easily on me today because it was never more than half my life at any time in the past. It was a very important part, but it was never the sole source of my personal identity. In reflecting on how this situation came to be, I cannot attribute it to my own precocious wisdom in understanding the proper role of football in our culture and in individual lives. Football's impact on American culture was less when I was a child than it is now, but it was still powerful. Supportive but undemanding parents, intense but reasonable coaches, a school system and a community that saw an important place for football but a lower one on the scale of human achievement than world building or sainthood—all contributed to an environment in which I could pursue my passionate interest in the game without losing sight of other concerns. My relationship to football for most of the years I played bordered on the schizophrenic. Particularly in high school and college, I led two lives: my life on the football field and my social and educational life away from it. The two halves of my existence were mutually influential but still distinct and separate. In the classroom and about town I was preparing for life in the real world. On the football field I was playing out my fantasies and working through psychological needs. I did not think much, if at all, about what one part of my life had to do with the other.

It was after college that the two separate parts of my life merged. Outwardly, my existence was more clearly divided than ever before. From July through December I played football. I lived in Kansas City, was identified in the community as a Kansas City Chief, was engrossed in my physical well-being and my desire for more playing time. From January through June I was a graduate student in American literature, indulging my other, more lasting passion. I lived near Palo Alto, California, went to classes at Stanford, thought about and talked with my friends about William Faulkner's novels instead of Hank Stram's playbook. But within my own psyche I was coming more and more to understand myself as the single person who did both of these separate things.

The change did not happen instantly. During my first season in Kansas City, I felt unusual for my off-the-field interests. As a member of the taxi squad rather than the forty-man roster, I felt literally not quite a part of the team. But I also felt that my intellectual life isolated me in many ways. I felt that I was straddling a line with a foot in two camps that were suspicious of each other. Bob Stein's law-school classes were more acceptable to his teammates, I suspected, than my classes in Elizabethan drama and the Victorian novel. I read *poetry,* for God's sake! How could I justify such an aberration to 270-pound defensive tackles? That first off season, I felt the flip side of my dilemma. I started my graduate studies at the University of Washington in Seattle. Arriving in January instead of September, I felt disoriented from the beginning. But I also particularly felt that I had better keep my previous six months' activity to myself. *I* knew there was nothing perverse in my playing professional football, but I feared that it might be perceived by others as a slight step higher than molesting little girls.

In my second year the barbed-wire barriers between my two lives disappeared, as I discovered my own misconceptions. In Kansas City, I did not say much about my off-season activities except to my closer friends, but I began to realize that not only did my other teammates not despise me for them, most of them respected me, and some perhaps even envied my progress toward a genuine career outside football. And that off season, now at Stanford, I discovered that English professors have no prejudices against football players in their classes—so long as they can write intelligent papers about Mark Twain and Henry James. My graduate studies exalted me in the eyes of some of my fellow Chiefs, and my football career in the eyes of some of my teachers and fellow grad students. The combination, probably by virtue of its extreme diversity, fascinated many. By this time I had come to appreciate the intelligence of many of my teammates, and I had also encountered the athletic interests of several of my professors. Inside many an academic there lurks an NBA guard or NFL quarterback wanting to break out. In Kansas City, Dennis Homan, a wide receiver from Alabama, started calling me "Chaucer," and would recite for me a few lines from the Prologue to *The Canterbury Tales* in his Southern drawl. If you have never heard Chaucer's Middle English

> Whan that April with his showres soote
> The droughte March hath perced to the roote,

in the tones of a good ole boy, you have been denied a rare treat. At Stanford, I played intramural basketball with my fellow graduate students, coached by a professor of American literature who had written books on James Fenimore Cooper and Ezra Pound. And it was my Chaucer professor who first suggested I write my dissertation on American sports fiction.

During my years in Kansas City, my interest in football became simply a part of me—not "part" now as a separate compartment of my life, but as a shade with which all of my life was colored. Football was removed from the realm of fantasy and obsession, and became simply the game that I played for money during six months of the year. But it also became more fully incorporated into the person I was. When my career ended, I only stopped playing football games. What the experience had been to me continued to be a part of me, and will continue as long as I live.

My adjustment to leaving football was made easier by a number of circumstances. For one thing, playing professional football was always secondary to graduate school and an eventual career in teaching. I thought of myself as a graduate student who played football between terms, not a football player who went to school in the off season. I knew from the beginning that at most I would play football for several years, while I would teach until I was sixty-five. My passion for literature was a never ending one. I would exhaust my potential as a football player very young, but would continue to learn from the books I read until I died.

My football and graduate school careers never conflicted while I was playing; had they done so, I always knew I would opt for grad school. The administrators of my department at Stanford, and of the Danforth Foundation which funded my fellowship, accommodated my requests to stretch out my studies for the sake of my football playing. I never felt that my performance on the field suffered by my going to school. The only time school suffered was in 1972 when I had to take my comprehensive exams in September. The three four-hour exams covering all of British and American literature were to be given on a Friday, a Monday, and a Wednesday at Stanford. I had made arrangements to take them through the testing center at the University of Missouri at Kansas City. But to work around my schedule of football games, I had to take the exams on a Monday, Wednesday, and Thursday of the same week. Preparing for the exams had been difficult enough; collapsing in bed at night after double practices in Liberty, I felt little inclination to curl up with commentaries on *The Faerie Queene*. But writing for twelve hours in four days was even more difficult. I became so punchy on the third day that I had to start over halfway through that exam. Somehow I passed.

From my first day as a professional football player, football came second in my life, and what came first was not just a job that promised financial security but a professional career that would challenge and satisfy me. My modest accomplishments as a Chief further made football less important in my life—and made leaving it easier. Had I gone directly from Notre Dame to graduate school or other employment, my adjustment to leaving football might have been more difficult. The frustration of my pinched nerve and my relative anonymity as a center would have prevented my looking back on my collegiate days as a pinnacle in my life. But I had worked my way up from walk-on to starter, captain, and second-team all-American. I had become a part of Notre Dame's legendary history. I had realized a dream. Leaving all of that cold turkey might not have been easy.

But when I left the Chiefs, I was leaving a business—a very special business—but a business nonetheless. And it was a business in which I had not risen so high that I had a long way to fall. I was not leaving as a captain and all-pro but as a backup center and special-teams player. Yet I was not unfulfilled. By playing at all I had achieved what I demanded of myself. No longer equating my self-worth with my accomplishments on the football field, I felt no deep-rooted failure. I wonder sometimes if I could have been more successful as a pro had it been important enough to me. If I had been desperate to be a starter, could I have fought my way into the lineup or forced a trade to a team that would play me? Although through my years of bench-sitting I came to question my ability, I saw many centers around the league whom I felt I could outplay. But I never knew for sure. There is a myth in America that we can succeed at whatever we are willing to work for hard enough. I don't believe it. But I do suspect that we are not likely to accomplish anything difficult that we do not want badly enough. A freak injury to Jack Rudnay could have dropped the starting job in my lap. But my lack of a burning need to be a starter made such an accident the only way it would happen. If I had warred against my own teammates, approached each practice as a desperate chance to prove myself against them—as I had done on the prep team in college—I might have forged a different career for myself. But I did not. And the fact that I did not feel the same way about professional football as I had about college, made leaving the game much easier. How ironic it is that the better players and the players for whom football has greater personal importance must pay a penalty in a more difficult adjustment to retirement. Blessed are the mediocre . . . for they shall inherit the future.

The one event I was not prepared for was being cut by the Chiefs in September 1974. I had planned to play six years, finishing my Ph.D. and my football career at the same time (and qualifying for my pension, which required five years—my first

year on the taxi squad not having counted), then moving on to
university teaching. This was *my* plan, but Hank Stram planned
differently. If my football career had ended with Stram's announcement, I would have adjusted, but I am sure I would feel
residual bitterness, dissatisfaction, even unfulfillment that would
color my memories of that long and important phase in my life.
Finishing out the season in Canada and leaving football after
eighteen years by my own choice gave me the final satisfactions
I needed. I had a sense of completeness, of an appropriate ending for the beginning and middle of my career. I had a sense of
final success rather than failure, of ultimate capability rather
than ineptitude. And I felt that I controlled my life. I could even
look back on Hank Stram and realize that he was no Machia-
vellian autocrat, but a man who did his job. He made mistakes
as we all do, but in treating me as an employee he betrayed only
my own naïveté, not the essence of professional football. I *was*
his employee, after all. In fact, during most of my career he
treated me better than a mere employee. I disliked the manner
in which I had been cut loose, but that end to my playing in
Kansas City became but another key episode in my overall career, not its culmination. My career ended two months later with
an outstanding performance against the best defensive end in
Canada. After eighteen years I walked away feeling contentment
rather than bitterness. Retirement is a "little death," but it can
also be a prelude to rebirth.

But still adjustment was necessary. As prepared as I was—
both psychologically and practically—for a career outside football, I gave up something as all ex-football players do.

I sometimes regret the loss of the physical pleasures of my
football-playing days, and even a few of the pains. Remaining
physically fit continues to be vitally important to me, but in my
hour of squash or tennis several times a week I cannot match the
physical conditioning of my football years. I will never again be
as strong, as fast, as able to endure prolonged physical strain as
I was when I played football. I have lost a physical mastery that
I can never regain. I will also never again, even for brief times,
live in so entirely a physical world—in which the fine-tuning of

my body has the central importance in my life, and pampering it and caring for it are my greatest pleasures. I have traded this physical world for a more intensely intellectual one—traded for the better, my culture would say, but with a distinct loss, too.

I retain a certain pleasant security in the knowledge that I played football all those years. I am still the same person who went toe to toe with 280-pound opponents, who did on football fields what many boys and even men only dream of doing. I have not entirely lost that experience; it will always be a part of me, making me more comfortable with myself, more self-assured than if I had not played the game. For maybe six years after I retired, I told myself periodically that if I really had to, I could play football again. I had lost twenty pounds fairly quickly and had stopped lifting weights and running so hard. But as I sat at my desk, I found a certain comfort in telling myself that I was young enough and fit enough to go back to the weights and running if necessary—that I was still capable of playing professional football. But around thirty-two I began to realize this was no longer true. My contemporaries in the NFL were now the old farts in the league. I was in good physical condition for an English teacher—but not for a professional football player.

Professional football creates a prolonged childhood in many ways. Living in a largely physical, sensuous world; obeying strict rules handed down by a patriarchal coach; viewing conflicts as we and they, good and evil—this is more like a child's world than the adult reality we all must deal with. Retirement is a sudden thrust back into the adult world where marriages and businesses fail, work brings no immediate and intense rewards, the rules by which one lives are not simple and unambiguous but complex and uncertain. I value the profession I have entered, but like all adults I occasionally regret the passing of childhood. When I do become nostalgic about Kansas City, I have only to remind myself about Liberty, about being owned, about the frustrations of not playing. I am relieved to be doing what I do now, but still . . . every now and then . . . I remember certain moments. . . .

In July 1975, eight months after I retired, Julie flew home from Stanford to visit her parents while I stayed to work on my dissertation. On one of the nights she was gone, the College All-

Star Game, in its last year, happened to be on television. I had
not watched an All-Star Game in six years. I had felt for some
time that it was a silly farce—a collection of rookies thrown together for a few weeks playing against the best team in professional football in an inevitably boring, badly played contest. But
this night I watched the game through to the end. And afterwards, feeling restless, I left the apartment to walk down to a
local drive-in for an ice-cream cone. As I stepped outside, I experienced a profound shock. The weather was uncharacteristically humid for Palo Alto. As I walked down Stanford Avenue
I had the eerie feeling that I was in Kansas City or Liberty. It
struck me that just one year ago I had been in training camp,
perhaps walking into the Dairy Queen after a grueling day of
two practices. And I was amazed to discover that I felt sad—
with an inexpressible sadness that I could not account for. What
could I possibly miss from Liberty? I realized for the first time
that never again in my life would I walk off a football field with
that intense satisfaction of knowing that I had just been pushed
further than most men could endure, and had survived. Walking
down the street on this muggy evening I was finishing off a day
of writing and watching a football game on television. A year
ago I had been completing a day on which I had proved once
again that I could do something few men were capable of. This
evening I had the satisfaction of having written a few pages of
my dissertation. A year ago I had had the satisfaction of having
triumphed over an ordeal.

In the years following that night in Palo Alto, when I have
thought about football I have most often remembered first of all
the tortures of training camp and the frustrations of being
owned, and have felt relieved to be no longer a part of that
world. But every now and then I have been assaulted by more
pleasant memories—not of games or plays, but of teammates or
of physical and emotional sensations I will never experience so
intensely again. Fortunately, those moments of nostalgia are
brief and infrequent. When I retired in 1974, I let go of football
and football for the most part let go of me. My football career
ended as fortunately as it began. I bear some physical scars from
my many years of playing, but no psychological ones. I have a
neat half-moon slash on the inside of my left knee from my first

injury in the seventh grade. One end of it is intersected by a four-inch scar from my high school surgery for torn cartilage. If I jerk my head too quickly, my pinched nerve will remind me of my legacy from Notre Dame. And two oddly bent fingers, plus periodic aches in various joints, remain from Kansas City. But my psyche is undamaged.

Football has been so often hysterically attacked and outrageously applauded that we can lose sight of what it really is: a much more varied experience than either extreme implies. I would be a hypocrite to deny its possible benefits to those who play, but a fool to ignore its potential harm. It brings pleasure and pain, glory and tragedy. It is like a potent medicine: used carefully and wisely it can invigorate and heal; used incautiously it can become a deadly poison. Football has had too many different meanings for the many thousands who have played it and the millions more who have watched it for me to arrive at any pat conclusions about its value in America. If it were packaged for purchase on supermarket shelves, some would argue that the wrapping should read:

"Warning: the surgeon general has determined that football playing is dangerous to your health."

That seems a little strong. I would prefer something simpler: "Handle with care."

Index